Soccer For Dummies®

The Field Of Play

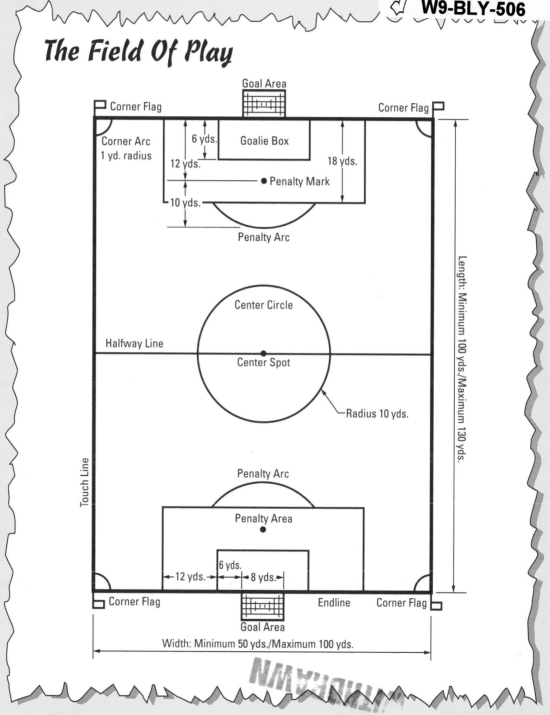

Goal Area

Corner Flag

Corner Flag

Corner Arc
1 yd. radius

6 yds.

Goalie Box

18 yds.

12 yds.

● Penalty Mark

10 yds.

Penalty Arc

Length: Minimum 100 yds./Maximum 130 yds.

Center Circle

Halfway Line

Center Spot

Radius 10 yds.

Touch Line

Penalty Arc

Penalty Area

●

6 yds.

12 yds.

8 yds.

Corner Flag

Endline

Corner Flag

Goal Area

Width: Minimum 50 yds./Maximum 100 yds.

For Dummies: Bestselling Book Series for Beginners

Soccer For Dummies®

The 11 positions

Each team has 11 players — one goalkeeper and 10 field players.

Goalkeepers: The keeper is the only player allowed to use his hands, and that activity is restricted to an 18-yard by 44-yard area called the penalty area. If a goalkeeper handles the ball outside of the box, he should be awarded a red card and the attacking team given a free kick from that spot.

Defenders: They play in front of the goalkeeper, and their primary duty is to stop the opposition from scoring or getting shots — quality and quantity. Their assignments and responsibilities can vary from man-to-man coverage or zone defense, in which they defend a particular area. Outside fullbacks play on the left and right wings and patrol the flanks and rarely move from their sides of the field. Central defenders play in the middle of the field and usually cover the opposition's leading goal scorer or center forward(s).

Midfielders: These players are the link between the defense and attack. Midfielders must be the most physically fit players on the field because are expected to run the most in a game. They should be able to penetrate deep in enemy territory on attack and make the transition to defense when the opposition retains possession of the ball. Midfielders can specialize as an attacking player or defensive midfielder.

Forwards: Their primary job is to score goals or to create them for teammates. There are several types of forwards. Wings play on either the left or right side and usually run up and down the sides of the field. They can either take the ball into the penalty area for a shot or keep it on the flank and try to pass it to a teammate in the area. Center forwards play in the middle of the field, but they are allowed to wander if open space is there. A center forward, also known as a striker, should be a team's leading goal scorer and most dangerous player up front.

Soccer Do's and Don'ts

- ✔ Do learn to dribble with your head up.
- ✔ Don't be a ball hog. Pass to your teammates.
- ✔ Don't talk back to a referee. You can get a yellow card, and if it's your second yellow, you will be ejected from the game.
- ✔ Do make sure that your shoes fit well. They are the most important part of your equipment.
- ✔ On the bench, be alert and watch the play. You never know when the coach will call on you or a teammate will be injured.
- ✔ Do avoid touching the ball with your hands — unless you are the goalkeeper in the penalty area. It can result in a yellow or red card.
- ✔ Don't tackle from behind. You could get red-carded.
- ✔ Do find time to practice on your own or with teammates or kids on your block.
- ✔ Do show some sportsmanship after a match — win, lose, or draw — by shaking the hands of the opponent.
- ✔ Never come back from an injury too early.
- ✔ Do make sure that you are always in good physical shape.

For Dummies: Bestselling Book Series for Beginners

Praise For Soccer For Dummies

"We've seen soccer, especially the women's game, grow so much in the last ten years. As soccer gets more popular at all levels, more and more people want to find out what this game is about. This book will help people understand why soccer is the world's sport and why we love it so much."

> — Tiffeny Milbrett
> U.S. Women's National Team Forward

"Usually, unable to resist the opportunity to jest with my good friends, the referees, I would suggest (due to the title) that this book be made mandatory reading for all whistle blowers.

"However, there is much more to really understanding the beautiful game then knowing where to kick, how to kick, when to kick, how far to kick, or even who to kick. This book will broaden your knowledge of the game and hence increase your enjoyment, whether it be as a participant, a spectator, or administrator. I give it two thumbs up."

> — Ron Newman
> Hall of Fame Coach

"*Soccer For Dummies* is entertaining, very informative, and essential for parents, fans, and players who want to learn about the world's most popular game. And, best of all, it's not just for beginners. Read and enjoy."

> — Tony DiCicco
> Head Coach '96 Olympic and
> '99 Women's World Cup Champions

"Soccer is the simplest game, and the most beautiful, and *Soccer For Dummies* makes it even simpler and more beautiful. Fans will love it, and those who want to become fans will devour it."

> — Bob Ley
> ESPN/ABC Broadcaster

 TM

References for the Rest of Us!®

BESTSELLING BOOK SERIES

Do you find that traditional reference books are overloaded with technical details and advice you'll never use? Do you postpone important life decisions because you just don't want to deal with them? Then our *For Dummies*® business and general reference book series is for you.

For Dummies business and general reference books are written for those frustrated and hard-working souls who know they aren't dumb, but find that the myriad of personal and business issues and the accompanying horror stories make them feel helpless. *For Dummies* books use a lighthearted approach, a down-to-earth style, and even cartoons and humorous icons to dispel fears and build confidence. Lighthearted but not lightweight, these books are perfect survival guides to solve your everyday personal and business problems.

"More than a publishing phenomenon, 'Dummies' is a sign of the times."

— The New York Times

"...you won't go wrong buying them."

— Walter Mossberg, Wall Street Journal, on For Dummies books

"A world of detailed and authoritative information is packed into them..."

— U.S. News and World Report

Already, millions of satisfied readers agree. They have made For Dummies the #1 introductory level computer book series and a best-selling business book series. They have written asking for more. So, if you're looking for the best and easiest way to learn about business and other general reference topics, look to For Dummies to give you a helping hand.

Wiley Publishing, Inc.

5/09

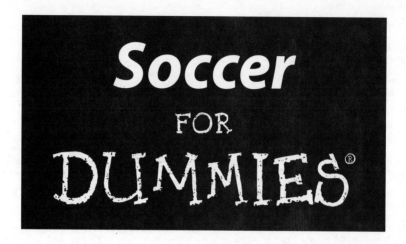

by United States Soccer Federation, Inc. and Michael Lewis

Foreword by Alexi Lalas

WILEY

Wiley Publishing, Inc.

Soccer For Dummies®

Published by
Wiley Publishing, Inc.
909 Third Avenue
New York, NY 10022
www.wiley.com

Copyright © 2000 by Wiley Publishing, Inc., Indianapolis, Indiana

Published by Wiley Publishing, Inc., Indianapolis, Indiana

Published simultaneously in Canada

No part of this publication may be reproduced, stored in a retrieval system, or transmitted in any form or by any means, electronic, mechanical, photocopying, recording, scanning, or otherwise, except as permitted under Sections 107 or 108 of the 1976 United States Copyright Act, without either the prior written permission of the Publisher, or authorization through payment of the appropriate per-copy fee to the Copyright Clearance Center, 222 Rosewood Drive, Danvers, MA 01923, 978-750-8400, fax 978-646-8700. Requests to the Publisher for permission should be addressed to the Legal Department, Wiley Publishing, Inc., 10475 Crosspoint Blvd., Indianapolis, IN 46256, 317-572-3447, fax 317-572-4447, or e-mail permcoordinator@wiley.com

Trademarks: Wiley, the Wiley Publishing logo, For Dummies, the Dummies Man logo, A Reference for the Rest of Us!, The Dummies Way, Dummies Daily, The Fun and Easy way, Dummies.com and related trade dress are trademarks or registered trademarks of Wiley Publishing, Inc., in the United States and other countries, and may not be used without written permission. All other trademarks are the property of their respective owners. Wiley Publishing, Inc., is not associated with any product or vendor mentioned in this book.

For general information on our other products and services or to obtain technical support, please contact our Customer Care Department within the U.S. at 800-762-2974, outside the U.S. at 317-572-3993, or fax 317-572-4002.

Wiley also publishes its books in a variety of electronic formats. Some content that appears in print may not be available in electronic books.

Library of Congress Cataloging-in-Publication Data:

Library of Congress Control Number: 99-69714

ISBN: 0-7645-5229-5

Manufactured in the United States of America

10 9 8 7 6 5 4

1O/SX/QS/QT/IN

About the Authors

United States Soccer Federation, Inc.: Based in Chicago, IL., the United States Soccer Federation is the sport's national governing body (NGB) in the United States. In addition to a U.S. National Teams Program, which includes 11 teams ranging from the Under-16 age level to the full men's and women's teams, the Federation is also responsible for the administration and development of coaches, referees, youth soccer, and amateur soccer throughout the nation.

U.S. Soccer's mission statement is very simple and very clear: to make soccer, in all its forms, a pre-eminent sport in the United States. As for the goals of its national teams, U.S. Soccer has developed separate initiatives for the men's and women's team for the new millennium. For the men, the goal is to be in position to challenge for the FIFA World Cup by the year 2010 and is appropriately named "Project 2010." For the women, "Project Gold" is built on the women's national team goal to "win forever."

Founded in 1913, U.S. Soccer became one of the world's first organizations to be affiliated with FIFA, the Federation Internationale de Football Association, soccer's world governing body. U.S. Soccer has continued to grow in the 87 years since, and now has the largest membership among U.S. Olympic Committee national governing bodies.

In the last 15 years, U.S. Soccer served as the host federation for two Olympic soccer tournaments (Los Angeles 1984 and Atlanta 1996) and the two most successful World Cup tournaments ever: World Cup USA 1994 (men's) and the FIFA Women's World Cup USA '99.

Currently, more than 100 U.S. Soccer employees work to administer and service the membership located in all 50 states. Known originally as the U.S. Football Association, U.S. Soccer's name was changed to the United States Soccer Football Association in 1945 and then to its present name in 1974.

U.S. Soccer is a nonprofit, largely volunteer organization with much of its business administered by a national council of elected officials representing three administrative arms: Youth (with approximately 3 million players 19 years of age and under); Amateur (with over 300,000 senior players over the age of 19; and Professional (with affiliated pro leagues at three different levels).

In addition to developing the game at a grassroots level through the U.S. Amateur Soccer Association and the U.S. Youth Soccer Association, U.S. Soccer also manages nine full national teams. Beginning with the full Men's National Team, the men's programs include the Under-23 (Olympic) team, the Under-20 team, the Under-18 team, the Under-17 team, and the Futsal (Five- A-Side) team. On the women's side, the teams include the full Women's National Team, the newly renamed Under-21 team, and the Under-18 team. Two developmental national team programs include the men's and women's Under-16 teams.

The national teams program has achieved tremendous success in recent years, highlighted by two Women's World Cup titles and an Olympic gold medal for the U.S. Women, the U.S. Men continuing to improve their place on the world stage, and virtually every youth level producing very promising results in international competitions.

U.S. Soccer's umbrella also covers the sports coaching and referee divisions, which are among the most active and fastest-growing in the world. Coaching schools are held regularly throughout the U.S. where participants can gain certification at six progressive levels. U.S. Soccer has more than 80,000 coaches, including almost 10,000 that are nationally licensed. The referee program makes up an integral part of the United States soccer scene, with more than 100,000 referees currently registered.

Michael Lewis: One of the pre-eminent soccer writers in the United States, Michael has covered every level of the game since 1975 — from 4-year-olds playing their first game, to the World Cup, to 50-year-olds running around at the Metropolitan Oval in Queens, New York. The author of three books, Michael is the soccer columnist with the *New York Daily News* and soccer columnist for www.CNNSI.com, among other ventures. Michael, former editor of *Soccer* magazine, has covered four World Cups, three Olympics, one Women's World Cup, numerous international games and competitions, the NCAA Division I men's tournaments since 1992, and every Major League Soccer Cup.

Michael also has won 45 awards, including the college category in the 1999 National Soccer Coaches Association of America writing contest, and has served as president of the Professional Soccer Reporters Association since 1998.

He lives in Coram, NY.

U.S. Soccer's Acknowledgments

U.S. Soccer would like to thank the following people for their extraordinary contributions to this great project: Michael Lewis (for his wit and wisdom in masterfully dissecting the sport he knows and loves), Bobby Howe (for his coaching expertise and unrivaled passion for the game), J. Brett Whitesell (for his skill behind the lens), Greg Drozda (for his marketing savvy and internal project management), and Bryan Chenault (for his editing, public relations efforts, final internal editing, and project management).

In addition, U.S. Soccer and HMI would like to thank John Ellinger, his coaching and administrative staff, and the players on his U-17 National Team: Meredith Benson, David Chun, Maureen Davila, Becca Edwards, Danny Fiore, P. Gray Griffin, Jordan Harvey, Gillian Hatch, Edward Johnson, Paul M. Johnson, Chris Lancos, Kelsey Lau, Quinn Reynolds, Zach Riffett, Chefik Simo, Jordan Stone, and Sarah Thomas.

We'd also like to thank U.S. Soccer staffers Pam Perkins, Brian Fleming, Jim Moorhouse, Aaron Heifetz, Rich Schnieder, Erin O'Connell, Amy Brennan, and Daiga Kirsten for their assistance and Jeff McRaney for securing 'talent.'

Most importantly, thanks to Stacy Collins, Lisa Roule, Kelly Ewing, and everyone at HMI for making this wonderful and long overdue book a reality.

Michael's Dedication

For Rachel and Jacob and their wonderful parents.

Michael's Acknowledgments

I'm no dummy. I realize that this book was written by one person, but it could not have been accomplished without the help of many thoughtful and talented people.

First of all, I must thank my project editor, Kelly Ewing, for her patience, persistence, superb editing, and questions. Kelly made sure that I wasn't too close to the forest. Another hearty thank you to acquisitions editor Stacy Collins for her vision and insights and coordinator Lisa Roule, who made sure that things did not fall through the cracks. On the opposite side of Kelly was Alfonso Mondelo, coach of the Project 40 team that plays in the A-League. He was the technical reviewer and made sure that I didn't forget anything from the forest.

This book could not have been written without the help of the U.S. Soccer communications department, particularly department head Jim Moorhouse, Bryan Chenault, Rich Schneider, and Aaron Heifetz, and Erin O'Connell of the National Team department. I certainly can't forget Peter Sawyer of the Fifi Oscard Agency of New York, who made sure that all the i's were dotted and the t's were crossed in my contract, and Marc Reiter of IMG, who approached me with the idea for the book.

I certainly could not have done the book without a list of talented and articulate players and coaches who took timeout to give some invaluable tips. They include Kristine Lilly, Michelle Akers, and Tiffeny Milbrett of the U.S. Women's National Team, Chris Armas, Ben Olsen, Jeff Agoos, Brian McBride, Kasey Keller, Claudio Reyna, Eddie Lewis, and Eric Wynalda of the men's team, and former U.S. international Tab Ramos of the New York/New Jersey MetroStars. The impressive list to thank goes on — U.S. Women's National Team coach April Heinrichs, former U.S. Women's National Team coach Tony DiCicco, U.S. Soccer director of coaching Bobby Howe, and Los Angeles Galaxy coach Sigi Schmid and writer Dan Herbst.

Dan Courtemanche, Trey Fitz-Gerald, and Carie Goldberg of the Major League Soccer communications department were always there with information when I needed it, as was Scott Creighton of the United Soccer Leagues.

And last, but certainly not least, a big tip of the hat to president Peter Collins and the Long Island Junior Soccer League and president Peter Masotto and the Eastern New York Youth Soccer Association, who both gave me the opportunity to re-establish my connection to the sport at the grassroots level, learn and understand the youth game, and forge my own passion about this beautiful game.

Publisher's Acknowledgments

We're proud of this book; please send us your comments through our online registration form located at www.dummies.com/register.

Some of the people who helped bring this book to market include the following:

Acquisitions, Editorial, and Media Development

Project Editor: Kelly Ewing

Senior Acquisitions Editor: Stacy S. Collins

Acquisitions Coordinator: Lisa Roule

General Reviewer: Alfonso Mondelo

Photographers: International Sports Images; J. Brett Whitesell, Chief Photographer; and Pam Whitesell, Photographer

Editorial Director: Kristin A. Cocks

Editorial Adminstrator: Michelle Hacker

Reprint Editor: Bethany André

Production

Project Coordinator: Emily Wichlinski

Layout and Graphics: Brian Massey, Barry Offringa, Tracy K. Oliver, Heather Pope, Brian Torwelle

Proofreaders: Corey Bowen, Rachel Garvey, John Greenough, Susan Moritz, Charles Spencer

Indexer: Liz Cunningham

Special Help
Donna S. Frederick, Ian Skinnari

Publishing and Editorial for Consumer Dummies
Diane Graves Steele, Vice President and Publisher, Consumer Dummies
Joyce Pepple, Acquisitions Director, Consumer Dummies
Kristin A. Cocks, Product Development Director, Consumer Dummies
Michael Spring, Vice President and Publisher, Travel
Brice Gosnell, Publishing Director, Travel
Suzanne Jannetta, Editorial Director, Travel

Publishing for Technology Dummies
Richard Swadley, Vice President and Executive Group Publisher
Andy Cummings, Vice President and Publisher

Composition Services
Gerry Fahey, Vice President of Production Services
Debbie Stailey, Director of Composition Services

Contents at a Glance

Cartoons at a Glance

By Rich Tennant

page 143

page 297

page 59

page 5

page 193

page 233

Cartoon Information:
Fax: 978-546-7747
E-Mail: richtennant@the5thwave.com
World Wide Web: www.the5thwave.com

Table of Contents

· ·

Foreword

· ·

Soccer tends to seek people out. It usually sneaks up, gently taps you on the shoulder, and then, without your permission, proceeds to invade every facet of your life. It can happen in so many different ways: Your friends want you to join their club team, your son needs you to coach, your daughter wants tickets to the Women's World Cup, or you're unable to contact a business associate across the pond in London because everyone in the country is at a pub watching the F.A. Cup Final.

But there you are asking, "Who is this Pelé person, and why doesn't he have a last name?" The blank stares of your friends, kids, or spouse say it all. Face it — you are a soccer dummy.

But you want in. Like some new dot.com stock about to go public, you want to be a part of this explosion that now only serves to confuse and humiliate you. You want to understand this game to the point where, come the next cocktail party, you raise your glass and, in a voice reeking of confidence, say, "The 3-5-2 formation is heavily dependent on the work rate of your defensive midfielder!" Well, my friend, you have come to the right place.

The good news is that the reason soccer is the most popular sport in the world is because of it's simplicity, and therefore it won't take you long to develop a basic understanding of the game. The bad news is that a basic understanding of the game doesn't always enable you to immediately recognize the beauty that exists in the time between when the goals are scored. That comes with time, and despite devoting my life to the game, I'm still learning something new with every game I play or watch.

Soccer is a game that can be as frustrating as golf, as physical as football and hockey, as sporadic as baseball, and as graceful as basketball. It can also be addicting. Whether you're a player, coach, or fan, as you become more immersed in the game, you will start to find yourself seeing things beneath the surface. You will feel the rhythm of a game change, you will respect the patience that is essential to success, and you will come to marvel at the beauty of something as simple as trapping the ball. I think that you will find that getting to that point is half the fun.

So all I can say is welcome to the ever-growing soccer family. If the game gives you half as much pleasure as it has given me, then you're in for an enormous treat. Now go forth and kick some grass!

Alexi Lalas
Defender, U.S. World Cup Team ('94 and '98)
Defender, U.S. Olympic Team ('92 and '96)
First American player to play in Italy's Serie A
Trademark goatee wearer

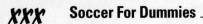

Introduction

Welcome to *Soccer For Dummies*.

We wrote this book for every soccer level, from the novice player to the inter-mediate coach to the most enthusiastic fan. In fact, veteran fans might discover a thing or two about the game as well.

The best thing about soccer is that it is such a universal sport. Virtually all ages can play soccer. You can find leagues for all age groups, from age four to Over-50 leagues, with Over-60 leagues on the horizon as the baby boomer generation ages.

We hope you enjoy reading it as much as we enjoyed writing it.

Why You Need This Book

No other book offers such a comprehensive view of the world's most popular sport, whether it's coaching, playing, or viewing tips or information about the top teams in the world. This book literally has something for every soccer fan.

Playing, coaching, or watching soccer may change your life, and it can open doors that you did not know that were there. A number of years ago, Michael was taking a taxi to Heathrow Airport outside of London when he struck up a conversation with the cab drive who couldn't believe an American not only could talk about soccer, but knew the key players in England.

Hopefully, *Soccer For Dummies* will start you on your way toward not only understanding this great sport, but enjoying it and developing a passion for it as well.

How to Use This Book

This book is relatively easy to use. You don't need to start at the first chapter to understand what's happening in later chapters. However, if you are a novice or a beginner in the sport — player or coach — you may want to read the glossary in Appendix A so that you can understand the language of the sport before starting the other chapters.

Although designed for the beginning to intermediate participant or fan, *Soccer For Dummies* will entertain or inform the most seasoned enthusiast, player or coach. We literally tackle every important aspect of the sport under the sun — from the very basics to tactics to the youth, pro, and international game, all the way to the World Cup. We do it without getting too technical and with the help of photos, charts, tips from the top American players, and interesting anecdotes and historical perspectives of the game.

How This Book Is Organized

Soccer For Dummies is broken into seven parts, from the basics of the game to the professional and spectator end. In each chapter, we start with the basics and go on from there. Whenever a point needs further clarification, we cross-reference another chapter for easy and quick reference. That way, you don't need to read the book from cover to cover.

Part I: Getting Started (Before the Opening Kickoff)

This part gives you information on what you need to get started — uniforms, balls, positions, and the rules — without getting too technical. You find out all about the soccer field, each position, and the laws of the game.

Part II: Fundamentals of the Game

This part deals with the basics of playing the game, like dribbling, heading, passing, shooting, and goalkeeping. We also take on attacking strategies, free kicks, and corner kicks and the various formations a team can use.

Part III: Calling All Soccer Moms and Dads

We wrote this part for the parents who are fans and who want to coach their sons and daughters. It gives you important background on how to behave as a game spectator, plus some important tips on how your children can stay in shape with proper conditioning, practice, and diet. We also look at First-Aid issues and some of the more frequent injuries in soccer.

Part IV: A Spectator's Guide

This part is for everyone. You can discover the best places to get your daily dose of soccer information (newspaper, television, magazines, books, or the ever-growing Internet) or find out more about the various U.S. National Teams or the rest of the planet's passion and fascination with this beautiful game.

Part V: From Saturday Soccer to the World Stage

The sport goes well beyond youth soccer all the way to senior citizens. In between, you can play in high school and college and as an amateur, professional, and, if you are talented and fortunate, for the National Team.

Part VI: The Part of Tens

No *For Dummies* book is complete without a Part of Tens. These short, fun chapters give you an understanding of some of the greatest names to wear the uniform — in the U.S. and overseas as well. They also remind you that the rest of the world plays this game at a very high level, highlighting the greatest feats, games, and goals by players on this planet.

Part VII: Appendixes

If you don't understand the language, you won't understand the game. The glossary in Appendix A can broaden your soccer vocabulary. Appendix B is a contact list for all the 55 state soccer associations — youth and amateur — plus the professional leagues as well and several worldwide organizations.

Icons Used in This Book

To help you navigate through this book more clearly, we placed icons — little pictures that point to a particular tip — in the margins. Here are the icons in this book:

Want others to know that you really know about the game? Use these words to master soccer speak.

This icon marks information that can help prevent you from making a bonehead play on or off the field.

Look for this icon when you want some wise advice, insight, or a shortcut.

Beware! This situation can be dangerous.

This icon means you are about to read an interesting anecdote about the sport.

Part I
Getting Started (Before the Opening Kickoff)

The 5th Wave   By Rich Tennant

In this part . . .

Have you heard a lot about soccer lately and wondered what all the fuss is about? Then this part is for you. In this part, we introduce you to the basics of the sport. You discover just what players wear, where they should be on the field, and the rules they must follow to play the game.

Chapter 1

The Bare Minimum You Need to Know about Soccer

In This Chapter

▶ Tracing soccer's roots

▶ Playing the game: Basic rules and positions

▶ Understanding why soccer is the greatest sport in the world

Soccer — or football as most of the rest of the world calls it — is the most popular sport in the world. It has been around in some shape or form for thousands of years. In fact, there have been times when more countries have played it than there are in the United Nations.

While men have dominated the game as players and spectators in the 20th century, women are poised to gain a larger foothold as a new century and millenium dawns.

In this chapter, we give you an overview of the game, including its beginnings, the laws and rules of the game, positions, and why it is such a popular game. Like a soccer game, this chapter is only the kickoff of the book.

Soccer in the United States

For a nation that has prided itself as the melting pot of immigrants, especially ones from soccer-playing countries, the sport of soccer has gone through many fits and starts in the past 100 years.

It is believed that some form of soccer was played in the Jamestown, Virginia, settlement as early as 1609.

The first soccer game in the United States was played at the college level between Princeton and Rutgers on Nov. 6, 1869, in an encounter based on the London F.A. rules.

There have been countless attempts to establish a long-lasting professional league. In modern times, the North American Soccer League, which boasted 24 teams at its height, enjoyed a 17-year run from 1968 to 1984, when it folded.

In 1996, Major League Soccer was formed. MLS, which was created as the legacy from the 1994 World Cup, which the United States hosted, has expanded from its original 10 to 12 teams and is considering expanding to 16 teams over the next five years.

There has been progress made internationally as well. The U.S. reached the semifinals of the 1930 World Cup and upset England, 1-0, in the 1950 tournament.

After 40 barren years of watching the World Cup from the outside, the U.S. Men's National Team qualified for the world's most prestigious tournament for the first of three consecutive times in 1990.

The U.S. Women's National Team, on the other hand, or should we say foot, is a world power, winning two of the first Women's World Cups championship in 1991 and 1999 and the first-ever Olympic gold medal in 1996.

Regardless of how pro soccer fares, there has been a major youth soccer boom in progress since 1975, or since Pelé came to these shores to play with the New York Cosmos in the NASL. More than 4 million boys and girls between the ages of 4 and 19 play the game in organized youth leagues and in public schools and high schools as well.

Origins of the game

It is not known who actually "invented" soccer, although the game's roots go back thousands of years. The earliest known version of the game occurred in 1697 B.C., when Chinese Emperor Huang-Ti supposedly invented tsu-chu, which was played with the feet and a leather ball.

At one time, there were early variations of the game played in Japan, Greece, Rome, South America, and even some Pacific islands.

In many tribal societies, soccer had its roots as a way to celebrate a victory as warriors used the severed heads of rival chieftans for a ball. While beheading is a rather primitive way of providing a ball, today, many coaches have to beware of losing their heads in another form — or in some cases, their jobs — if they are not successful.

The game did not start to take on its modern form until the English started playing various forms of soccer, and even that took centuries of evolution and overcoming bans from kings and queens to get accepted.

A major milestone occurred in 1863, when the owners of several soccer teams produced the first Laws of the Game, sanctioned by the London Football Association.

Soccer around the World

Soccer did not become organized on a global scale until FIFA — Federation Internationale de Football Association — was formed by seven European countries in 1904. It took another 26 years before a world championship was established.

The first World Cup was played in 1930 and has become the most important single sporting event in the world. (See the section "The World Cup," later in this chapter, for more on this spectacular event.) As many as five billion people will watch the World Cup, which is played every four years, with Europe and the Americas usually alternating as host. The 2002 World Cup, however, literally will break new ground as Asia will organize the games for the first time. Japan and South Korea will host the venue, the first time two countries will act as cohosts of the 32-team tournament.

When National Teams aren't competing, the players perform in leagues whose teams can last as long as ten months. The most lucrative leagues in the world are based in Europe — Italy, England, Spain, and Germany. Many of the top South American players perform in Europe because of the lucrative contracts offered.

National Teams

Just about every country in the world has a *National Team,* essentially an all-star team or a group of the best players who represent their nation in various competitions, including the World Cup. These players perform for their club teams and then get together several times during the year to play in *international friendlies* — exhibition matches — and qualifying games for the World Cup and Olympics. Players are allowed to play for only one country. They were either born in the country they play for or have become naturalized citizens. (For more on National Teams and the World Cup, see Chapter 20.)

Soccer: The Basics

Soccer is a relatively simple and easy game to learn and follow (especially if you have this book). The object of the game naturally is to score more goals than the opposition by putting the ball past the goalkeeper and into an 8-foot by 8-yard goal.

Except for the goalkeeper inside the penalty area, players are not allowed to touch the ball with their arms or hands. They can, however, use any other part of their body to move, pass, dribble, or shoot the ball, including their heads (see Part II).

A typical field, shown in Figure 1-1, is usually is 75 yards by 110 yards. The 17 Laws of the Game — the rules (see Chapter 4) that govern the conduct of the players on the field — allow fields to be as narrow as 50 yards and as wide as 100 yards and as short as 100 yards and as long as 130 yards.

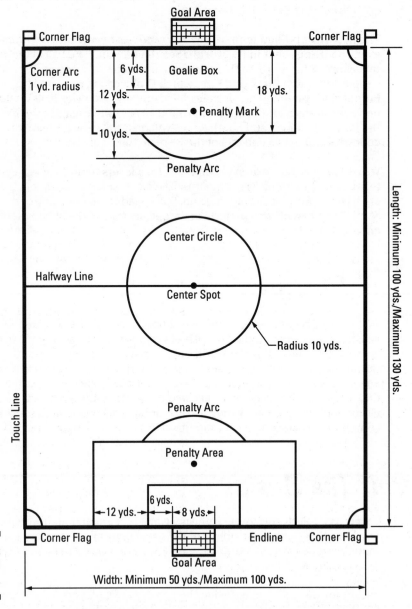

Figure 1-1:
A typical
soccer field.

The most basic rule is that the ball must pass completely over any of the lines — *touchline* (sideline) or *endline* (goal line) — to be out of bounds or a goal.

In other words, a ball can hit the crossbar of the goal, bound down on the line, and be partially on the line and still considered in play. But if the ball is still touching the line, it is not a goal.

The same can be said for a ball on the endline or touchline. A player, however, can be out of bounds dribbling the ball, as long as the ball is not totally over the line.

A typical adult soccer game takes 90 minutes to complete — 45 minutes in each half with as long as a 15-minute rest period between the halves. The length of a youth match, however, varies depending on the age group. The game kicks off when the referee whistles. A player of the team who won the coin toss has the option of kicking off or picking which end of the field it wants to defend in the opening half. One team kicks the ball from the center mark — to either a teammate or opponent.

At the professional and international level and in many high-level amateur and older youth league matches, stoppage or injury time can be added onto the match at the end of each half. This additional time is determined by the referee based on whether time has been lost due to injuries, arguments, or time-wasting tactics by either team.

Players come in all shapes and sizes

When Tiffeny Milbrett is on the field, size doesn't matter. She is 5-foot-2, but thanks to her quickness, speed, agility, and instinct, Milbrett has scored more than 60 goals for the U.S. Women's National Team and is getting close to 150 international appearances.

"This amazes me that I even need to talk about it. People come up to me and say, 'Oh my gosh, you're not very big. You're so teeny. How are you so good out there against them all?' I never even thought about it until people said it. Yeah, I'm a short person. In all my years of soccer, I have never thought that it's amazing that I can go out there and do so well. It never occurred to me it was any different.

"Because people in this country aren't big soccer fanatics, they don't realize you don't have to be big to be the best athlete. When they think of being the best athlete, they think of 7-foot-2 and 6-foot-8 — those basketball guys or football guys, the 300-pounders.

"Soccer is completely different. Sure, you're going to have the taller people, the 6-foot-4s who might be goalkeepers. People who are on the soccer field tend to be quicker, smaller, agile. You have to be. That's the kind of player soccer recruits — somebody who is able to move any direction in any given second."

Depending on which league or level you play, there may or may not be *extra time* — that's soccertalk for overtime. In some competitions and leagues, ties are decided by a penalty-kick tiebreaker.

The *tiebreaker,* which is generally used to determine which teams advance to the next round in tournaments, involves five players from each team. They take their shots from the penalty spot, which is 12 yards from the goal. If the tiebreaker is tied after both teams have attempted five shots, the process enters *sudden-death,* meaning that the process continues round by round, kicker by kicker, until one scores and the other doesn't. Because opposing players must be at least 10 yards from the ball on all penalty and free kicks, there is a semicircle atop the penalty box called the penalty arc, which is 10 yards from the penalty spot and 22 yards from the goal to help referees police the rule.

Players can be penalized for *fouls* — when they knock down or trip an opposing player or impede play — in which free kicks are awarded. If a player is called for a severe foul, the referee can give him a yellow card. If a player receives two yellow cards (see Chapter 4) in a game, the equivalent of a red card, that means ejection from the match. Red cards also can be given for dangerous plays and fouls. If a punishable foul is committed in the penalty area, the referee will award a penalty kick as well as a red card.

The game is officiated by one referee and two assistant referees, or linesmen as they were called until a few years ago.

How Soccer Is Played: The Positions

Each team fields 11 players. There are four basic positions in soccer — goalkeeper, defender, midfielder, and forward. They can be arranged in a number of tactical formations. For more on these positions, see Chapter 3.

The most popular formation is called the 4-4-2. When talking about formations, soccer coaches, players, and media count from the goal up. In other words, this particular setup includes four defenders, four midfielders, and two forwards. There are several other basic formations, from the ultra-conservative 4-5-1 to the attack-minded 4-2-4 (see Chapter 9).

The goalkeeper is never listed in those formations, since that position is a given in every situation.

Ten Reasons Why Soccer Is the Greatest Sport in the World

There is a reason why the great Pelé has called this sport "the beautiful game." Actually, there are ten reasons.

The World Cup

The World Cup is the Super Bowl, World Series, and Kentucky Derby all rolled into one. There isn't another tournament like it in the world for any single sport. The passion of the fans and players is second to none. Yes, the Olympics are a two-week celebration of sports — 33 sports among dozens of countries. However, the World Cup focuses on one sport over five weeks once every four years with 32 teams representing every continent.

If you are ever fortunate to attend one — the 1994 tournament was hosted by the United States — your senses will experience sights and sounds they never had before. You might remember the Brazilian fans who samba from the opening kickoff to the final whistle, or the fervent nationalism of a country's supporters (especially before and after matches), or you just might enjoy cheering on some of the world's greatest players as they display their talents. The next World Cup, to be cohosted by South Korea and Japan, is in 2002. If you have the time, energy, and money, you must attend a World Cup, no matter what country hosts it. It will be an experience of a lifetime.

Goal celebrations

Whether it's a player ripping a shirt off in exuberance, diving onto the field, running to the stands, or performing a backflip, there is nothing like the jubilation or joy of scoring a goal. Who can forget U.S. defender Brandi Chastain ripping off her jersey after her game-winning penalty kick earned the Americans the Women's World Cup '99 title?

Goooooaaaallll!!!!!

The next best thing to watching a goal celebration is listening to famous announcer Andres Cantor or a South American broadcaster describe a goal and literally climax it with his signature call. These goal calls originated in Latin America. Some announcers have been timed as long as 16 seconds on their goal calls.

The most colorful fans in the world

American soccer fans saw it up close and personal at the 1994 World Cup, when foreign spectators painted their faces and the rest of their bodies in the colors of their country. Most recently, they saw it and got in the middle of the act as young girls painted their faces in red, white, and blue in honor of their heroes at the 1999 Women's World Cup. (If you want to join in on the fun, make sure you check out Part IV.)

The universal language

There is nothing quite like having soccer open up a few doors for you. If you are overseas or with someone from another country, you probably can start a conversation anywhere in the world and get instant respect.

Sing-a-longs

The passionate fans of some teams, particularly ones overseas, will serenade their heroes with colorful songs and chants. If the team is doing well or winning big, the lyrics will be upbeat. If those same teams are losing or playing poorly, some of those words . . . well, you might be prepared to cover your ears and get ready to blush. Many supporters take popular tunes and add their own lyrics for their chants and songs, such as "When the Saints Come Marching In."

You can take the entire family

Without sounding like a commercial for pro soccer, tickets are very reasonably priced, and you can bring your entire family without taking out a mortgage. Tickets range from less than $5 for a college game to an average ticket price of less than $15 for Major League Soccer, the top league in the United States.

Any kid can play it

In soccer, size truly doesn't matter. A boy or girl doesn't necessarily have to be 6-foot-5 and 300 pounds to excel. The world's greatest players combine skill, speed, and vision to dominate matches. Remember, the fabulous Pelé was only 5-foot-9 and 165 pounds. And kids can play as early as age 4 or 5, making soccer the first organized sport most every child plays.

Accommodating players

At most pro soccer games in the United States, players will stay on the field after games to sign autographs or are willing to do so at the players' parking lot. In fact, a victory lap by the home team, despite a win or loss, is usually customary in America as a way of thanking the fans for their support. At least in America, soccer could be the last major professional sport not tainted by ego and overblown salaries or questionable off-field behavior.

It doesn't last forever

Unlike some sports we won't mention, which can take as long as four hours to finish, soccer games usually last two hours. If there is a shootout or extra time, you might want to add another half hour. In other words, there is a good chance you will be home well before midnight and still be able to catch the end of a baseball game on TV.

Chapter 2

The "Wear" of Soccer

This chapter looks at the bare necessities of soccer — uniforms, shoes, accessories, and balls. You can't have an organized game without the right equipment.

Getting the Right Look: Uniforms

Compared to other sports, dressing a soccer player is relatively inexpensive. In youth soccer, the shirts and shorts are usually supplied by the team or club, while Mom and Dad have to buy the cleats, socks, and shin guards. Add a ball, and the players can have a ball playing the game and the parents don't have to go to the poor farm.

Uniforms may not make a fashion statement or a statement about the quality of play from a team. But some teams are superstitious on what uniform they might wear. Years ago, English power Manchester United wore its gray jerseys for a rare game and lost. Not surprisingly, they never wore those colors again.

Styles of uniforms can range from one basic color to some flashy, multicolored fashions, as though they just came out of Paris or Milan. And we're not talking about the European pro soccer teams Paris St. Germain or A.C. Milan, either.

Every youth soccer team must wear the colors of its club, although many teams do have home and away uniforms. One of those sets is usually white. If the colors are not commonly used, such as maroon and gold, teams may just switch the priority of the colors on the second set of uniforms.

At the pro level, Major League Soccer teams are allowed to choose their own style and colors, although their uniform suppliers can have the final say on the exact style. If MLS teams want to change their colors, they need permission from the league.

The following items are mandatory for play at all levels of soccer:

- **Socks:** Basic white socks go with everything just fine, although the color may change depending on your team or club. Socks are more sanitary in the, ahem, long run, just in case you pop a blister on your foot.

- **Shin guards:** Every player — youth, amateur, college, professional, or National Team — must wear shin guards. There are no exceptions.

- **Shirts:** Jersey styles have changed dramatically over the years, although today it seems that anything goes. Some clubs and teams prefer the traditional look, even with collars and long sleeves, while other teams prefer the nouveau high-fashion look. (Shirts have undergone a metamorphosis. They were first made of thick wool in the early 1900s before going to cotton, then to double-knit nylons in the '60s and '70s, and finally to lightweight polyester.)

- **Shorts:** Shorts aren't as fashionable as jerseys, but they should fit in with the correct style and color so that they won't clash with the shirts. Some teams prefer to have the same color as their tops, while others opt for white, basic black, or another color.

- **Shoes:** Shoes or cleats are the single most important part of a soccer player's equipment. If they're too tight or too loose, they can hinder a player. (For more on shoes, see the next section.)

Why shoes can make or break your game

On occasion, former New York Cosmos star Giorgio Chinaglia talked to his shoes before games, trying to give them a "pep talk." How well did it work? Chinaglia led the old North American Soccer League in scoring five times and was the league's all-time scoring leader (193 goals in 213 matches). Okay, it was very likely that Chinaglia scored most, if not all, of his goals from his skills. But that was the type of respect he had for his shoes.

While the correct style may make a fashion statement, wearing the right shoes on your feet could help you make a much more important statement on the field. Many pro players like a tight shoe because it gives them a good feel on the ground and with the ball.

But much has changed over the years as the soccer shoe business has become very, very big business. Today, soccer shoes are made out of leather — kangaroo has become popular — and are closer to the ground. Cleats and *outsoles,* or the bottoms of the shoes, have been redesigned on many new models.

The long and shorts of it

While soccer shorts don't have the long and sometimes controversial history of jerseys, they still have played a role in the sport at times:

✔ As he converted a penalty kick in Italy's 2-1 semifinal victory over Brazil in the 1938 World Cup, captain Giuseppe Meazza almost lost his shorts, whose elastic was torn earlier in the match. With one hand he placed the ball down at the penalty spot, and with the other he held on to his shorts. With his shot, the shorts fell to the ground as his teammates gathered around him, and a new pair was found.

✔ Former Scottish international forward Willie Johnston, then with the Vancouver Whitecaps (North American Soccer League), claimed his shorts accidently dropped in front of the Seattle Sounders bench during a shootout in 1980. Vancouver won, but Johnston was a loser; he was fined $750 by the league and suspended for two games.

Besides traditional black, a player can choose from a rainbow of colors, from red to blue to green to white. During a postgame press conference at a World Cup qualifier in 1996, former U.S. international midfielder-defender Thomas Dooley was not only asked questions about his and the team's performances, but also about his signature red shoes.

Many players have endorsement deals with certain manufacturers and literally go through shoes like underwear. Due to the pricey nature of the shoe business, this is something I do not recommend. However, if financially feasible, you should have a pair of shoes for practice and another for games. In case one gets ripped or worn down, you will always have a backup.

There are dozens of styles and brands from which to choose, and we're not going to recommend any. What is comfortable and works for one player is totally different for the next.

However, when it comes to shoes, the most important factor is comfort. If the shoe is just right — not too tight or not too loose — the player should play at maximum potential without any complaints.

For beginning players, sneakers suffice quite nicely. As a player grows older, he may want a more sophisticated soccer shoe that allows him to turn faster and do more things with the ball.

Slowly, but surely, English and European soccer jargon has caught on in the United States. In the United Kingdom, soccer shoes or cleats are known as *boots*. An entire uniform set is also known as a *kit* over there.

How soccer uniforms are numbered

Numbers are mandatory on the back of all jerseys, according to rules set up by FIFA (Federation Internationale de Football Association), the sport's worldwide governing body.

Traditionally, names did not appear on shirts because teams supposedly had no individuals and the only name that matter was that of the team. Today, many professional teams and clubs put the names of players on the back of the jerseys for obvious fan identification. Some youth clubs and coaches like the names on jerseys because it gives the players an opportunity to feel like the heroes from professional soccer that they are trying to emulate on the field. Others don't like it because they feel it clutters up the shirt.

Traditionally, professional soccer teams are numbered by position. Assuming that you're using a 4-4-2 formation (that's four defenders, four midfielders, and two forwards; see Chapter 9 for more on formations), the goalkeeper is No. 1. The defense are numbers 2 through 5, the midfielders are 6 through 8 and 10, and the forwards are 9 and 11. The midfield general or creative midfielder usually is given No. 10 as a sign of respect and leadership. Substitutes get numbers 12 and higher. Of course, there have been exceptions.

Nowadays, the numbering doesn't matter as much at the youth level, although the low numbers generally go to the defense, and goalkeepers generally get the numbers 1, 0, 00, or even 18.

Some players prefer a high number for the year they were born or settle because they couldn't get the low number they wanted.

The first time numbers were used on shirts in World Cup play was in 1938.

What about advertising?

Other than the occasional team sponsor, advertising shouldn't appear on any youth soccer uniforms, but pro uniforms are another story.

While uniform advertising has been part of the European soccer scene and culture for years — sponsors names can be much more prominent than the actual team name or logo on the jersey — it really didn't get a start in the United States until the early 1980s, when the Pennsylvania Stoners (Allentown) of the American Soccer League contracted Alpo, the dog food company, as a sponsor. It helped the club pay some bills, although opposing fans taunted the Stoners players by barking at them.

Some interesting shirt tales

To most Americans, Brandi Chastain has left an everlasting image of ripping her shirt off to celebrate the U.S. clinching the 1999 Women's World Cup. But taking off shirts or using shirts to send a message has been around for years.

Some of the most memorable incidents or situations:

✔ When the U.S. was trying to qualify for the 1972 Olympics, former Cosmos goalkeeper Shep Messing faced an Honduran player in a penalty-kick tie-breaker after regulation; the winner would go to West Germany. In an attempt to intimidate the opposition, Messing said some things to his foe and took off his shirt and whipped it around several times, as though he was a mad man. The player kicked the ball over the net, and the U.S. qualified.

✔ Players have thrown their shirts as methods of protest. Former Manchester United star George Best threw his shirt at the feet of Fort Lauderdale Strikers coach Ron Newman during a North American Soccer League match in 1977.

✔ In a more productive, but definitely a more costly way of using a shirt, Dallas Sidekicks forward Tatu would take off his jersey after scoring a goal in an indoor game and throw it into the crowd in celebration.

✔ Brazilian star Tostao gave his shirt and World Cup winners medal to the surgeon in Houston who had performed two operations on a detached retina before the 1970 competition.

✔ After France dropped a 2-0 decision to West Germany in the 1986 World Cup semifinals, French stars Michel Platini and Jean Tigana, instead of trading shirts with the victors, threw their jerseys into the stands in Guadalajara, thanking fans for their support.

✔ To celebrate a goal he scored against the Netherlands in the 1998 World Cup quarterfinals, Argentina's Claudio Lopez pulled up his jersey to reveal an undershirt that said, "Felize Cumpleanos Viejo" — Happy Birthday Father.

Today, advertising is more accepted. In Major League Soccer, each of the 12 teams has a sponsor. The sponsor names is visible in three places — on the left arm, right leg, and back of the uniform.

The Richmond Kickers of the A-League have taken it yet another step. The Kickers have advertising on the front and back of the shirts and shorts and even on the sleeves. Each spot has a different sponsor. While multiple sponsors may clutter the uniform, the extra money brought in by all that advertising helps the Kickers pay for travel expenses.

If you have a favorite European team and buy replica jerseys, be forewarned: Many clubs like to change the style of their uniforms, so fans have to buy new ones every several years. The reason is money. Manchester United, arguably the world's most famous soccer team, changed its shirt style and colors several times in the 1990s. It even happens in the states as well. The New York/New Jersey MetroStars unveiled their third design entering their fifth season in 2000. The San Jose Earthquakes, who changed their name from the Clash after the 1999 season, had their third uniform change as well. (See the sidebar "Adventures in shirt trading.")

Why goalkeepers don't match the team

Goalkeepers are known as the peacocks of soccer, and for good reason. Because they must wear a different color from their teammates, goalkeepers can wear virtually any type of color under the sun. It wasn't until 1913 that keepers were mandated to wear a different color than the rest of the team, and it wasn't until the 1980s that they could wear a color other than green, yellow, or white.

So, goalkeeper fashions can range from a basic solid color shirt to one that is so outrageous that you need sunglasses to look at it. Former Mexican international goalkeeper Jorge Campos, who played for the Los Angeles Galaxy and Chicago Fire in MLS, wore some outlandish outfits, including a yellow fluorescent one and another that looked like it was a crazy quilt made from all of the colors of a rainbow (see Figure 2-1).

Figure 2-1:
Jorge
Campos and
one of his
outlandish
outfits.

International Sports Images, J. Brett Whitesell

One of the most ingenious designs was one with an archery target on it, obviously giving the opposition a target to shoot at instead of around or over the keeper. The two trains of thought are that if you're wearing a solid, the shooter will have more difficulty seeing the keeper and, if you're wearing bright or outlandish colors, the shooter is more likely to shoot at the keeper.

Why referees are no longer the men in black

Referees used to be known as the men in the black, because that was all they were allowed to wear. In the 1980s, teams began to use black uniforms, which clashed with the referees' attire. Rulings by FIFA, the sports worldwide governing body, have allowed game officials — referees and assistant referees — to wear colors other than black.

In 1999, U.S. Soccer mandated that the official national referee uniform be a gold jersey with black pinstripes, black collar, black cuffs (long sleeves) or no cuff (short sleeves), black shorts, black socks, and black shoes. The alternate jerseys are black and red. The U.S. Soccer referee committee said the current jerseys, black and fuchsia, can be worn through Jan. 1, 2002, to allow referees to accommodate to the change.

Even the liberalization of colors has led to some problem and mix-ups. In the United States' 2-1 upset of Colombia in the 1994 World Cup, referee Fabio Baldas of Italy changed from a silver-gray jersey to a purple one because his original shirt was too close in color to the denim blue and white worn by the Americans. (Of course, Baldas did not receive a yellow card for an unnecessary delay of game.)

Accessories: Things That Might Come in Handy

To some players and coaches, soccer is more than just a game; it can be a lifestyle. Bringing more than your uniform and shoes to a game could mean a major difference between feeling comfortable and playing well and feeling out of it.

- **Sports bras:** Brandi Chastain made the female sports bra famous by whipping off her shirt after converting the winning penalty kick at the 1999 Women's World Cup. But it's been around for almost ten years.

  Actually, a sports bra is not as provocative as you might think. Depending on the style, it can look like a mini-halter top or the top part of a two-piece bathing suit (no, not as small as a bikini).

Women and girls should not choose sports bras on style, but rather on how comfortable they are and how they support a player.

✔ **The bag:** Depending on the level of player, the team or club may supply each player with a bag so that he or she can store and organize accessories. If not, these bags can be purchased at sporting goods stores. They run from approximately $30 to $75, depending on size, quality, and needs.

✔ **The little stuff:** For the traveling player, it never hurts to have extra shoe laces (in case yours break while tying them), extra studs — aluminum or rubber, depending on your shoe — and a stud wrench, just in case.

✔ **Warm-weather gear:** If you play in November or early March with a frost or snow on the ground, you may want to try a long-sleeved undershirt and some gloves specifically designed for field players. You won't be called a wimp for using them. For a World Cup qualifying match against the United States in Foxboro, Massachusetts, in November 1997, virtually the entire El Salvadoran team wore gloves to keep warm.

✔ **Another type of footwear:** If you play in tournaments and want to give your feet a rest from your soccer shoes between matches, why not try a sandal? Like shin guards, you can choose from many styles, sizes, and colors.

✔ **First-Aid kits:** Whether you're a coach or player, bringing along a First-Aid kit for bumps and bruises at practices and games certainly doesn't hurt. While the team or club may have a larger selection of medical supplies or even a trainer at the field, a First-Aid kit bought in a drugstore may suffice in an emergency situation.

Keepers are a different breed and, of course, need different types of equipment. Goalkeeping gloves are a must, unless you want to come home with several blisters after every practice and home game. The other important items are elbow pads to protect against the shock of hitting the ground.

If they have to stare into the sun for a half, some keepers prefer a hat or eye or sun glare resistance, that black substance that is put under the eyes to cut down the glare. Keepers also like to bring bottles of water in the net and take water breaks when their team is on attack. Some goalkeepers even like to bring a good luck charm into the net. Former Canadian National Team and NASL goalkeeper Tino Lettieri liked to bring a stuffed parrot, Ozzie, into the goal for games. But pssst! That's a secret. Please don't tell anyone about that.

Adventures in shirt trading

One of the most unique traditions of soccer is shirt trading after matches, especially important games (see figure). No one knows when this custom actually began, although Professor Julio Mazzei, former coach of the New York Cosmos and confidant of Brazilian superstar Pelé, believed that it started at the 1954 World Cup in Switzerland.

"Since then, it has become a tradition," Mazzei said. "Some players start collecting special shirts from special idols, such as Pelé. After some games, players fought for Pelé's shirt, so Pelé decided not to play politics and gave it to the first player who asked for it."

International Sports Images, J. Brett Whitesell

When Pelé's Santos team went on tour, the club took as many as 100 jerseys with the famous No. 10.

"That wasn't only for exchange after the game, but for dignitaries," Mazzei said. "It was incredible. One time his shirt was used for a raffle for charity.

Mazzei estimated that Pelé gave away more than 20,000 shirts in his career.

Santos and Pelé experienced a scare before a match against the Japanese National Team at Olympic Stadium in Tokyo in May 1972.

"We were concerned about the security," Mazzei said. "There was no fence around the stands to keep the spectators out.

"Santos came onto the field wearing their traditional white shirts. Santos was just joining on the field when fans started to run onto the field to take Pelé's shirt. When this happens, Pelé likes to take his shirt and throw it far away. It gets the mob away from him.

"In the process of taking off his shirt, someone grabbed it and started suffocating him. Our goalkeeper, Claudio, who was playing his first game since returning from a severe knee injury, saw that and jumped into the middle of the crowd. In the process, he broke his thumb. He saved Pelé, but could not start the game. It took 35 minutes to clear the field."

That's the Way the Ball Bounces

The ball is supposed to be a player's best friend. If a player is serious enough about the sport, he will have several balls around his house (or garage or basement) and will find an excuse to kick it around even in the snowiest of winters.

Face it. Without a ball, you don't have a game. And without developing skills on a ball, you don't become a decent player.

While growing up in Brazil, Pelé and his friends did not have a soccer ball to kick around and to play games. Instead, they wrapped rags into a ball. Some other children have tried newspapers.

In fact, a number of U.S. players, including Eric Wynalda and Cobi Jones, prefer to kick a tennis ball or a ping-pong ball to develop those special skills needed to shoot and pass the ball.

For years, the traditional soccer ball had been brown or black and made of hard leather. Looking back, it seems a miracle that more players did not go to the hospital after heading the tough rawhide ball.

Today, balls are made out of plastic and synthetic leather and, depending on the manufacturer, have unique designs on them.

Traditionally, soccer balls have 32 panels, although newer models have as few as six to cut down wind resistance. The most basic models, which should be used for the beginning player between the ages of four and seven, are plastic. For the intermediate and advanced player, hand-stitched balls are more appropriate.

Virtually every league and competition, including the World Cup, seemingly have official balls.

Size does matter

Depending on a players' age, you have three different sizes:

- **The No. 3 ball:** This 10-ounce ball is recommended for players between the ages of 4 and 7 because it is small enough for small feet. Using this size ball allows children to learn to dribble, shoot, and do throw-ins.

- **The No. 4 ball:** This 12-ounce ball is recommended for players between the ages of 8 to 12 as they grow.

- **The No. 5 ball:** This ball, which the pros use, is for players 13 and up. It is 14 ounces and 27 to 28 inches in circumference.

The cost factor

Depending on the quality of material and type of construction, the prices of soccer balls vary greatly.

The lower priced basic balls can range from $15 to $25. Mid-quality ones are priced around $40, and top-of-the-line balls, which are used by professional leagues and serious international competition, run $75 and up.

Entry-level balls usually have a butyl bladder and an outside casing that uses processed rubber, not unlike the one found on a car's tire. These balls retain their air and shape very well, but have a much harder feel, especially when it comes to heading.

As the quality of the ball increases, so does the material. In the middle and top models, polyurethrane is used as the casing. These balls usually have more stitches and softer surfaces and are aerodynamically superior as well.

Many soccer store managers and owners recommend using the less expensive balls for practice, and the higher price models for games.

Dealing with child labor

In recent years, a tremendous furor over child labor producing soccer balls in Pakistan made national and international headlines. It was estimated that as many as 250,000 children work. (Child labor usually refers to children 14 or younger.)

Pakistan produces more than 75 percent of the world's market in soccer balls, which produces more than $1 billion in revenue annually.

"The whole thing is a cottage industry," said U.S. Women's National Team player Julie Foudy, who visited the city of Sialkot in the Punaj province of Pakistan to witness the situation up close in 1997. "There is one city that does the stitching, and there are villages around it. They drop off bags of soccer panels and stitches. Nothing is monitored. They literally have their kids stitch to process more soccer balls a day."

Several years ago, an agreement between the Sporting Good Manufacturers Association, the World Federation of Sports Goods Industry, the International Labor Organization, UNICEF, and Save the Children Fund, prevented children under the age of 14 from producing soccer balls and helped make changes in community and family attitudes in accepting the laws of child labor in the industry. According to SGMA officials, this agreement has been followed and enforced.

Chapter 3

The "Where" of Soccer

Soccer has four basic positions — goalkeeper, defender, midfielder, and forward. While each one has a specific duty, every position is called upon to take on the responsibilities of another position at some time or another in a game. In this chapter, we look at each position and examine the duties of each one. You may be surprised.

The Four Basic Positions

Soccer has four basic positions — goalkeeper, defender, midfielder, and forward (see Figure 3-1). But each position is not limited by its specific duty. For example, forwards have been known to defend in certain situations. (Just remember how far Mia Hamm, the all-time leading scorer in women's soccer, came back to defend against the Chinese in the Women's World Cup championship game.) Many times, defenders join the attack and are able to dribble great distances because of confusion in the opposition's defense. And even goalkeepers, who make their living primarily with their hands, have been called on to dribble the ball up the field or pass the ball to a teammate after they are not allowed to use their hands after a *backpass* — a pass from one of their defenders.

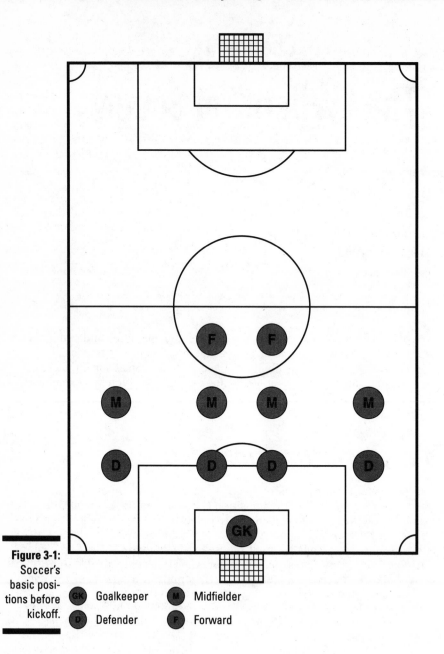

Figure 3-1:
Soccer's
basic posi-
tions before
kickoff.

U.S. National Team and D.C. United midfielder Ben Olsen feels that youth players should play different positions when they are younger so that they can figure out which position is right and most comfortable for them.

"It is very important because you get different looks of the game. You learn all the techniques. You learn shooting. But you play a little defense, you learn defensive heading. Playing out wide, you learn crossing. It helps you become a complete player. It also helps you to get on the field. You want to be on the field to play at a good level. At a young age, it is very, very important to play different positions.

"At one time or another I played every position on the field. I remember playing sweeper, right back, left back, in goal, too. I remember getting scored on one or two times. This was state team stuff, so I wasn't that young. I definitely am a better player for it because I have done that (playing every position)."

But as a player gets older, she should learn how to specialize in one position, according to National Team midfielder Eddie Lewis.

"One of the most important things — and I think Americans haven't done a good job of this, coaches included — is sort of specializing on a particular trait on the field. There are a lot of good Americans who are very good all-around players on the field, but aren't really specialists at a particular position, like Chris Armas, a defensive midfielder. He has the unbelievable knack of filling holes and clogging things up. He does it better than anyone. It's probably the best thing he can do. I think players definitely should know what they do well, whether its strikers, defenders, balls in the air, it doesn't matter. Do it and make sure you do it really well."

Goalkeepers

The *goalkeeper* is the last line of defense. They are the ones that protect the goal and are the only players allowed to use their hands on the field — inside the 18-yard by 44-yard penalty area. If a goalkeeper handles the ball with her hands outside of the box, she is awarded a red card and the attacking team is given a free kick from that spot.

Goalkeepers can run anywhere on the field, but they don't want to wander too far up field and be caught out of position, leaving the net unattended when the opposition gains possession of the ball. They usually stand in the middle and in front of the net, although many keepers will walk to the top of the penalty area and even beyond when their team is on attack. They do that to follow the action so that they can be prepared just in case the opposition gets a counterattack and moves down the field quickly.

A goalkeeper may not handle the ball for long stretches of the game and then may wind up under intense pressure for several minutes. They must be alert and have a strong personality to be able to handle criticism and blame because every goal is their fault, even when it isn't.

While size shouldn't matter, more and more professional teams opt for larger keepers. In the end, what it comes down to is quickness and vision. If a keeper can react quickly and force the opposition to shoot wide without ever touching the ball, then she has done her job.

If you want to impress your soccer buddies, always call the position a goal-keeper or keeper. If you call it a goalie or goaltender, they'll definitely know you're a novice. For more on the goalkeeper position, see Chapter 8.

U.S. National Team goalkeeper Kasey Keller has more big game experience than any other American keeper over the past decade, performing for Millwall and Leicester City in England and for Rayo Vallecano in the Spanish First Division.

"There are no secrets. It's basically all about a few basic things. It's different ways to get the same job done — not to let the ball into the net. You have to have quite bit of a thick skin to be a goalkeeper. You have to be able to put everything else aside. When you've made an error, you might have a lot of the game left. If you conceded a bad goal, your team might score two. If you've gone into a shell and have a nightmare of a game, all of a sudden your team is trailing, 3-0. You have to live with that and tell yourself that the next game you have to play better."

Defenders

Defenders play in front of the goalkeeper and are responsible for stopping attacks by the opposition or at least limiting them or slowing them down. Like goalkeepers, defenders must be ready to accept the blame because they can play a marvelous 89 minutes, let down for 30 seconds, and allow the opposition to score the winning goal.

Teams usually use four defenders, although the number of players on the back line depends on the formation. If a coach wants an attack-minded forma-tion, he might use only three defenders. If the coach wants to play conserva-tively and not allow many scoring opportunities or goals, five defenders or as many as six — which is quite rare — may be deployed.

Defenders must be team-oriented enough to play within a system but must be flexible as well to play man-to-man marking or zone defense:

- *Man-to-man marking* is when a defender follows his man closely, wher-ever he goes on the field and never leaves him unless otherwise instructed by the coach. The advantage to this defense is that the defender knows which player he will cover the entire match, so he won't miss or mix signals when the opposing team attacks. He knows what his job is. The disadvantage is that you can match up well with three or four defenders, but have a serious mismatch in the fourth or fifth one, due to speed, experience, or height.

✔ *Zone defense,* or *zonal marking,* is when a defender picks up a player when she comes into her area. The advantage is less pressure than on man-to-man coverage. The disadvantage is miscommunication in that two players go for the same forward, leaving another uncovered for several seconds, which just might be enough time to score or set up a dangerous play.

Because of the different formations (see Chapter 9), the responsibilities of defenders can change.

There are primarily two types of defenders:

✔ **Outside fullbacks:** They play on the left and right wings (sides) and patrol the flanks and rarely move from their sides of the field.

✔ **Central defenders:** There are several different variations of using central defenders, the most common being two central defenders playing alongside each other. Some teams have moved away from the sweeper-stopper combination in the center of defense that was popular for so many years and use two players who perform next to each other in the middle of the defense. A *sweeper* is not unlike a free safety in football, in which he is the last person in front of the goal. In front of the sweeper is the *stopper,* who usually must cover the opposing center forward, although assignments can vary depending on the strength, weaknesses, and speed of the players.

More and more, defenders have been called on to become part of the attack. This is called *overlapping,* in which a left or right fullback overlaps from his position into the attacking half. Overlapping can surprise the opposition on occasion, especially when they are not looking for it.

U.S. National Team defender Jeff Agoos, who also performs for three-time Major League Soccer champion D.C. United, feels that you cannot be a free spirit to play defense well.

"Part of a defender is born inside of you. It can be developed as well. You have to read the game and know where the ball is in a team concept. You're not an individual as a forward, where you can do your own canvass. You have to be more organizational and be more in tune with the goalkeeper behind you and the midfield in front of you.

"There are two basic types of defenses — man-to-man and zone. Playing man-to-man gives you more accountability. You are against another guy. Players run all over the field. If one man beats you, he can beat the whole team. In a zone defense (playing in a specific area on the field), you keep a little better shape, and you also can go forward. It is very important to remember to communicate. You don't want to stick to the mentality 'It's not my guy, it's your guy' because (attacking) players are running from one zone to another."

Midfielders

No player runs more in a game than a *midfielder*. Not only must the midfielder be the most fit player on the field, but she should have the ability to go on the attack and defend. She is the ultimate link between defense and attack. Teams generally use four midfielders, although the number utitlized in a game can vary from three to as many as six, depending on strategy.

Many games are "won in the midfield," which means if the midfield has a superior game or outplays the opposition, then its team has an excellent chance of winning. If a midfield is weak or is experiencing a poor match, teams sometimes opt to ignore the midfield — that is, defenders try long passes to the forward line. Unless the team has the right type of players to pull over this type of manuever, this tactic doesn't always work.

Defensive midfielders

Defensive midfielders also are known as stay-at-home midfielders.

Teams usually use one in a match. But depending on the formation used, a team can have as many as two defensive midfielders, which is rare. The U.S. National Team used two defensive midfielders in the 1998 World Cup.

Because American sports fans are accustomed to following the ball, they sometimes have difficulty to appreciating the midfielders, although their coaches, teammates, and opposition certainly do.

The best defensive midfielder has the ability to take on the opposition's top player, break up plays by picking off errant passes, quickly start the transition from defense to offense, and sometimes even become part of the attack.

Attacking midfielders

The prototype *attacking midfielder* was the great Diego Maradona, a player who not only can find a teammate with a well-placed pass, but one who can dribble around defenses and score himself. These types of players are few and far between and the truly great ones only come about once every ten or 20 years.

If an attacking midfielder excels at one of those attributes, you have a special player. A midfielder with superior skills who can pass without getting intercepted many times is one of the most sought-after players in the world. Called No. 10s, after the number they usually wear, they are, not surprisingly, the on-the-field leaders who can organize a midfield or attack. They want the ball in tough situations, whether it is trying to get the ball out of their defensive end or to set up a teammate for a tying or winning goal late in the match.

PLAYER'S TIP

The best of the best

The best defensive midfielders in Major League Soccer today are members of the U.S. National Team — the Chicago Fire's Chris Armas and D.C. United's Richie Williams. They have different styles, but they both get the job done quite efficiently. Armas is as complete a defensive midfielder as the U.S. has had, while Williams will drive the opposing team crazy, almost like a gnat or mosquito that doesn't want to go away.

Michelle Akers, who defined the forward position for women a decade ago, is now defining what a defensive midfielder does. Her work ethic and skills have made her the best women's defensive midfielder in the world.

Armas has become a MLS all-star in his role as defensive midfielder for the Chicago Fire and has established himself as a vital member on the U.S. National Team.

"The defensive midfielder anchors the midfield. It is the link between the defense and forwards and other attacking players. A defensive midfielder has to definitely win (50-50) balls, break up plays, and start attacks. When you are in a 3-5-2 formation, you are the fourth defender. You are in the center of everything."

If a defensive midfielder is doing his job, then the opposition's ends, and his team's offensive push begins with him.

"Some of the best balls are early balls because if you can look for Claudio (Reyna, U.S. National Team midfielder) or Peter Nowak (Chicago Fire midfielder), the quicker things are going to happen. You need vision to be able to see things. The faster you see things, the less times you'll lose the ball," Armas added.

D.C. United midfielder Marco Etcheverry of Bolivia, Major League Soccer's Most Valuable Player in 1998, fits that mold perfectly. Los Angeles Galaxy's Mauricio Cienfuegos of El Salvador and Tampa Bay Mutiny's Carlos Valderrama also play that role for their teams very well. Not many American players have been called on to play that role in MLS because coaches would rather go with more skilled and experienced players, and many coaches don't have enough confidence in U.S. players yet.

Claudio Reyna, who performs for the Rangers in Scotland, is the closest thing to a great American hope as an organizing midfielder. While he has showed some flashes of brilliance, Reyna still has yet to reach his full potential in this most difficult position.

There are other types of offensive-minded midfielders as well. If a midfielder has the ability to fire accurate, long shots, he could wind up playing the role of a withdrawn forward. These players may not possess the same playmaking ability as an Etcheverry, but they have a dangerous long-range shot from just outside the penalty area.

Attacking midfielders also can be used on the left and right wings. New York/New Jersey MetroStars midfielder Tab Ramos, before he suffered a pair of devastating knee injuries, was a superb midfielder on the right side. His dribbling ability allowed him to penetrate deep on the wing and either cross or pass the ball to a teammate or take a shot himself.

Despite their incredible success internationally (two World Cup championships and an Olympic gold medal entering 2000), the U.S. women don't have a true No. 10 organizing their attack. Carin Jennings was the creative force before back problems forced her to retire in 1996. Since then, it has been attacking midfielder by committee and teamwork between midfielders Julie Foudy, Kristine Lilly, occasionally Michelle Akers, and Tisha Venturini off the bench.

U.S. National Team midfielder Claudio Reyna fears that the creative midfield general, the No. 10, may become a thing of the past at the international level.

"Just in general, all over the world, I think No. 10s are disappearing more and more each year. Soccer teams are being built around the team concept. The modern midfielder has to be able to attack and defend as well. Sometimes players have great ability at a young age — 17, 18, or 19 year-olds — but coaches tend to leave them out because they don't defend well. I think that's the way tactics of coaches develop around the world. I think you see more faster, athletic teams. And with that I think the No. 10 position has suffered. Until I became a professional, I basically played my whole career behind the forward and only worried about attacking. Once I got to Europe, I found out I had to work on my defending. I think there are still some classy No. 10s around the world, like Zinedine (Zidane of France) or (Argentina's Ariel) Ortega, who still do it well."

The working or all-around midfielders

The all-around midfielders are the workhorses of a team, running up and down the field playing offense and defense equally well. Doing both is not easy. Some working midfielders sometimes turn into decent defensive midfielders because of their work ethic.

The best example of a working midfielder is Kristine Lilly of the U.S. Women's National Team. She literally never stops running in a game and is a force at both ends of the field. Remember, Lilly was stationed at the right place at the right time on the goal line as she headed a shot away to deny China a goal in overtime of the Women's World Cup championship game that was won by the U.S.

Forwards

The primary responsibility of forwards is to score or help another teammate to score. In short, forwards get all the glory. But just as they can be seen as heroes for scoring an important goal, they can quickly be turned into scapegoats when the team isn't producing goals.

Strikers

Not all forwards are strikers or center forwards — players who usually get paid the most money in the world to fill the net. Strikers are probably the most opportunitistic players on the field, ready to pounce on a loose ball in the penalty area and turn it into a goal. Sometimes it is a matter of being in the right place at the right time.

A great striker scores an average of one goal per game in professional leagues. In international and World Cup competition, a strike rate of once every other game or a third of the matches is considered decent.

In lower levels of competition, scoring rates of more than one goal per game is considered superior.

A striker must be able to handle the ball and be quick in tight quarters, score under pressure, and take physical abuse and fouls from the opposition. He also must be someone who can bounce back from failure; a striker who scores once out of every five shots has an excellent rate.

Wings

Players who play on the right and left flanks are called *wings*. Their primary responsibilities include ball possession, dribbling, and crossing — sending the ball into the middle of the penalty area for the striker or center forward and stretching the defense by playing as wide as possible. This responsibility doesn't preclude them from scoring, although they are not known as great goal scorers. Some midfielders have become superb wing players, such as former San Jose Earthquakes midfielder Eddie Lewis, who has developed this talent of penetrating deep on the left side and sending crosses and passes into his teammates in the middle.

The great American scoring hopes

Eric Wynalda, the U.S. Men's National Team's all-time goal scorer with 34 goals in 106 matches, wasn't a traditional striker. He preferred to play a lot on the left wing.

In many respects, the United States is like many countries in the world in trying to find that consistent goal scorer up front. A number of players have done well in MLS, but have yet to step to the forefront internationally.

PLAYER'S TIP

Getting free

Every forward has his way of getting free from his marker. Some use their speed, while others utilize their guile or experience. Former German international striker Juergen Klinsmann used to literally run in circles — albeit huge circles — so that defenders could not figure out the path he would take to the goal. In fact, in one game with Tottenham Hotspur in the English Premiership, Klinsmann was on the move so much that he played on the left and right sides and also in the middle.

U.S. National Team forward Eric Wynalda, who has scored more goals than any other U.S. men's player at the international level, understands a forward will experience more failure than success and must have a certain resiliency.

"You never know when the ball is going to bounce your way. You have your instincts, and you're wrong more often than you're right. You do the best you can. When it finally happens, you could have gone out there and tripped all over yourself for some 90 minutes and for that one split second, you knew how to do it and you've won the game. That's how our lives are. We know we're going to take criticism. We know we're going to get beat up. We're going to get kicked more than anyone else on the field. That's one guy's job — to destroy everything that I create. It's a lot easier to knock the blocks down as opposed to building them up. It's something that you've got to have. You have to be able to block everything out and stick to your guns, so to speak."

Roy Lassiter, who was traded to his third team (from D.C. United to the Miami Fusion) during the off-season, is the league's all-time scoring leader entering the 2000 season. While he has been prolific in the league, he is not one who can create his scoring chances, but rather someone who needs a great midfielder to set him up. He has yet to prove himself internationally, although Lassiter may be an asset coming off the bench late in matches thanks to his speed.

Brian McBride has established himself as the target man because of his superior heading ability. He was the only American to score a goal in the 1998 World Cup. He is adept at *finishing* — scoring — with head shots up front for both the National Team and the Columbus Crew.

Dallas Burn Jason Kreis may wind up being the man U.S. men's national coach Bruce Arena has been looking for up front. Kreis enjoyed a breakthrough season in 1999, becoming the first player to crack the 15-15 barrier, scoring at least 15 goals and assisting on 15 others in a season. He finished with 18 goals and 15 assists. He was named the 1999 MLS Most Valuable Player.

Perhaps the next great American international goal scorer will come from Landon Donovan, who earned MVP honors at the Under-17 world championship in 1999, Chicago Fire forward DaMarcus Beasley, who finished second, or Fire teammate Josh Wolff.

The U.S. Women's National Team is overflowing with outstanding goal scorers. At the top of the list is Mia Hamm, the all-time international scoring leader with 115 (at press time), although linemate Tiffeny Milbrett has forged a reputation as a dangerous goal scorer. During her prime as a striker, Michelle Akers was considered the best on this planet and stands with 104 in her career.

Chapter 4

Laws of the Game

*S*o, you want to be a referee — or simply understand what's happening on the playing field?

Soccer rules are basic, although they can seem to be complicated to the beginner. In this chapter, we give you the rules you need to know to call the shots in soccer. Their official title is the Laws of the Game, which is derived from the English, while virtually every other sport has a rulebook.

The rules, ahem, laws of the game, have been modified over the years. Every February or March, the International Football Association Board (IFAB), which is comprised of members from England, Scotland, Wales, Northern Ireland, and FIFA, the sport's worldwide governing body, meet to decide proposed rule changes and experiments.

In some years, very little or nothing changes. In others, there are several modifications. For example, after a rather boring 1990 World Cup in which scoring was at an all-time low for the competition, the board adopted several rules to speed up the pace of the game and give some advantage, albeit small, to the offense. One change was to force the goalkeeper to distribute the ball six seconds after making a save. Before that, some keepers were holding the ball for a good 30 seconds. Another modification was restricting *back passes* (from defenders and midfielders back to their own goalkeepers) to force teams to move forward with the ball.

U.S. Soccer, the sport's governing body in this country, abides by the decisions of the IFAB, although local youth leagues can modify the rules for younger players.

Law 1: The Field

Any field must be longer than its width. For professional, amateur, college, and youth teams 16-years-old and higher, the minimum and maximum field dimensions range from 45 by 100 yards to 100 by 130 yards. For international matches, the dimensions can range from 70 by 120 to 80 by 120. Fields as small as 60 yards by 110 yards are used in Major League Soccer.

The penalty area, the area in which a goalkeeper is allowed to use his hands, is 18 yards in length by 44 yards wide. The best way to remember the size of a goal is 8 by 8, as in 8 yards wide and 8 feet high.

For youth soccer, the field sizes vary depending on the age group of the players. The U.S. Youth Soccer Association recommends a field of 25 by 20 yards for Under-6 players who play in a 3 versus 3 competition, 50 by 30 yards for Under-8 players in a 4-a-side competition, and 70 by 30 yards for Under-10 players in an 8-a-side competition. Many competitions for players under the age of 8 do not have penalty areas.

While not specifically covered in the laws, many, if not all, game officials, make a pregame inspection of the field to make sure that the dimensions and markings are correct.

In their A-League franchise opener at Downing Stadium in New York City in 1995, the New York Centaurs had a rather embarrassing situation. The left side of one of the penalty areas was shorter than the right side. Because there was not enough time to realign the field, the game was played under those rather dubious conditions. Fortunately, there were no fouls or potential penalty kicks in that area as the Centaurs dropped a 1-0 decision to the Montreal Impact.

Basketball games have been delayed after a player has shattered an artificial glass backboard. While it certainly is a rare occurrence in soccer, a game was delayed by a broken crossbar. While celebrating a goal during the 1980 North American Soccer League season, New York Cosmos forward Mark Liveric hung on to the crossbar, bringing down the goal. Even though he scored, Liveric received a yellow card for delay of game.

Law 2: The Ball

The ball must be made of leather or a similar substance, have a circumference of between 27 to 28 inches, and weigh between 14 to 16 ounces. At the professional level, it is advised to have several backup balls to help speed up play, or in the case of youth soccer, if the ball is kicked into a wooded area.

Because there was no official World Cup ball at the time, there was a controversy over which ball would be used at the championship match between Uruguay and Argentina at the very first World Cup in 1930. Referee Jean Langenus allowed Argentina to use its ball in the first half, the Uruguayans in the second. Using their ball, the Argentines took a 2-1 halftime lead. The Uruguayans rallied with 3 second-half scores using theirs en route to a 4-2 victory.

Law 3: Number of Players

Teams start each match with 11 players (10 field players and a goalkeeper) although teams can play with as few as seven. If the number of players drops below seven, the referee stops the match and files a report to the league.

Teams are limited to three substitutions in official international matches, although there are exceptions at various levels and leagues. In Major League Soccer, for example, teams are allowed three substitutions and a fourth for the goalkeeper. The laws allow up to as many as five subs per match, as long as both teams agree and the referee has been informed before the match. Once a player has been substituted for, he cannot return. An assistant referee signals a substitution by holding his flag at both ends over his head (see Figure 4-1).

Figure 4-1:
The assistant referee signals to the referee that it's time for a substitution.

Players are not allowed to leave the field or return to it without the permission of the referee. If they do, they are subject to a yellow card.

Of course, the younger end of youth matches — 4- and 5-year-olds — can use as few as 3 players.

If a team has more than 11 players on the field, the referee will stop the game and then caution (yellow card) the extra player. If a team with an extra player scores before the referee figures out the infraction, the goal stands. However, the referee could be in hot water with his superiors because he will have to file a report about the incident.

The referee was forced to stop the 1988 NCAA Division I men's second-round match between Seton Hall and Brooklyn College after the latter team was reduced to six players with a minute remaining, due to five red cards in what was a violent confrontation. Seton Hall, who was leading at the time 5-2, was awarded the victory and advanced to the next round.

Law 4: Player Equipment

The basic equipment includes a shirt, shorts, socks, shin guards, and foot gear (see Chapter 2 for more details). Shin guards, thanks to a fairly new law, must be worn, be covered entirely by the socks, be made of rubber, plastic, or a similar substance, and provide a reasonable amount of protection.

Players are not allowed to wear anything that a referee considers dangerous to the player or an opponent, such as jewelry. Jewelry can get tangled with another player, or the opposition can grab it to impede the player.

Goalkeepers must wear colors that distinguish them from the rest of the players and game officials.

In many instances, referees do prematch inspections of players' equipment, making sure that teams comply with the laws and that studs on the bottom of shoes, or *cleats* as they're called in America, are plastic and not metal.

India had to drop out of the 1950 World Cup qualifying competition because FIFA refused its request for its players to play in their bare feet.

Law 5: The Referee

In many respects, the referee is God on the field. Even if he is wrong or mistaken, what he says is final. The laws of the game state, "The decision of the referee regarding facts connected with the play are final."

The referee is called the man — or woman — in black or the man or woman in the middle. "Middle" can be interpreted as to the middle of the field, middle of arguments, or middle of controversy.

Referees don't run indiscriminately up and down the field. They usually follow a diagonal system from one end of the field to the other. They will either whistle for stoppage and start of play, mostly for fouls, or signal for direct and indirect kicks and penalty kicks.

There is no steadfast rule that prohibits a referee from talking to the players. Whether they do may depend on their interpretation of the laws or their personalities. Some referees never say a word, while others actually like to talk and banter with the players, keeping the lines of communication open.

The referee's duties include enforcing all laws. That includes making decisions on abandoning — or calling off — a match, making decisions on whether an injured player should be removed from the field, ensuring the safety of the participants (for example, whether the field is playable or whether the players are wearing the correct equipment), being the timekeeper, and keeping a record of the match. After a game, the referee must file a match report with the proper authorities, detailing any disciplinary action he or she may have taken.

Not all referees are perfect or make the right calls all the time. During a North American Soccer League playoff game in 1977, referee Henry Landauer awarded Rochester Lancers midfielder Francisco Escos two yellow cards, which is the equivalent of a red card and automatic ejection. Landauer had booked so many players that he apparently had forgotten about Escos's first yellow. Escos remained in the match until he was substituted. The Lancers went on to prevail over the Toronto Metros-Croatia in a shootout, 1-0. Toronto protested the yellow card decisions (or lack thereof), but the league turned it down.

Law 6: Assistant Referees

If the referee is God, then assistant referees must be his or her angels. Their duties are entirely different than the referee's. Assistant referees, with flags in their hands, run up and down either side of the field, following even with the path of the ball. They signal which team gets possession of the ball when it goes out of bounds and results in a corner kick, goal kick, or throw-in. They also notify the referee when a play is offside — keeping in line with the last defender so as to be in a good position to make an offside call. They alert the referee when a foul is committed out of the view of the ref.

For years, assistant referees were called linesmen, but FIFA, wanting to be politically correct and gender correct, changed the designation to assistant referees.

Although the position's responsibilities are not officially defined in this section of the laws, the fourth official usually sits on the sideline in the middle of the field and handles the game's paperwork. Those responsibilities include regulating substitutions, ensuring that there is decorum on both teams' benches, posting any added injury or stoppage time, and being ready to be called on in case the referee or one of the assistant referees does not show or is injured during the game.

Because of the dearth of game officials at the youth level, many players' parents are called on to be the assistant referees. Their primary responsibilities include determining whether a player is offside and ball possession when it goes out of bounds. Don't be surprised if you are called on to be an assistant referee someday. (For more on youth soccer, see Part III.)

Once in a while, you may see an assistant referee standing with his or her flag extended to get the attention of the referee. The assistant referee may be signaling that a goal was offside, that the referee missed a committed foul, or that he or she has some other important communication.

Law 7: Duration of the Match

In every major pro league in the world and in all international matches, games last 90 minutes, which are broken into a pair of equal 45-minute halves, with a halftime interval not more than 15 minutes. Before a match, teams can agree to alter the time — if there is not sufficient light, for example.

Again, the length of a game may vary for youth soccer. The younger the team or age group, the shorter the game length. Under-10 leagues schedule 60-minute games (30-minute halves), while Under-12 matches last 70 minutes (35-minute halves).

What separates soccer from other timed sports is *stoppage time*. Stoppage time, which is also known as injury time, is time added on by game officials at the end of a half or game to make up for wasted time, substitutions, injuries, players arguing with the referees, or game officials explaining a ruling to coaches. In other words, there is a mystery as to when a half or game will be actually finished.

Brazil discovered that the hard way during a first-round match of the 1978 World Cup against Sweden. With the score tied at 1-1, Brazilian Zico sent a corner kick that eventually went into the net. Referee Clive Thomas of Wales, however, whistled the end of the match before the ball entered the net. It cost Brazil the win.

For the first time, Major League Soccer will introduce stoppage time and extra time for its 2000 season. That means the league will keep time like the rest of the world. In the final minute of each half, the fourth official will hold up a sign designating the number of minutes that will be added on. It usually varies between one and four minutes.

Some leagues allow for *extra time,* or overtime. Extra time usually is decided through one or two 15-minute "Golden Goal" periods, meaning the first team to score is the winner.

Law 8: The Start and Restart of Play

Actually, a game doesn't start with the kickoff, but rather the coin toss, which allows the winner of the toss to either kick off or defend a goal. This procedure takes place in the center circle between the captains of each team. The winner of the toss has the option of kicking off or deciding which goal it will defend.

Kickoffs are done at the start of the game and second half, after goals are scored, and at the start of each extra-time period.

One of the rarest plays in soccer is the *dropped ball,* which restarts a game after a temporary stoppage for any reason not mentioned anywhere else in the laws. The referee drops the ball between a player from each team at the place where the play was stopped.

There are some interesting twists to this law. A player can score a goal directly from a kickoff, but that same player can't kick the ball twice until another player has. If a player commits that infraction, an indirect free kick is awarded to the opposition at the spot of the foul.

Depending on the weather conditions, picking the right direction in the opening half could determine a team's fate. If it's a windy day, a team might want to play against the wind in the first half to get the difficult part of the game out of the way. Many teams have scored and taken leads while playing against the wind, giving them confidence and an advantage entering the second half.

Law 9: The Ball in and out of Play

This law is straight and to the point. The ball is out of play when it has fully crossed the goal line or sideline (touchline). It is considered in play after the ball rebounds off a referee or assistant referee standing on the field or after hitting the crossbar, goalposts, and corner flags.

The player with the ball may stand out-of-bounds dribbling the ball while it is in play.

Law 10: Method of Scoring

Using Law 9 as a precedent, it is easy to determine what is a goal and what is not. The entire ball has to pass over the goal line between the posts and under the crossbar to be considered a goal. As long as there have been no committed fouls by the attacking team, the goal will stand. If the attacking team is called for a foul, the goal is negated and the ball is given to the defending team.

The most famous and controversial instance of whether the ball was totally over the goal line was England forward Geoff Hurst's extra-time goal that determined the 1966 World Cup championship in a 4-2 victory over Germany. With the score tied at 2-2, Hurst fired a shot that bounded off the crossbar and into the goal. Or was it? The Germans claimed it wasn't a goal, saying that part of the ball touched the goal line. But linesman Tofik Bakhramov of the Soviet Union ruled the ball had crossed the line. The referee agreed and the goal stood.

Law 11: Offside

The offside law is the most controversial, confusing, and misunderstood of all the laws by players, coaches, fans, and even some game officials. The offside law was instituted to prevent "goal hanging" or "cherry-picking" by forwards near the opposition's goal, although some critics of the modern game feel that it restricts the offense. A referee raises his flag when a player is offside, as shown in Figure 4-2.

A player is offside when he or she is nearer to his or her opponent's goal than both the ball and the second-to-last opponent, when the ball is played. A player is not offside if he or she is not in his or her own half of the field or level with the last defender.

You should remember that it is not an offense to be in an offside position. The player has to be interfering with play, interfering with an opponent, or gaining an advantage by being in that position. There is no offside if the player gets the ball directly from a corner kick, throw-in, or goal kick.

If offside is called, the defending team is awarded an indirect free kick from where the infraction occurred.

Figure 4-2:
The
assistant
referee
holds his
flag upright
and then
straight out
to signify
that a player
is offside.

The key phrase is "when the ball is played." Sometimes a play or pass happens so quickly that it is difficult to determine if a player is onside when the ball is played. Game officials have been instructed that if there is any doubt about a player being offside, not to call it. It's that simple.

Law 12: Fouls and Misconduct

Two types of fouls exist:

- ✔ **Serious offenses that result in a direct free kick.** Direct kick fouls are awarded when a player kicks, trips, charges, jumps at, strikes, or holds an opponent, or handles the ball with his or her hand. (See Law 13 for more on direct kicks.)

✔ **Technical offenses that result in an indirect free kick.** Indirect kicks are given if a player performs in a dangerous way, obstructs an opponent, or stops the goalkeeper from releasing the ball from his hands. Conversely, a goalkeeper can be called for an indirect free kick if he or she takes more than four steps before releasing the ball, touches the ball with his or her hands after it was thrown or kicked by a teammate, or wastes time. (See Law 13 for more on indirect kicks.)

For the really more serious offenses, there are yellow and red cards, which are awarded by the referee by standing near the offending player and raising the proper card over his head (see Figure 4-3).

✔ **Yellow cards:** Called cautions, yellow cards are awarded for several offenses. The list includes demonstrating unsporting behavior, showing dissent (verbal or nonverbal), continually fouling players, actions that delay free kicks or corner kicks, failure to give the opposition 10 yards on free kicks or corner kicks, or re-entering the field of play without the referee's permission.

✔ **Red cards:** Very serious and violent actions can result in a red card. Those fatal offenses include if a player is guilty of a serious foul or violent conduct, spits at an opponent, denies the opposition a goal or an obvious goal-scoring opportunity by a physical foul or a hand ball, uses really offensive, insulting, or abusive language, or receives a second yellow card in the same match.

Figure 4-3:
The referee gives either a yellow or red card for a dangerous or violent action.

The best way to remember yellow and red cards is to compare them with traffic lights. If you get a yellow card, you are being warned or cautioned to slow down. If you receive a red card, you are being told to stop, as in stop playing.

You can describe a red card in several ways. The American way is an ejection, or seeing red. Overseas, it is a player receiving his marching orders or having a player sent off.

Not every foul results in a free kick. It is left up to the referee's discretion to whistle a foul or allow play to continue if the attacking team has a good chance of scoring or placing a shot on goal. A foul would work against that team. It is called the advantage rule. To demonstrate that he or she realizes a foul has been committed, the referee will make a sweeping movement (see Figure 4-4) with both hands, telling the player to "play on." Sometimes, if play is stopped after a serious foul, the referee will award the offending player a yellow card.

Despite all these fouls, infractions, and cards, there still is fair play in soccer. The ultimate act of fair play comes when Team A has the ball, and a player on Team B is injured. A Team A player kicks the ball out of bounds to stop play, so a trainer or doctor can examine the injured Team B player. After play resumes, Team B will throw the ball back into play to a Team A player. In fact, FIFA and many leagues — professional, amateur, and youth — hand out an annual Fair Play Award to players and teams who exhibit the best acts of sportsmanship.

Figure 4-4:
The referee tells the players to "play on" even after he realizes that a foul has been committed.

Some players go their entire career without receiving a red card. Others collect them like they are baseball cards. Take the case of former Brazilian World Cup star Branco, who incurred a Major League Soccer record of three red cards in only 11 matches while performing for the New York/New Jersey MetroStars during the 1997 season. That is equivalent to eight ejections per season. There are no maximum number of red cards allowed, although leagues have the authority to suspend or ban a very violent player.

In international tournaments such as the World Cup, receiving a red card in a game will suspend a player for the next game in that competition, sometimes two games.

Law 13: Free Kicks

There is a slight but important difference between free kicks. A direct kick needs to be touched only by the kicker before a goal can be scored, while an indirect free kick must be touched by at least two players (it could be an attacker and/or the defending team) before it can become a goal. If an indirect kick goes directly into the opponents' net, a goal kick is awarded to the defending team. If an indirect kick goes directly into the attacking team's goal, a corner kick is awarded to the defending team.

There are two distinct referee signals for free kicks. For a direct kick, the referee holds his arm out, perpendicular from his body before whistling for the play to begin (see Figure 4-5). For an indirect kick, the referee holds his arm up over his head (see Figure 4-6).

Regardless of the type of kick, the defending team must give the kicker at least 10 yards from the ball, only if the attacking team asks for 10 yards. If not, the referee can award the offending player a yellow card. Referees sometimes fail to enforce this, giving only seven, eight, or nine yards. That becomes an advantage for the defending team. If a team chooses to do a quick free kick, the required distance does not need to be enforced.

Even the greats sometimes forget the difference between a direct and indirect free kick. Belgian star Enzo Scifo did it in his team's 2-2 draw with Paraguay in an opening-round match of the 1986 World Cup. He apparently scored a goal off a free kick for a 3-1 advantage late in the match — or so he thought. It was nullified because the call actually was a free kick. Another player had to touch the ball before it went into the net. The same thing happened to Bulgarian midfielder-forward Hristo Stoitchkov in the 1994 World Cup. He thought he had scored a goal off a direct kick in a 3-0 loss to Nigeria. But it was disallowed because it was an indirect free kick.

Figure 4-5:
The referee
signals for a
direct kick.

The A-League, the Second Division of U.S. professional soccer, has mandated that opposing players give 15 and not 10 yards for free kicks, in an attempt to stimulate more shots on goal. And besides, if the referee gives 12 yards instead of the full 15, the kicker still has plenty of room to shoot.

Law 14: Penalty Kicks

A *penalty kick* is a free kick that is awarded in the penalty area. Immediately after the infraction is committed, the referee points to the penalty spot, as shown in Figure 4-7 (and probably gets ready to hear a mouthful from the defending team).

The attacking team shoots the ball from a white circle 10 yards from the goal called the penalty spot. The shooter must wait for the referee's signal before attempting the shot.

Except for the goalkeeper, players from both teams must stand outside of the penalty area, beyond the penalty arc, that semicircle located at the top of the penalty area 10 yards from the penalty spot.

Figure 4-6:
The referee
signals for
an indirect
kick.

Goalkeepers now are allowed to move laterally before and during a penalty kick, but they cannot move forward prior to a kick. If they do and save the shot, the referee will make the shooter retake the kick.

If the shooter doesn't score, but the defending team infringes — prematurely steps into the area — the attacking team will be awarded another try. If the shooter scores and one of his teammates steps into the area, the kick must be retaken.

If the goalkeeper saves the penalty kick, but can't maintain possession of the ball, the kicker or any of his or her teammates is allowed to score off the rebound shot. If the shot hits the post or crossbar, the kicker cannot score off the rebound, but his teammates can.

Figure 4-7:
The referee
points to the
penalty
spot,
signaling a
penalty kick.

Law 15: Throw-Ins

A *throw-in* is awarded when the ball crosses the touchline (sideline).
Possession is given to the opponent of the team that lost the ball out of
bounds. The thrower, who must be standing with both feet on the ground
behind the touchline or have both feet on the line, holds the ball with both
hands. He or she must start the throw from behind his or her head. If the
throw-in is not performed correctly, the referee can award the ball to the
opposition for a throw-in.

The throw-in has many of the attributes of an indirect free kick. The thrower
cannot touch the ball until it is touched by another player. A goal cannot be
scored directly off a throw-in, although many teams have started scoring
sequences from the restart. Opponents are also prohibited from jumping and
waving his or her arms to distract the thrower.

In college and in some U.S. pro leagues, players are literally allowed to go
head over heels on throw-ins, because the thrower is allowed to do a somersault before throwing the ball. It can look spectacular, but if the ball is off
target and does not go to a teammate, it is a wasted opportunity.

Law 16: Goal Kicks

A *goal kick* is given when the ball travels over the goal line and was last touched, shot, kicked, dribbled, or headed by the attacking team. Either a goal kicker or a teammate takes the goal kick, which must originate anywhere in or on the line of the 6-yard box.

Remember, the ball is in play on a goal kick when it is kicked beyond the penalty area. Opponents must remain outside the area on goal kicks. If the ball does not go beyond the penalty area, the kick is retaken.

Law 17: Corner Kicks

A *corner kick* is awarded to the attacking team when the defending team kicks or heads the ball over the goal line or the goalkeeper parries the ball over the crossbar. The referee will point toward the corner where the kick will be taken (see Figure 4-8). The kick is then taken from the corner of the side of the field where the ball went out of bounds. Players from the defending team must stand at least 10 yards away.

The kicker, also known as the *server,* is allowed to stand out of bounds before kicking the ball toward a horde of players jockeying for position in and around the penalty area. His teammates will try to score while the defending side will try to clear the ball out of the area. A player also can score directly off a corner kick, but it is very rare and takes a lot of skill and a bit of luck to make it happen.

Law 18: "Common Sense"

Okay, it's not one of the official rules or laws of the game, although game officials are called on by occasion to use common sense when formal rules do not provide a clear answer to a problem. This kind of thinking has alleviated and avoided many potential problems. Say that a corner kick flag might be broken, and a suitable replacement cannot be found. The referee would not call off the game, but he would find a way to make the corner visible with an appropriate object.

Figure 4-8:
The referee
signifies a
corner kick
by pointing
to the
corner from
where the
kick will
originate.

Part II

Fundamentals of the Game

The 5th Wave   By Rich Tennant

In this part . . .

Whether you're a player, parent, fan, or coach, this part gives you the inside scoop on the fundamentals of the game. You find out how to dribble, pass, receive, and head the ball, as well as how to successfully protect the goal. We also share with you some perfect plays and strategies.

Chapter 5

Some Amazing Feats with Your Feet

In This Chapter

▶ Finding out how to dribble

▶ Using more advanced moves

The most basic of all soccer skills is dribbling. If a player can't dribble a ball, then he cannot play the game. Every player, including the goalkeeper, must be able to dribble the ball at some level of competency. Some time during a game you will be called on to move the ball on your own, whether you have open space or all available teammates are covered closely by the opponent.

Discovering the Lost Art of Dribbling

Dribbling is a lost art these days. *Dribbling* is the ability to carry the ball past an opponent while being in control, whether by using is a series of simple taps or a fantastic move around a foe. Many coaches — youth, amateur, and pro — downplay the role of the individual and emphasize teamwork. There is certainly nothing wrong about passing the ball to a teammate. But, in a match, you may be forced to dribble in a tight situation or have the chance to take on an opponent to create a scoring opportunity or even score a goal.

Knowing when to dribble

Many times, knowing when to go off on a long dribble and when to pass to a teammate comes down to timing, awareness, and experience. If you dribble through two or three players and then lose the ball to a fourth, you're wasting your time. You have to know the strengths and weaknesses of the opponents before taking that kind of risk.

If you constantly take on an opponent by dribbling, they will know what's coming. If you add passing and teamwork into the equation, you will be that much more of a better player and your team will be much more dangerous. (See Chapter 6 for more on passing.)

The best players in world play as though the ball is part of their foot. Take a look at the way they dribble the ball. Dribbling is very natural to them, as if they were born with this skill. Saying that, even the greatest players needed to perfect dribbling over a period of years.

Dribbling: Easy to learn, difficult to master

Dribbling should be fairly easy to learn. But can you dribble in tight quarters with a player or perhaps two, literally on your back? Do you have a move or two in your repertoire that will allow you to break free of your coverage?

The best dribblers can move the ball swiftly, without looking down, and have a few tricks up their sleeves — or is that pant legs?

The key to dribbling is to kick the ball ever so lightly with both feet without losing control at a comfortable speed for you. You should touch the ball with the inside of your shoes, for the most part, for better control. But you can touch it with the outside of your shoe as well (see Figure 5-1). The very best players in the world can dribble the ball adeptly with both feet. Most people usually favor one of their feet as the superior skilled foot to dribble the ball in close quarters, although both feet also are used.

The most common mistake made by a beginner is constantly looking down and not knowing which direction you're going.

Figure 5-1:
The basic
dribble.

The greatest dribblers in the world

Everyone who plays soccer can dribble, but only a handful of players can do it with such accomplished skill or speed. Here are five players who literally could do amazing feats with their feet.

George Best: Best could do it all: jump high, score goals, set up teammates, and dribble past opponents. Unfortunately, because of his undisciplined lifestyle, his potential was never fully explored.

Johan Cruyff: Cruyff was gifted with an uncanny change of speed that allowed him to glide past opponents. The ball was never more than a few inches away from his body. This Dutch master was able to completely change directions at full speed, which is a rarity.

Stanley Matthews: Matthews was one of the great wing players of the English and international game, able to whisk down the right side

past an opponent thanks to his superior dribbling skills.

Diego Maradona: In his prime, Maradona was the best. His finest moments came during the 1986 World Cup, when he dribbled through the English defense over 60 yards to score what is considered the greatest goal ever. He added a similar score against Belgium in the semifinals several days later.

Pelé: Not only was Pelé exceptional in virtually every skill, but he was surrounded by superb players as well, especially on the Brazilian National Team. Opponents had to give Pelé his space because if they didn't, another player would hurt them.

As you become more comfortable with the ball, you will pick up speed and become more confident. Unless you are gifted, dribbling speed comes only with time.

As long as you follow the proper techniques, you can never do enough dribbling. The best thing about dribbling is that you can practice by yourself. If you practice enough, you may invent a move or two that suits your style or skill level. (See the next section for more on dribbling moves.)

We can't stress enough the importance of keeping your head up as you're dribbling. If you don't, you literally will run into trouble, whether it is the opposition or teammate. You won't know where you are on the field, and you won't have the ability to make quick decisions to help your team.

Jazzing Up Your Dribbling

A player who just dribbles up and down the field becomes very predictable. Teams are able to double-team you and strip you of the ball. You need at least one or two moves in your repertoire to keep the opposition honest. Who knows? You may invent a move yourself someday.

Former U.S. National Team and current New York/New Jersey MetroStars midfielder Tab Ramos, regarded as the best dribbler produced by the United States, said he did not learn that skill in practice, but rather on his own and playing by himself and with his friends.

"I grew up just playing in the streets. We played with no rules or no goals," Ramos said. "We played two against two or three-on-three. . . . I was one of those kids who didn't want to give the other kids the ball. I didn't want anyone else to have it.

"At my soccer camp, I don't emphasize passing. I want them to dribble. Once you're 17, it's too late to learn to dribble."

Once a player gets command and a feel of the ball, he can then take dribbling to the next level.

"The key to dribbling is when you make your move," Ramos added. "It's the explosion when you take off at the time when the defender isn't expecting it. It doesn't have to be a great fake or move. That's how you get the advantage. You can time it correctly when he's coming at you.

"Some guys have great fakes. What I do is slow down more and make the change of pace more dramatic. I don't know how to explain it. It's kind of a feeling more than anything else."

In the following sections, we share with you ways to improve your dribbling. We assume that the ball starts on the right foot. (In fact, if you're right-handed, you will feel more comfortable starting with your right foot.) To start with the ball on the left foot, just switch the directions.

Changing directions

Before attempting to change directions, you first need to make sure that you have enough space to turn with the ball. You should turn away from your opponent and then use the inside or the outside of your foot, depending where the pass is coming from and where the opponent is (see Figure 5-2). You must avoid exposing the ball to the defender or turning into the opponent. After performing the move, you must accelerate your dribble. As you dribble, always try to keep your body between you and your opponent.

The Cruyff move

Named after Dutch master Johan Cruyff, the Cruyff move is used to surprise the opponent by shifting your weight in one direction and running in another direction.

Figure 5-2:
Turning
the ball.

To do this move, fake like you're kicking the ball with your right instep and then step past the ball with your supporting foot (left foot). Then rotate your right foot so that your toes point downward. Then use the inside of your right foot to make contact with the ball so that it rolls behind the support foot before you play the ball with your left foot.

Scissors move

Like the Cruyff move, the scissors move is used to unbalance a foe. Use this move to switch the ball from one foot to another in an attempt to confuse the opponent.

The ball starts on your right foot. Step over the ball with your right foot as you shift your weight until the ball is under your left foot. Then dribble away with the outside of your left foot.

Zico move

Brazilian midfielder Zico originated this move, which also leaves a foe unbalanced and a step or two behind.

You fake to hit a pass with your foot. You then step over the ball with your right foot as it winds up in front of your supporting (left foot). Spin clockwise, while keeping your body between the ball and defender. Then use your instep to take the ball with your left foot before accelerating.

Shielding the ball

Sometimes you can't pass the ball when you want to because you're waiting for a teammate to get into position. That means you have to keep the ball away from the defender, as shown in Figure 5-3.

To shield the ball, stand sideways to the defender, keeping your body between the opponent and the ball. You also should extend your arm closer to the opponent for balance and to make more room between you and the defender. While doing all of this, keep the ball and your foot away from the opponent and your head up to see what options are open.

Figure 5-3:
Shielding
the ball.

Chapter 6

The Finer Points of Passing, Shooting, and Receiving

In This Chapter
▶ Passing or shooting the ball
▶ Getting fancy with your passes
▶ Receiving the ball

*I*n some soccer games, one player's outstanding performance may settle matters, but over the long haul, one-man teams don't succeed. In other words, as good a player as you may be, you cannot shoulder the burden alone. Even the great Pelé, when he brought Brazil an unprecedented three World Cup titles in 12 years, had a superlative supporting cast.

Even if you are a superb dribbler and shooter, you need your teammates' skills to excel in and win games. If you want to get the ball to take a shot, you must be able to receive passes and settle the ball down quickly. *Quickly* is the key word because big-time scorers have to develop the ability to take in a pass in tight quarters in the penalty area. The rewards can be great — a goal. If the player can't accomplish that task, the ball probably will be cleared by the defense.

The Three Basic Passes

There are three basic passes — forward, square, and back.

The *forward pass* is the most aggressive and most risky of all three because the attacking team moves the ball toward the goal. The length of the pass, the spot from where you attempt it, and the skills of the passer and receiver can all increase your chances of being intercepted.

A *square pass* is a relatively safe pass. Attempt this pass when you're trying to get out of a difficult situation — for example, two opponents are gearing in

Own goals: When passes go awry

The most embarrassing play in all of soccer is the own goal, when a player accidentally kicks or heads the ball into his team's own net. It can happen to the best of players. The best known own goal in recent memory was by U.S. defender Brandi Chastain (shown in figure) in the quarter-finals of the 1999 Women's World Cup. Chastain tried to pass the ball back to goalkeeper Briana Scurry. Instead of passing it to the outside of the goal and keeper, Chastain knocked it to the inside. The goal gave the Germans a 1-0 lead, but fortunately the U.S. rallied for a 3-2 victory.

Some other well-known cases when players have scored against their own team:

International Sports Images, J. Brett Whitesell

✔ **Sudden-death:** While trying to clear a cross by John Harkes in the 1994 World Cup, Colombian defender Andres Escobar accidentally knocked the ball into his own net, the first goal in the U.S.'s 2-1 upset. After a humiliated Colombia was eliminated in the opening round, Escobar was shot outside a Medellin, Colombia, nightclub a week after the team returned home.

✔ **Three in a game:** Democrata defender Jorge Xlino scored three own goals in a single game — in a 5-1 loss to Atletico Mineiro in Brazil in October 1982. Multiple own goals also happen at the highest levels. Leicester City defender Frank Sinclair scored not one, but two own goals, which decided the outcome of his team's opening two matches in the 1999–2000 English Premiership season, a 2-1 loss to Arsenal and a 2-2 draw with Chelsea.

✔ **Early goals:** Arsenal defender Steve Bould managed to score into his own net with his English First Division match with Sheffield Wednesday only 15 seconds old. The goal stood up as Wednesday won, 1-0.

✔ **The long shot:** Most own goals happen in the penalty area. In 1981, Tampa Bay midfielder Keith Bailey sent a 25-yard pass back to his goalkeeper that resulted in an own goal in a 4-1 loss to the New York Cosmos.

✔ **Fan interaction:** The Baltimore Blast fans tricked Cleveland Force forward Keith Furphy into scoring one during the Major Indoor Soccer League playoffs in 1982. They counted down the final seconds of the game. Believing the game was over, Furphy booted the ball into his own net. The referee, however, claimed that six seconds remained, and the goal stood as Baltimore registered a 10-5 win.

on you. In this case, you need to give the ball to a teammate who is open or to a better ballhandler.

The *back pass* is the most conservative of all passes. Use this pass to get out of a tough defensive situation — for example, when you have little or no room to pass the ball forward or you need to give your team an opportunity to regroup. If you're not careful, however, you can run into problems. When passing to a goalkeeper or another teammate, you need to remember where the enemy is because the opposition can run out of nowhere and steal or intercept the pass. Many back passes have been transformed into goals — as in the player scoring into his own net. (This is probably the most embarrassing of all plays in soccer.) You can solve most potential back pass and own-goal problems with proper communication and positioning, although the luck factor is always involved as well.

Making Forward Passes and Taking Shots

The most important pass players will make is a forward one. While there is a time and a place for back passes or square passes, try to move the ball forward most of the time, whether it is out of the defensive zone or into the attacking zone.

And when you get into the attacking zone and toward the penalty area, you face the decision of whether you should make a pass or take a shot.

When shooting or passing, the same follow-through and action is involved. However, a shot usually must have a lot more velocity when it's attempted.

The push pass or shot

The *push pass* or *shot* (see Figure 6-1) has two functions: You can use it to pass the ball over short and medium distances or as a shot. When shooting the ball, you need to remember that you need accuracy, not power.

If you're a beginner, keep in mind that the inside of your kicking foot must remain square — parallel — to the target as the toes of your kicking foot are slightly higher than the heels as the ankle remains locked. Your support foot should be pointed at the target as it is on the same plane as the ball, which must be struck through the middle or just above it.

The more experienced players do not necessarily have to align their body to attempt a pass or shot.

Figure 6-1:
The push
pass or
shot.

The instep pass

The *instep pass* (see Figure 6-2) is used to get the ball to a teammate over a huge distance in the air or on the ground.

When attempting a low, ground pass, approach the ball from a slight angle and then put your support foot alongside the ball, pointing toward the target. Then drive your kicking foot through the ball, hitting it with the inside of your instep.

Figure 6-2:
The instep
pass.

For an air pass, again approach the ball from a slight angle. This time, however, put your support foot alongside (but also toward the back) of the ball before you drive diagonally through the underside of the ball using the lower instep of your big toe. At the instant of contact, lean back ever so slightly to give the ball some loft.

The outside foot pass

You can use the *outside foot pass* to pass or shoot quickly (usually in the penalty area) in distances of 10 yards or less. Point your kicking foot down and in as your ankle remains lock and your knee is over the ball. While keeping your supporting foot behind the plane of the ball, kick the upper part of the ball to keep it low to the ground.

The chip pass or shot

If you can perfect the *chip pass* or *shot,* shown in Figure 6-3, you've added an important part to your repertoire. While most goalkeepers are aware of the possibility of a chip shot, sometimes they "fall asleep" in the goal. An alert attacking player can bloop the ball over the head of a goalkeeper who has come a bit too far out of the net. This technique is also called *lobbing* the keeper.

Figure 6-3:
The chip
pass.

The best way to attempt a chip pass or shot is to imagine that the ball is on a golf tee. You should kick under the ball to give it height and backspin. As you follow through, use your instep, hitting the ball with the inside of your shoe laces. Your kicking foot should jab into the ground because there is no follow-through. As you perform this manuever, you should put your arms out for balance.

Mia Hamm accomplished this feat against China in the Goodwill Games in 1998, and Mohammed "Nayim" Amar scored a marvelous 45-yard goal on a chip shot with only seconds remaining in regulation over goalkeeper David Seaman to lift Real Zaragoza to the European Cup Winners Cup crown in 1995.

Claudio Reyna, who plays his club ball with Rangers in Scotland, is the midfield general of the U.S. National Team, which means he handles and passes the ball a lot. So, he knows a thing or two about passing and finding the open man.

"When I was young, I went out and got a feel for the ball. To this day, I concentrate on passing well. It's a major part of the sport. I kicked the ball nonstop against the side of my house for hours until my mom yelled at me to come in. That's something that helps. You can get a good feel for the ball. You also learn from mistakes when you make a bad pass or when you kick it incorrectly, you know it's not the right way. You know the right way to feel the ball and how it comes off your foot and it feels right. It comes from a lot of years of practice.

"There are so many things involved in it, from the actual technique of it to how to hit a ball. I often try to make sure each pass is received by the next player in a way that they can do something with the ball and the right pace is put on it. Before you receive the ball, you have to know where you want to go with it. There are so many different things, whether you want to hit the ball on the ground or in the air and whether you want to use your left foot or right foot or inside or outside of your foot, which makes the ball curves in different ways.

"The most important thing is the weight of the pass, so your teammate can receive the ball and they can do something with it as easy as possible. With a pass, you're setting up your teammate for something. It's not giving the ball to someone else because they're open. It's giving it to someone so they can do something with it.

"Passing is a lot of practice, a lot of instinct. You also have to read how the other players are running and their speed as well so you can time the pass correctly. You realize that once you play with teammates, you get to know whether they are lefty or righty. Obviously, you want to play to their preferred foot. Before I pass the ball, I put out as many targets as possible and then find the one person I want to play it to when they're in the most dangerous position."

Back heel pass

The back heel pass is one of the simpler passes. However, it can look spectacular when done correctly, as the ball is played with the back of the foot — the heel — to a teammate. This pass is usually attempted on the run. The attacking player, who may be closely marked at the time, will suddenly flick the ball back to a trailing teammate who is open. If that teammate is not prepared to receive such a pass, he will look rather silly and could lose the ball. Former U.S. National Team player Roy Wegerle mastered this maneuver.

Shooting

Shooting at the goal can be a complicated process. Where do you want to shoot from? Are you at the correct angle? When will you shoot the ball? How much velocity do you put on the ball? Where do you want to place the ball? Into the upper corner? The lower corner? Far post? Near post? Or would you rather pass the ball to a teammate who is in a better position? A lot of this comes with experience, instinct, and even common sense.

Most shots are attempted in and around the penalty area. The closer you get to the goal, the better your chance of scoring. Not surprisingly, the closer you get to the goal, the more difficult it is to put a quality shot on net as defenders usually close down on you once you run into the area.

That's why so many players take shots just before they enter the area or step into the 18-yard box. Determining where and when you shoot depends on the situation or even the goalkeeper. How many defenders are between you and the goal? Can they block the shot? Or perhaps they will screen the goalkeeper, and he won't be able to see your shot until it is too late. Or maybe the goalkeeper has trouble picking up the ball on long-range shots outside of the penalty area.

There is no one way to score goals. Some players like to blast the ball, while others use finesse to beat the goalkeeper. The most important thing is accuracy. If you always fire the ball at 80 miles-an-hour and it lands over the net and in the stands, your shot might look impressive, but ultimately it is useless. However, if you hold back on the velocity to place the shot on net, you should score goals.

Some players, like D.C. United midfielder Marco Etcheverry, have the dribbling and technical ability to work their way deep into the penalty area before shooting. Others, such as Manchester United great Bobby Charlton, rely on a powerful shot from outside the area. Still others, such as U.S. Women's National Team forward Mia Hamm, can score from the right, left, or center of the field or close to the goal or 30 yards or more away from it.

Miami Fusion forward Eric Wynalda knows something about putting the ball into the back of the net. After all, he is the U.S. men's National Team's all-time leading goal scorer. He feels that it is more than just skill that makes a good goal scorer, but rather someone who has instinct and an innovative mind.

"It has a lot to do with getting yourself into positions to score. You have to have the instinct to be able to read the game and know where you need to be. It's just a feeling you get. It's something kids recognize. If somebody keeps finding the right place to be all the time, it's a gift. It's not luck if it keeps happening. It's very important in being a forward.

"Once you get into position, you'll find that people who score a lot of goals score them in a lot of different ways. Being predictable or being good at one thing usually doesn't cut it anymore. I'd say we've overcoached our kids, so we get these kids who are average at everything as opposed to being good at one thing. I was lucky growing up. They recognized that I knew how to be in the right place at the right time.

"I worked very hard on my technique. It's not a big power thing. You don't have to hit the ball very hard. The idea is to beat the goalkeeper. You go through stages in which you are infatuated with putting it into the upper corner. That doesn't matter. If the ball goes down the middle of the goal and still beats him, that's enough. That's what I think is the secret. I tell people that the secret to my success is that I aim for the keeper, and I miss. And I miss a lot. You never will want to put the ball exactly where you want to. When you are put in one-on-one situations with the goalkeeper, just try to get the ball past the goalie.

"You have to find different ways to score. If you go down the field four or five times and go to your right foot and shoot with your right foot, everybody will know what you're up to. You have to figure out different ways. I've had the most success by keeping the ball low. There are opportunities when you have to go high, which is to get over a wall or there is an obstacle. I think 80 percent of the goals I scored have been on low shots. Keeping it low is the hardest thing for a big guy to do."

Making the Ball Do Some Magic: Mastering Difficult Passes and Shots

Players can do more than just passing the ball straight toward a teammate. The more advanced player discovers how to redirect passes and take more difficult shots, score a spectacular goal with his back to the net, cross the ball to a moving target, and even bend balls around defenders and teammates into the goal.

Some memorable goal celebrations

The happiest moment in soccer is scoring a goal (see figure).

The goal celebration can take many forms. Millions of Americans remember how Brandi Chastain whipped off her jersey to reveal a black sports bra after she converted the winning penalty kick in the Women's World Cup final against China in 1999.

Pelé had a signature celebration. After he scored, he would throw a punch into the air with his right arm.

Dallas Sidekicks forward Tatu liked to throw something else. He used to take his shirt off and throw it into the crowd after indoor goals.

Miami Fusion and U.S. National Team forward Roy Lassiter, Major League Soccer's all-time scoring leader, usually likes to spread his arms out wide and run to mimic an airplane.

U.S. Women's National Team midfielder Tisha Venturini celebrates her goals with a backflip, which has become her signature.

International Sports Images, J. Brett Whitesell

D.C. United players have been known to gather in a circle hands in the middle while running in a circle.

Some scorers dance and celebrate in front of their fans, while others throw themselves onto the field stomach first. Other players run to the corner flag and run around it, while yet other goal scorers run to their own bench or coach to celebrate. During the 1994 World Cup, Nigerian players got on all fours, performing a "dog crawl" to celebrate a goal. Players have been known to dance in front of the bench of their former teams, as though they were rubbing it in.

After he scored against Argentina in the 1998 World Cup, Dutch striker Dennis Bergkamp fell to the ground on his back with his arm's outstretched as though he was thanking the heavens.

The volley

One of the most spectacular plays in all of soccer is the *volley,* shown in Figure 6-4, when you shoot or pass the ball in the air before it touches the ground. Timing is everything because you'll look foolish if you miss the ball.

Figure 6-4:
The volley.

As the ball arrives, you must get the knee of your kicking foot over the ball with your toes pointing down and then take a short stroke. (The speed of the ball supplies the power to the pass or shot.) You should make contact just above the center of the ball.

If time and space permits, the shooter should hit the ball while as close to the ground as possible.

The side volley

Like the volley, the *side volley,* if done correctly, can be one of the most beautiful moves in the game (see Figure 6-5). This ploy is used to redirect a pass or a cross on offense or defense.

For a side volley, move into the ball as early as possible, with your body facing the ball and your support foot pointed at the target. Then dip your front shoulder toward your target and at the same time move away from the ball. Before you make contact, your kicking leg should be at the plane of the ball and moving a bit downward. Your body then should rotate toward the target with the laces of your shoe barely above the center of the ball. You must remember to keep the volley as low as possible.

Figure 6-5:
The side
volley.

Bending the ball

Not every ball has to be a straight shot or pass. A player can find ways to literally *bend* the path of the ball around the opposition on shots, crosses, or free kicks.

Say that you usually use your right foot for shots and passes. Then use the inside of that foot to curve the ball from right to left. The opposite goes for left-footed shooters.

Approach the ball from an angle while concentrating your weight on the outside of your support (left) leg as it remains on the ground next to the ball. While leaning backward and away from the ball, point your toes slightly up and hit the outside of the ball with the inside of your right foot.

Eddie Lewis, who plays left midfield for the U.S. National Team and Fulham in England, has the uncanny ability of being able to cross the ball into the middle or to the right side to a teammate. Having the ability to cross the ball to a target, whether it is moving or stationary, has become a lost art, in many instances, in soccer.

"The three most basic crosses, the ones that I try to master, are the driven cross, the bending cross, and the dink or chip cross. The driven cross, more or less, gives the ball just back spin. I'm usually out wide near the touchline (side-line). When you see guys crashing the (penalty) box, you try to drive one in.

"Then you have a bending cross, which is probably the most common one. It is probably the most effective because you can lead a player a little bit. You can bend it behind the defense. A lot of times, defenders don't want to touch it because they are afraid of knocking it into their own goal because they are running toward their own goal. It's a real dangerous situation.

"And finally then there is the dink or the chip, which a lot of times if you get pushed into the endline and the whole defense is screaming back to get in front of the ball, you pop one back to the 18-yard line (at the top of the penalty area) to the second wave of runners. A lot of times, it is a very effective cross. So many defenders have pulled in close and you can put the ball over them. You get a late midfielder such as Claudio (Reyna) or (Chris) Armas running onto those type of balls.

"The most important part before you get technical or where you want to place the ball is your body positioning as you approach the ball for a cross. As you are dribbling north to south on the field, the cross is more east and west. The biggest challenge is how to adjust your body and not to try to hit the ball 90 degrees at a full sprint going forward. That adjustment and timing takes a lot of practice and lot of time to develop. Once you are able to sort of pull your run out a bit,you are approaching it with more of a straight-on run. As I take my last dribble, I take a couple of steps to the left and come in to the ball. I have a much easier angle to hit the cross. That is the most important thing in crossing.

"Probably the most difficult next phase is the ability to look up and look inside (toward your teammates) before you get back down to the ball, so you know where the players are going. Probably the biggest challenge to the player is that you have to know where the guys are going to be. As you learn to cross the ball, you know there are safer crosses than others. There are particular spots in the penalty box that I'll hit, and I don't have to hit with a ton of pace, regardless of where the runner is at that time. He can get to that ball. At times, a guy crossing the ball won't try to hit a player on the head and will aim for those spots, hoping one of the runners gets to it. That, again, comes with a lot of time and experience.

"I have hit a million great crosses that because the run or timing is not right they have not been able to get on the end of it. That's what makes the game so difficult."

The bicycle kick

While the *bicycle kick,* which is also known as the scissors kick, is for the more advanced player, it cannot be forgotten because it is one of the moves that makes soccer such a beautiful game. The kick combines control, power, balance, timing, and a sense of style.

You don't see many bicycle kicks because it is the most difficult of all shots and moves in the game. Like a volley, if it is done correctly, it will look majestic. If not, you can fall to the ground awkwardly (and injure yourself if you don't fall properly) and look rather silly in the process. Just ask Brazilian defender Roberto Carlos, who missed the ball completely when he tried to clear the ball out of the penalty area with a bicycle in a 3-2 win over Denmark in the 1998 World Cup.

To attempt a bicycle kick, stand with your back to the goal. As the lofted ball reaches you, fall backward parallel to the ground. Then lead with one leg and follow through with the other to snap at the ball. After you kick the ball, use your hands and arms to brace your fall and absorb the shock. You don't want to land on your back.

Bold beginners should be supervised when attempting this maneuver. In fact, the beach may be the perfect venue to practice a bicycle kick before you get the hang of it because the sand can brace your fall.

Ramon Unzaga from the Basque region of Spain reportedly used the first bicycle kick in 1914. He eventually migrated to Chile, and the Argentine press was so impressed with his kick that they called it the *chilena.* Brazilian star Leonidas da Silva perfected the bicycle kick in the 1930s and 1940s and several generations later, another Brazilian player, Pelé, made it famous. Mexican star striker Hugo Sanchez and Argentine great Diego Maradona became modern-day proponents of the bicycle. And yes, bicycle kicks can be spectacular, even when a player misses the target. During the U.S.'s 2-1 upset of Colombia in the 1994 World Cup, defender Marcelo Balboa attempted a bicycle kick that barely missed the goal by inches.

As it turns out, the best demonstration of a bicycle kick occurred during the movie *Victory,* when Pelé scored the tying goal for the prisoner-of-war team against the Germans in this fictional World War II film. Pelé's spectacular kick was shown up close and in slow motion from various angles. The price of renting this movie is just worth watching Pelé attempt the kick and convert the shot.

Receiving: The Other End of the Pass

Receiving the ball is just as important as passing it. After all, if you're going to be a good teammate and an all-around player, you not only have to pass the ball, but know how to receive and trap it as well and then run or take a shot. If you can't take in the ball within a reasonable amount of time and move quickly, the opposition will be all over you.

Depending on the height of the pass, you can take in the ball with your foot, chest, thigh, or head.

The foot

You can receive virtually every type of pass with your foot (see Figure 6-6). You can make life easier for yourself by assessing the situation before the ball arrives and determining how you will receive the ball. You should move into the path of the ball as early as possible. If your opponent is on your right side, then play the ball across your body. If your foe is on the left side, withdraw your foot upon contact to cushion and turn the ball. You also have the option of receiving the ball with the outside of your foot to keep it away from the opponent. Balls also can be controlled in the air with the inside of your foot. The moment the ball makes contact with the leg, you should withdraw it to cushion the ball.

The most common receiving mistakes include being too stiff when the ball arrives and not looking up until after the ball has arrived.

Figure 6-6:
Receiving the ball with your foot.

The chest

You can receive a ball with your chest when it bounces off the ground or when you're trapping the ball in the air.

For ground balls, lean forward from the waist up so that you are over the ball. Then extend your arms for balance, with your hands inward and thumbs pointing down while on the balls of both feet.

When the ball comes in through the air (see Figure 6-7), have your body weight concentrated on the balls of both feet. Extend your arms with your hands open and thumbs up to balance yourself. Instead of leaning forward for a bouncing ball, lean backward from the waist. As the ball arrives, withdraw from the contact a bit and relax your knees. When the ball falls to your feet, make sure to redirect the ball away. The key is to relax the body to absorb the speed of the ball.

Figure 6-7:
Receiving
the ball with
your chest.

The thigh

You should use your thigh to receive a flighted ball that is lower to the ground. These balls can be line drives or land around thigh level.

To do so, extend your hands for balance and angle the receiving thigh a bit downward. While on the balls of your support foot, use the fleshy part of the thigh to take in the ball and then withdraw your leg, as shown in Figure 6-8.

Figure 6-8:
Receiving
the ball with
your thigh.

The head

Use your head to receive the ball when it's high in the air. As in other trapping maneuvers, you must be on the balls of your feet with your arms extended for balance. As when taking a head shot, you should hit the ball with the hairline of your forehead. As the ball arrives, lean backward from the waist down.

Forward Tiffeny Milbrett, one of the leading goal scorers for the U.S. Women's National Team, doesn't score her goals by accident. Many times, she will get a cross from the right wing from teammate Mia Hamm. In international soccer, the slightest hesitation or wrong move means the difference between keeping possession and taking a shot on goal or losing the ball. That could be the difference between winning or losing a world championship.

"It's one of the most important things because that's what keeps your team having possession of the ball," Milbrett said. "To be able to do that, you should know where your defender is, so you know whether you have to stop it (the ball) completely or keep moving it. When you receive the ball close or a few yards away from you, you want to keep it moving. You want to either sweep it back or to one side or the other to keep that defender away so they can't camp on you.

"At any level, you must be aware of where your defender is, whether they are really tight on you on one side. That way, when you are preparing to receive the ball, you can receive it away from the defender. If they are tight on you behind, you can receive the ball and knock it straight back to yourself away from the defender."

Chapter 7

When You Have to Use Your Head

In This Chapter

▶ Heading the ball

▶ Flicking the ball

▶ Taking up medical concerns

*W*hile not used as much as dribbling, heading the ball can play a vital part of team's game in many areas. A player can head the ball as a pass to a teammate. Or he can use it to win a *head ball,* or air ball, at midfield. Or the midfielder or forward can use it as a weapon as a shot on goal. Or, on the other side of the ball, a defender can head a high ball out of harm's way in front of his net.

However, the medical community has concerns about heading. In this chapter, I tell you how to head correctly and discuss the concern of injury.

Mastering Basic Heading

Heading must be done properly. If a player heads the ball off the top of his head and not his forehead, he will look rather silly and probably will not help his team one bit.

To head the ball properly, the player must assess the flight of the ball and time his leap to head the ball at the highest part of his jump. With his eyes open and mouth closed, the player should strike the ball with the hairline of his forehead. To accomplish that, he should lock his neck and keep his upper body rigid and thrust forward from his waist (see Figure 7-1).

Figure 7-1:
The correct
way to head
the ball.

To head the ball down toward the ground, the player must strike through the top half of the ball. To head the ball in the air, such as clearing the ball out of the penalty area, the player should hit below the middle of the ball.

You should literally keep your eyes on the ball when heading. You should only close your eyes at the moment of impact because you might head the ball with your nose or the top of your head.

You also should avoid running backwards when heading the ball. You will not get enough power to control the header.

Taking a head shot

When using a header as a shot, you should not take it outside the penalty area. You're most likely to be successful around the 6-yard goalkeeper box off of crosses, corner kicks, and successive headers. Anything more than an 8-yard shot usually loses its velocity and accuracy.

Heading off some misconceptions

Most people assume that the tallest players are the ones that control all air balls, but that isn't necessarily so. Sometimes a smaller, more athletic player can out-jump a taller player for the ball. For example, Pelé was all of 5-foot 9-inches, yet many of his goals were scored off of head shots.

Many times, players will execute diving headers when shooting at the goal because of the velocity generated. If you decide to try this technique, you need to throw out your arms in front of you, below your shoulders. Then hit the ball with your forehead while bending your knees and relaxing your arms to cushion his fall, as shown in Figure 7-2.

Figure 7-2: Shooting a goal with a head shot.

Using glancing or flick headers

A *glancing* or *flick header* is used to change the path of the ball a bit, yet to keep it traveling in the same direction.

To flick the ball, extend your arms and snap your head when the ball arrives while keeping your eyes open and mouth closed. Then make the bottom of the ball glance off the top of your forehead, as shown in Figure 7-3.

Figure 7-3:
Brian
McBride
heads the
ball.

International Sports Images, J. Brett Whitesell

Columbus Crew and U.S. National Team forward Brian McBride is considered the best at heading the ball in the United States. He demonstrated his unique ability by scoring off a head shot and setting another up during the CONCA-CAF Gold Cup in February 2000. Actually, the goal he set up against Colombia was more spectacular. Goalkeeper Brad Friedel booted the ball from the U.S. penalty area to McBride, who was standing outside the Colombian penalty area. McBride then headed the ball to Chris Armas in the area, and the mid-fielder hit the ball on a volley past the goalkeeper. Even though his 6-foot-1 height has helped make him dominant in the air, McBride stressed that a player doesn't have to be tall to excel at this skill.

"You always want to head the ball with your forehead," McBride said. "If you head it with the side of your head, you're bound to have more headaches. When the ball is coming at you, keep your eyes open and watch it into your head. You always want to attack the soccer ball. You always want to hit it. Don't let the ball hit you. The main thing is to head the ball with strength.

"When you get that down, when you have enough of a touch, you can start doing other things, such as flicking the ball.

Some basic heading drills and games

Unless a player finds a solid wall to practice heading the ball against (the side of your house is not an option; just ask your parents), heading is best done in groups of two or three players. Among some of the best-known drills:

✔ **Basic drills:** Basic drills come in several variations. If you're practicing in pairs, stand 10 to 12 feet apart and throw the ball back to each other so that your partner makes a standing jump to head it back. If you want to practice running toward the ball, stand 15 yards apart and repeat.

✔ **Heading volleyball:** The only drawback to this exercise, which you should use only for players age 11 and up, is that you need a net or something similar to separate the sides. But this drill may improve your heading. Treat it like a volleyball game — the object of the game is to head the ball back and forth over the net — and give points when a team is unable to head the ball over the net.

Handling the ball is not allowed, unless it is for serving. Unlike volleyball, in which the taller players are sometimes at a greater advantage, the better skilled players with their heads can dominate. You can do a variation of this drill in which only feet are involved.

✔ **Heading for the goal:** Use this drill with four regulation-sized goals, which you place in a square in a 40-x-40 yard area. At each goal, you have a header (the attacker), goalkeeper, passer (or server), and a player who chases the ball. The ball is either tossed or kicked to the attacker who tries to score via a header. Each player gets five tries before switching positions.

✔ **Heading juggling:** Have pairs of players compete heading the ball back and forth to see which one can complete the most exchanges without the ball falling to the ground.

"I learned to head the ball first at practice. When I would do drills warming up at indoor soccer, I got sick and tired of kicking the ball against the wall. I tried heading it. It felt comfortable. Since then, it's been an important part of my game."

Heading and Head Injuries

Over the past several years, a few reports and concerns from the medical community have raised the possibility of head injuries from heading and concussions (when players hit their heads together). In 1999, a study in the Netherlands published by *The Journal of the American Medical Association* (JAMA) raised concerns that heading, concussions, and continuous strikes by the head would lead to chronic traumatic brain injury to amateur soccer players.

Remember, that study was done in the Netherlands. Doctors in the United States have not come out against heading.

If done correctly, soccer coaches and officials say that injuries should be nonexistent or kept to a minimum. If a player continues to head the ball the wrong way, then injury can occur. Players who want to develop their heading skills should work on it in practice with their coach. If they literally want to get a head up on everyone else, they might consider going to a soccer camp to get special one-on-one instruction on that particular skill.

Chapter 8

Protecting the Goal

• •

• •

Goalkeepers are definitely a different breed. They need to have good reflexes, nerves of steel, and soft hands. They also must have a certain level of mental toughness to be a goalkeeper because that position is the last line of defense. Allowing a goal is your fault, even when it isn't actually your fault. You can make ten incredible saves in one game and give up the winning goal in the final two minutes and be the scapegoat. Saying that, it could be one of the most rewarding positions on the field. Many goalkeepers take on leadership roles and can later further their careers as coaches.

Goalkeepers are considered to be among the most colorful soccer players — in personality and fashion. Some observers feel you have to be "a little crazy" to play that position. But keepers will be the first to tell you that its just part of that mental toughness. Others consider goalkeepers the peacocks of soccer because they can actually wear different jerseys than their team-mates. In fact, they have to differentiate themselves from their teammates, so that there is no confusion as to who is handling the ball with their hands in the penalty area. The on-field fashion show can range from basic solid colors to a fluorescent green and/or yellow jersey, similar to the one that Mexican Jorge Campos wore at the 1994 World Cup.

Why Should You Be a Goalkeeper?

At one time or another, a player should play every position on the field to get a real feel for the game. That includes goalkeeper, even if it is for only half a game or a scrimmage. Who knows? You may surprise yourself, and you may like it and wind up being proficient in it. Many goalkeepers — pro and youth — don't start out standing between the posts. They are usually field players, either a defender, midfielder, or forward, who gravitate to the position or are put in there in an emergency situation. It's funny how some of those temporary assignments become lifelong careers.

Sometimes even the most unlikely players wind up in the nets. For the final 11 minutes of the U.S.'s 3-3 draw with China in the first round of the 1995 Women's World Cup, star forward Mia Hamm was called into the net on an emergency basis after Briana Scurry was red-carded by the referee. She held her own and did not give up a goal.

Remember, goalkeepers are the only players allowed to use their hands — in the penalty area. If they touch the ball while standing outside of the box, they are punished as though they are any other field player — with a red card, depending on the severity of the infraction. (See Chapter 4 for more on soccer rules and regulations.)

They Come in All Shapes and Sizes and Ages

In today's modern game, the bigger the goalkeeper, the better; they can cover more ground in front of the net. But they must be quick and nimble as well. The best ones in the world are six feet or taller, though there certainly is room for the smaller set like Jorge Campos, who is just 5-foot 9-inches.

There are essentially two types of goalkeepers — the ones who stay at home and others who like to handle the ball and go up field. The traditional keepers are the ones who stay close to the goal and don't wander outside of the penalty area or race into the midfield with or without the ball and wind up as part of the attack. A new generation of keepers are so adept at handling the ball that they become part of the attack. And yes, some goalkeepers have scored goals — during the run of play, although most of them have come through penalty kicks and free kicks.

Some say goalkeepers are like wine, meaning that they get better with age. The more experienced they become, the more knowledgeable about the game they are; most professional keepers, in fact, don't hit their prime until they are into their 30s. For example, instead of coming out of the net to make a spectacular save, a veteran goalkeeper may know how to cut down the angle on a forward — in other words, come out of the goal to give the attacker less room to shoot at — and force that player to shoot wide, without ever having to make physical contact. That type of play doesn't show up in the statistics as a save, but long-time observers of the game appreciate that kind of pre-emptive thinking. It's all about positioning. The less pounding a body takes, the better. And besides, your mom will love you a little more because your uniform won't be as dirty as it could be.

Saving Graces: Stopping the Opposition

The most important and obvious responsibility of a goalkeeper is to stop the ball from going into the back of the net. The last thing a goalkeeper needs is a bad back from stooping down to pick up the ball after the opposition scores. You can deny your opponent a goal in several ways, which are called *saves*.

You can also describe a goalkeeper's performance in different ways. Goalkeepers who excel are said to "stand on their head" or "stonewall" the opposition. In England, a shutout is called "keeping a clean sheet," which is the ultimate, ahem, goal for a goalkeeper.

Catching the ball

Making saves isn't just knocking the ball out of harm's way. If a keeper can hold onto the ball, the opposition has no way to score. It is an unwritten law that if a goalkeeper can touch the ball, he can save it.

When the opposition is attacking, the keeper should be prepared to grab the ball out of the air or pounce on it. For starters, the keeper should be standing with his hands at his side and palms facing the ball while his feet should not be wider than his shoulders. The goalkeeper's center of gravity should be low, and his weight should be on the balls of his feet when the shot is taken (see Figure 8-1).

Here are some common catches:

✔ **The diamond catch:** This catch is also known as the W catch. The goalkeeper catches the ball when the shot is wide or over the head of his body, as shown in Figure 8-2. The name comes from the fact the goalkeeper forms a diamond behind the ball with his thumb and index fingers. It is vital to get as much of the body behind the ball as possible, so that the ball, just in case it pops loose, can hit the body and the keeper can fall on it. After the keeper catches the ball, he should bring the ball into the chest.

Figure 8-1:
The proper
way to
stand in
goal.

Figure 8-2:
The dia-
mond catch.

✔ **The chest catch:** When the shot is right at the keeper, the keeper needs to get as much of his body behind the ball as possible. As the ball arrives, the keeper should surround his arms around it with his elbows close together to trap it against the chest, as shown in Figure 8-3.

Figure 8-3: The chest catch.

✔ **The scoop catch:** For a low shot or one that is rolling on the ground, the keeper should place his hands on the ground with his palms facing up, as shown in Figure 8-4.

✔ **The full-extension dive:** This method is used when a shot is placed toward one of the corners of the net and the keeper has to extend himself to the fullest. The goalkeeper should make his first stride as long as possible with arms extended and away from the face to see the ball as clearly as possible. The body must remain parallel to the ground while the keeper catches the ball, as shown in Figure 8-5.

✔ **The collapse dive:** This type of save is used when low shots are only one or two feet to the side to the keeper. The goalkeeper's feet should not be greater than a shoulder's width apart. As the ball reaches the keeper, the foot on the ball side should kick in the opposite direction of the shot. The player's body goes to the ground with his hands down first as the ball is caught in front of the chest of against the chest. If this isn't done properly and the goalkeeper gets his hands and body down later, the ball could roll under the keeper.

✔ **When it's one-on-one:** The object of this save is to deny a player on a breakaway. This is the most dangerous of all saves because the goalkeeper puts his body and face at risk as he tries to take the ball off the attacker's foot. The keeper should stay on his feet as long as possible, putting pressure on the opponent. As the player with the ball nears, the goalkeeper moves forward with his hands low and palms exposed to the ball. The keeper then moves forward when the attacker doesn't make contact with the ball, diving into the opponent's feet to smother the ball.

✔ **The cross:** Going up for crosses is all about timing and confidence — confidence his teammates have in the goalkeeper and vice versa. The purpose here is to stop the opposition from scoring off a head shot, usually from a corner kick. To get the best possible jump, the goalkeeper should jump off one leg and lift the knee that is facing the play to add to his leap. The keeper should attempt a diamond catch while moving toward the ball before cradling it into his chest, as shown in Figure 8-6. If a catch is not possible, the keeper's only option is to punch the ball away from the goal.

Figure 8-4:
The scoop
catch.

Figure 8-5:
The full
extension
dive.

Figure 8-6:
Catching
high
crosses.

Punching the ball

While going for the ball in a crowd, sometimes goalkeepers don't have the luxury of catching the ball. The next best thing to do is to punch the ball as far down field as he can. If a keeper attempts to catch the ball and misses it, the results can be quite embarrassing. Again, it comes down to timing. A keeper should leap as though he is about to catch the cross. However, instead of catching the ball, the goalkeeper makes two fists and punches the ball out of harm's way, always to the side, so as not to leave the ball in a direct scoring position (see Figure 8-7).

Figure 8-7:
Punching
the ball.

Parrying the ball

Sometimes goalkeepers don't have time to catch the ball. Sometimes they can only react with their reflexes. Knocking or deflecting the ball over the crossbar or around the post (all kind parrying the ball) are ways of saving a goal. It takes timing and jumping ability. While it should be a routine play, it could look like one of the most spectacular moves by a goalkeeper, as shown in Figure 8-8.

Figure 8-8:
Parrying the
ball over the
crossbar.

Saving penalty kicks

Thanks to a 1999 FIFA directive, goalkeepers can move on penalty kicks, giving them a much better shot at stopping the shot. Keepers are allowed to move from side to side, but not out of the goal, although some goalkeepers have gotten away with that tactic. In fact, U.S. goalkeeper Briana Scurry (shown in Figure 8-9) admitted that she moved forward to save Liu Ying's attempt in the penalty-kick tiebreaker of the Women's World Cup championship game. But the referee did not call an infraction or make Liu retake the kick.

Internataional Sports Images, J. Brett Whitesell

Even with the new rules, the shooter still has the advantage because he knows where he is going to put the ball. A goalkeeper should do several things, including looking at the shooter as he walks up to the penalty spot. Is he looking toward one side? Has the keeper faced this shooter before? Is the shooter just right-footed or left-footed? The smallest indication can give the goalkeeper a legitimate advantage and an opportunity to block the shot.

There is also the psych-out factor, as in making the shooter think about the shot by taking too much time or saying something. Most referees do not allow this, but there are exceptions to every rule.

Sometimes a goalkeeper is left to guessing, leaving a thin line between success and failure. Sometimes they'll guess left, and the shooter deposits the ball to his right, making the keeper look very silly. But if the keeper guesses correctly, then he or she looks like a genius.

Positioning: Being at the Right Place at the Right Time

A goalkeeper can save his teammates and coach a lot of grief and needless contact by learning how to position himself. Not every save has to be a spectacular one. In fact, the best ones are when the goalkeeper doesn't even touch the ball, making the difficult seem routine. Usually, positioning is accomplished by timing, patience, and experience, but some keepers are fast learners.

The best save a goalkeeper can make is by forcing the attacker to shoot wide or high without touching the ball. He can do this by cutting down the angle by coming out of the net.

A goalkeeper should stay on the goal line most of the time. When the ball is to your left, you should be toward the left side of the net to cut down the angle at the near post. When the ball is to your right, you should favor the right side of the net. The near post is always the goalkeeper's responsibility, and he is expected to make the save on a shot. Shooting at the far side of the goal, although not impossible, is more difficult.

On corner kicks, the goalkeeper should be ready to leave the goal line to either catch the ball or punch it out of harm's way. Timing is important here. A bad decision — missing the ball entirely or hitting it poorly — can result in a shot on goal, or worse, a shot into the goal.

Every situation is different, but this is where experience comes into play. When your team is attacking deep into opponent's territory, a keeper should stand at the edge of the area to watch for a sudden counterattack. If the defending team manages to move the ball forward, the keeper has an option of staying in goal or coming out to get to an errant pass or cut down the angle.

But some words of caution: A goalkeeper who strays too far out of the net can be susceptible to *chip shots* by the opposition, a floating ball that is looped high in the air over the keeper's head and difficult to recover or stop.

A goalkeeper must always be on his toes, especially when the ball is yards away from the goal. Two recent examples of a goalkeeper not staying alert and not on the goal line have helped decide key games. In the 1995 European Cup Winners Cup, Mohammed Nayim lofted a 50-yard floater that eluded Arsenal goalkeeper David Seaman for a goal in the final minute to lift Real Zaragoza (Spain) to a 2-1 victory over the English club. In the 1998 Goodwill Games, U.S. forward Mia Hamm beat Chinese goalkeeper Gao Hong with a marvelous, 35-yard chip shot.

When your team has the ball for long periods of time, you need to stay alert. You can easily lose concentration when no action is coming your way. Too many times in the past, a defending team retaliates with a quick counterattack and burns a goalkeeper who is "taking a nap" between the posts.

The goalkeeper should have the first and last word with his or her defense. A keeper has the best vision of the playing field because all of the action is in front of him. Communication lines should always be open between him and his defense, or disaster will result, which usually means a goal.

Yes, You Have to Use Your Feet as Well

One of the most vital, yet understated and underscored responsibilities of a goalkeeper is the ability to distribute the ball in a timely, orderly fashion. After making a save, a keeper has six seconds to get rid of the goal under FIFA's mandate to speed up the game.

Distributing the ball

The goalkeeper has several options when it comes to distributing the ball. Each method has its plusses and minuses.

✔ **Booting the ball into midfield:** Because the goalkeeper is the first attacker when he has possession, his first choice is to find a teammate in a 1-on-1 situation, preferably a forward, so that he can accurately punt the ball, as shown in Figure 8-10. If the keeper is an accurate punter or has a teammate who is exceptional in the air heading the ball, this is an excellent way to distribute the ball. Punting gets the ball up field faster, especially when the keeper's team is trailing late in the game and needs to score quickly. If his team is average in the air, it may retain possession only half the time.

✔ **Throwing the ball to a teammate well up the field:** A quick, accurate throw to a defender (usually one on the left or right flank) can start the team's buildup on attack and maintain possession. If the keeper sees a teammate open farther up the field, she may want to throw the ball overhand or javelin style, as shown in Figure 8-11.

✔ **Rolling a short pass to a defender who is better at dribbling with the ball:** Giving the defender the ball in the area will work over the short term, but it telegraphs to the opposition that the keeper has mediocre or even poor distribution skills, as shown in Figure 8-12. The opponents may try to pressure him or her in a key situation. Sometimes goalkeepers will throw the ball to a teammate who is running away from the play and while not looking at him. A turnover in the defensive third can result.

✔ **Dribbling the ball up the field:** This method isn't advised unless the goalkeeper is blessed with superior feet skills, has some courage, and has a teammate, preferably a defender, who is willing to stay behind and cover for her.

Figure 8-10:
The goal-
keeper
punts the
ball upfield.

It's not always feet first with keepers

When he was younger, U.S. National Team goal-keeper Kasey Keller admits that he wasn't very good with his feet.

"I've never been a tremendous player with my feet," he said. "But I'm a safe player with my feet.

"It's an important part of the game. It's something that every goalkeeper needs to learn, something which I didn't do."

So, Keller worked on his weakness, which isn't considered a weakness anymore. "You have to work on your strengths and you have to improve on your weaknesses," he said. "If you do that, the more rounded you will get."

A goalkeeper being able to play the ball well with his feet will help his team determine certain strategies.

"Do your teammates feel comfortable giving you the ball?" Keller said. "Can they play a little bit further up the pitch?"

Figure 8-11:
Another way to distribute the ball is an overhead or javelin pass.

Figure 8-12:
The keeper rolls the ball to his teammate.

Whatever works for you and your coach

When does a goalkeeper give a teammate a short pass or boot the ball into midfield? Sometimes it isn't his decision. Sometimes it depends on the coach or manager of a team.

In fact, Kasey Keller plays for two teams that have coaches and managers who have different philosophies on distributing the ball, and it certainly keeps the goalkeeper on his toes trying to remember which style he has to use, depending on for which team he is playing.

"My manager (at Rayo Vallecano in Spain) doesn't want me to play the ball short very often," he said. "With the National Team the coach (Bruce Arena) wants me to play the ball short and I'm used to punting it out of the other end.

"When you're punting it, your first advantage is that the ball is not in your area. The disadvantage is losing possession. When you're distributing the ball (on a short pass), you retain possession, although I have seen it very often when a team connects for 15 passes and scores a goal.

"The first and foremost thing for a goalkeeper is safety, getting the ball out of the danger area. Once you're safe, that's all that matters. Whatever you do past that is a bonus."

Goalkeepers can score, too

While it is rare, goalkeepers have been known to set up and score goals. The most common way for a goalkeeper to get an assist is to boot the ball way up field to a speedy forward, who instantly puts a shot on net and scores.

Another way is a bit more risky, as some keepers have been known to dribble dangerously into the midfield and, heaven forbid, into the attacking half of the field. While this tactic surprises many teams (and allows the keeper to roam freely up field), because they have no plans to mark the goalkeeper, it has some potentially disastrous drawbacks. While out of the penalty area, the goalkeeper can lose the ball. Even if the wandering goalkeeper's team has a defender staying home in the nets — he still can't use his hands — a quick counterattack by the opposition may occur and, worse, a goal may result.

Just ask Colombian goalkeeper Rene Higuita, who ventured too far out of the net in a 1990 World Cup second-round match against Cameroon. He lost the ball, and Roger Milla scored an easy goal in a 2-1 win for the Africans.

When their teams are losing in the waning minutes of a match, goalkeepers have been known to run up the field and become part of the attack because there is nothing to lose. In fact, on occasion a goalkeeper has scored during a scramble in front of the opposition's net.

There are other ways to score — through free kicks and penalty kicks. Paraguayan National Team goalkeeper Jose Luis Chilavert has perfected this method, having score more than 50 goals in his career. In fact, he was believed to have become the first goalkeeper to record a hat-trick, scoring three goals, for his Argentine club Velez Sarsfield (November 1999).

There is, however, one major drawback to this method. If the goalkeeper is unsuccessful on the attempt, there is always the possibility of a quick counterattack by the defending team. So, if the keeper misses, he should be ready to high-tail it back to his net and make sure that he doesn't commit the ultimate goalkeeper irony — surrendering a goal after trying to score one himself.

Two of the most famous goalkeeping blunders in U.S. soccer history happened on the same part of the field at Foxboro Stadium some 2½ years apart:

- ✔ During a World Cup qualifying match in April 1997, Kasey Keller inadvertently sent a goal kick directly to Mexican forward Carlos Hermosillo. The ball hit Hermosillo in the head, and the Mexican quickly used his head to score a goal. While a tragedy, it wasn't the end of the world or World Cup because the Americans rallied for a 2-2 tie and eventually qualified for the World Cup.

- ✔ For Los Angeles Galaxy goalkeeper Kevin Hartman, however, there was no tomorrow in MLS Cup '99, Major League Soccer's championship game in November 1999. Under pressure from D.C. United forward Roy Lassiter at the top right of his penalty area 3 minutes into injury time in the first half, Hartman stumbled a bit and miskicked the ball to an onrushing Ben Olsen (shown in Figure 8-13). Olsen then lofted an 18-yard shot into an unattended goal. The score gave United a 2-0 lead, which turned out to be the final score.

The Greatest Saves of All-Time

Virtually every fan, player or coach has his or her favorite all-time goal. But what of the goals that fail to hit the back of the net? Here's a short list of the most memorable saves and goalkeeping performances:

The save of all saves

It just wasn't the fact that English goalkeeper Gordon Banks dived from one end of the goal to the other to deny his opponent a goal in the 1970 World Cup. It was *who* he accomplished the memorable feat against — Brazilian superstar Pelé, who was still very much in his prime. Pelé headed the ball toward the corner of the net, and Banks, standing at the far post, miraculously knocked the ball out of harm's way with one hand. Does anyone remember that Brazil won the game 1-0?

Figure 8-13:
Ben Olsen.

The scorpion kick

Even though it was in an international friendly, Colombia goalkeeper Rene Higuita produced one of the most memorable saves in recent times against England at Wembley Stadium in England in 1995. With his back to the goal, Higuita dived forward and kicked his legs behind his back, looking like the tail of the scorpion.

Saves of a lifetime

Yes, even an American has gotten into the act. Kasey Keller certainly has made more than his share of saves, although none might have been more dramatic during the U.S.'s 1-0 upset victory over Brazil at the U.S. Cup in 1998. Keller produced ten saves in that match, denying former World Cup star Romario on several point-blank attempts. In fact, Romario went out of his way to say that it was an honor playing on the same field as Keller, adding that it was like he could read his mind.

The Black Panther strikes again and again and again

There are no official statistics on who has made the most saves or made the most stops in penalty kicks. But it is estimated that that Soviet Union goal-keeper Lev Yashin, nicknamed the Black Panther — he always wore black and made saves thanks to his catlike reflexes — stopped more than 150 penalty kicks in his illustrious career, which is considered a world record. To many coaches, players, media and fans, Yashin was the greatest goalkeeper to play the game.

Peter's principal saves

Even though some people knew the result before they watched the game on tape, they were still astounded by the overall play of Danish goalkeeper Peter Schmeichel. Schmeichel's marvelous saves help to hold off the favored Germans in the 1992 European Championship final, 2-0. It may have been the most magnificent job by a keeper in a championship game.

Communication: Getting the Word Out

The best goalkeepers are not shy. Some keepers are known to shout at their defense after a close call or goal. Depending on a player's psychological makeup, that type of tactic with teammates might not be the best route to take. The best goalkeepers communicate with their defense regularly — before there is a problem.

The worst type of goal is when there is a miscommunication or no communication. A goalkeeper should learn when to call for the ball with a simple "Keeper!" If the ball is a defender's, the keeper should have a word that is understandable to the defender, such as yours, or the defender's name. When the goalkeeper wants the ball cleared, he should shout, "Away."

The goalkeeper has responsibility for other important parts of communication as well, such as making sure that all his teams are positioned properly on free and corner kicks (see Chapter 9).

The difference between shouting and screaming

Having played more than 600 games for three European teams since 1992, U.S. National Team goalkeeper Kasey Keller knows when it's the right time to shout and the right time to keep his mouth shut.

When a ball is heading his way in the penalty area, he lets the entire defense know it's his. Since he plays for Rayo Vallecano in the Spanish First Division, he doesn't yell "Goalkeeper," or "Keeper" but rather "Puenta," which is Spanish for those words.

"You shout it, and they know it's your ball," he said. "Nobody wants to get a knee in the chest from the goalkeeper or get punched in the back of the head."

And nobody wants to be yelled out by his own goalkeeper after making a fatal mistake or giving up a goal. Keller said that he doesn't scream at his defense because, as professionals, they know when they have made a mistake.

"Rarely do you see me berate my defense," he said. "It's common courtesy. That's all someone needs, getting screamed at and everyone in the world knows it."

Specialty Training and Camps

Training goalkeepers is a weakness in youth soccer because a coach must spend his time in practice with 15 or 16 field players. In many cases, a goalkeeper workout will consist of him standing in the net and facing shots, which hardly covers the wide range of keeper responsibilities.

But there is a way to solve this dilemma — specialty coaches and camps. Virtually every Major League Soccer team has a goalkeeper's coach, although that might be an extremely rare luxury in youth soccer. However, more and more camps are devoted to goalkeepers, where they can hone their skills and craft.

Before committing to any camp, a few words to the wise: Check out several camps, ask questions, and make sure of the goalkeeper coaches' reputation and staff as well because some of these camps are not cheap. Getting the most out of your money is important.

Remember that attending a goalkeeper's camp won't turn you into a Kasey Keller or a Brad Friedel overnight. It is better entering the camp knowing that you will work on one or two skills that are weaknesses, such as catching crosses in traffic or ball distribution with your feet. (See the section "Saving Graces: Stopping the Opposition," earlier in this chapter.) If you come out a better goalkeeper, especially in one particular area, you can chalk up the camp as a positive experience and work on another part of your game at the camp next year.

They excel at their profession

Just who are today's best American goalkeepers? Kasey Keller, who spent 1993–1999 in England, usually has been the first choice of the U.S. Men's National Team since 1996. Brad Friedel, the former Columbus Crew star who is trying to break into the Liverpool lineup in the Englishship Premiership, is considered No. 2.

After that, it's a scramble for the third slot, depending who is hot and who is performing well. When he is healthy, Kansas City Wizards goalkeeper Tony Meola is among the best goalkeepers in Major League Soccer. Juergen Sommer of the Crew, who missed the 1999 season with a knee injury, was the third-string goalkeeper in the 1994 and 1998 World Cups. Zach Thornton is like a middle linebacker in the net for the Chicago Fire, he is so difficult to move. The Los Angeles Galaxy's Kevin Hartman and Dallas Burn's Matt Jordan are among the up-and-coming keepers in the league. Marcus Hahnemann, who helped the Colorado Rapids to a fast start in the 1999 season, was sold to Fulham in the English First Division.

And who are the best goalkeepers in the world? Paraguay's Jose Luis Chilavert probably will be the first to tell you that he is. The funny thing is, he usually can back up his boasts as an excellent shot blocker and goal scorer, usually from free kicks and penalty kicks. Denmark's Peter Schmeichel anchored Manchester United's great teams in England before he moved to Sporting Lisbon in Portugal. It isn't a mistake that Vitor Baia's teams usually don't allow many goals with him in the nets, because he is so technically sound. While the Netherlands is best known for its attacking players, Edwin Van Der Sar has emerged as one of the top goalkeepers in the world. For the future, Italy's Gianluigi Buffon has one as bright as anyone. In fact, the Italians have enjoyed a long tradition of fine goalkeepers, which include Dino Zoff, who anchored the 1982 World Cup win, Walter Zenga, and Gianluca Pagliuca, among others.

The women's game, still in its infancy internationally, has three candidates to be called the best in the world — the United States' Briana Scurry, who made the big saves when it counted in the 1999 Women's World Cup, China's Goa Hong, who has made some fine acrobatic saves, and Sweden's Ulrika Karlsson, who is as steady as they come.

Chapter 9

Perfect Plays and Strategies

• •

• •

*U*nlike other sports where teams have regular stoppages (huddles in football, for example) or can take timeouts, soccer is a free-flowing game of constant action.

But soccer does have some stoppages — on fouls and when balls go out of bounds — and these stoppages can give a team a unique advantage, especially if they have players gifted in taking free kicks and corner kicks. These stoppages are known as restarts, dead ball situations, and set plays. Teams have won championships taking advantage of these set plays, particularly free kicks and corner kicks.

And while pro soccer teams don't huddle like gridiron football teams, they do come into a game with a game plan. If they're at home and the favorite, sometimes the plan is to play an attacking game. If they're the underdog or on the road, sometimes it's a defensive game to hold the score down and perhaps register an upset.

In this chapter, I look at soccer strategies — both preplanned and ones that literally have to be put together while on the run.

Kickoffs: It All Starts Here

Kickoffs are done at the beginning of games, the second half, overtime periods, and after goals. Play begins with a *kickoff,* which is when a designated player stands over the ball at the center spot and kicks it.

Unique kickoffs

Some teams like to see whether the opposition is awake on kickoffs. The Carolina Lightnin', 1981 American Soccer League champions, once in a while started the game like gridiron football. The entire team, except for the goalkeeper, would line up for a football kickoff. The ball would sail in the air to the opposing goalkeeper, who, if he wasn't on his toes, dropped it and created a possible scoring situation for the Lightnin' — or worse, let it fly over his head into the goal.

It shouldn't be surprising that the Lightnin' was coached by former English great Rodney Marsh, nicknamed the Clown Prince of Soccer for his unusual and comic behavior and antics on the field. Yet, some of his innovations are still around today.

Perhaps the best known kickoff sequence occurred at the 1974 World Cup final. The Netherlands kicked off and put a string of 14 passes together, culminating in Johan Cruyff being taken down in the penalty box. The Dutch converted the kick and led 1-0 without Germany ever touching the ball.

Of course, teams that kick off should be aware and awake as well. I remember one North American Soccer League game in 1983 between the Toronto Blizzard and Vancouver Whitecaps when the Blizzard kicked off. Instead of moving the ball up the field, the Toronto players lazily kicked the ball backward toward their own goal. Then Carl Valentine swooped in and intercepted for Vancouver. He fed the ball to English international Peter Beardsley, who scored only 10 seconds into the game. And his team did not even kick off! Toronto coach Bob Houghton called the goal "unforgivable." He probably had a few other choice words that can't be printed in this book.

Moreover, his team learned a hard lesson. Hopefully, your team won't learn that way.

Unlike girdiron football, the team kicking off in soccer retains possession of the ball until it is stolen, intercepted, kicked out of bounds, or a goal occurs. So, kickoffs aren't as strategically important given the "transient" nature of the sport. The most important thing is that your team has the ball at midfield.

Taking Advantage of Free Kicks

Free kicks are awarded to the attacking team after a player has been fouled. There are two types of free kicks:

   ✔ **Direct kicks** are awarded when a player kicks, trips, charges, jumps at, strikes, or holds an opponent or handles the ball with her hand. A direct kick needs to be touched only by the kicker before a goal can be scored.

The greatest free-kick takers

Having someone who can convert free kicks is a godsend. The following are some of the greatest free-kickers.

Ronald Koeman: Koeman had average skills and speed, and the Dutch National Team had to "hide" him at sweeper because he didn't have to run as much as a fullback or midfielder. But Koeman had the unique ability to consistently put the ball behind the goalkeeper on free kicks.

Pelé: What couldn't Pelé do? The Brazilian superstar used skill, power, guile, and his marvelous understanding of the game to beat opposing goalkeepers on a regular basis.

Branco: Branco, who liked to get a 10-yard head start, was another Brazilian who excelled at free kicks. Perhap his most famous was his 25-yarder that lifted Brazil to a 3-2 victory over the Netherlands in the quarterfinals of the 1994 World Cup.

Roberto Carlos: Today, Brazilian international defender Roberto Carlos, who plays for Real Madrid (Spain), is recognized as one of the best free kick takers in the world. In fact, his powerful and impressive free kick for Brazil in a 1-1 draw with France in Le Tournoi de France in 1997 (dress rehearsal for the 1998 World Cup), which swerved around the defensive wall, is considered the ultimate masterpiece.

✔ **Indirect kicks** are given if a player performs in a dangerous way, obstructs an opponent, or stops the goalkeeper from releasing the ball from his hands. An indirect free kick must be touched by one other player besides the kicker (on either the attacking or defending team) before it can become a goal. If an indirect kick goes directly into the opponents' net, a goal kick is awarded to the defending team.

No matter what type of kick is occurring, the defending team must give the kicker at least ten yards from the ball, which is placed at the spot of the foul. If not, the referee can award the offending player a yellow card. Referees sometimes fail to enforce this rule, giving only seven, eight or nine yards, which becomes an advantage for the defending team. Players cannot run toward the kicker at all on direct or indirect kicks.

Direct kicks

Free kicks can be awarded anywhere on the field, but the ones that get the most attention are those that are 30 yards from the goal. There, free kicks become scoring opportunities. (See Figure 9-1.)

A player with the ability to put the ball on target with a strong shot or pass should be the first choice to take free kicks. It doesn't matter which player takes them, whether it is a defender, midfielder, forward, or even a goalkeeper.

Paraguayan National Team goalkeeper Jose Luis Chilavert, who has scored many goals from penalty kicks, occasionally takes free kicks. Yes, he has scored off some of them.

There is no one way to take a free kick if a team is proficient at turning them into goals. Sometimes players and teams like to cross or pass the ball to a teammate rather than shooting. There is no one right way to take a free kick.

If you have a player who has a howitzer for his right or left foot, it would be wise to let him fire away on a direct kick. Former Dutch international Ronald Koeman used to score free kicks this way.

Other players, such as Pelé and his Brazilian colleagues, are more finesse shooters and like to bend the ball around the defensive wall of opposing players. These shots are called *banana kicks* because of the way the ball dips and curves.

If you don't have a player who can either finesse or power the ball, you may want to use your head and come up with a free-kick play. They range from the very basic to the very imaginative. Many teams have two or three variations of these free kicks to keep the opposition on its toes. And not every kick has to be aimed at the goal.

- ✔ **The option:** Two or three players stand near the ball, not allowing the defending team to know which one is going to take a kick. One or two offensive players may run over the ball — not touching it — trying to confuse the opposition. Then the final player quickly shoots at the goal.

- ✔ **Audibles:** Sometimes players or coaches notice a weakness in the way a team lines up. Argentine coach Daniel Passarella noticed one during his second-round match against England in the 1998 World Cup. Passarella ordered his players to execute a special play 38 seconds into stoppage time in the first half. Instead of taking the kick, Gabriel Batistuta ran over the ball and Juan Veron shuffled off a short pass to his right to Javier Zanetti, who was standing at the edge of England's five-man wall. Zanetti scored off a 10-yard shot.

- ✔ **Distraction plays:** Two players stand over the ball "arguing" who is going to take the kick, trying to get the defending side to let its guard down for a couple of seconds. If the defending team does, the attacking team may find a hole in the wall or some extra space to shoot the ball. During the "argument," one of the players fires the ball on goal. While some teams might catch on to this type of ploy, some teams have variations of these distraction plays.

  Other creative free kick plays include a team breaking a huddle and running up to the ball, confusing the defending team, or various players running up to the ball and creating a screen for the shooter in front of the defensive wall. And there probably are other plays just waiting to be invented by a coach or player with an innovative mind.

✔ **Long free kicks:** Kicks from more than 30 to 35 yards don't need a wall because more often than not the kick will be more of a looping pass to a teammate down field or in the penalty area. However, there are exceptions. I remember the final seconds a high school game in 1987 when Irad Young, the son of former New York Cosmos forward Roby Young, powered a free kick from a good 40 yards out that ricocheted off the crossbar. A teammate got to the ball and knocked in the rebound to salvage a 2-2 tie.

✔ **Quick restarts:** Sometimes a player is fouled and instead of waiting for the defensive wall to set up, he or she takes what is called a quick free kick. If such a kick is allowed by the referee, there is a good chance the defense will be out of position, giving the attacking side an advantage.

Indirect kicks

When taking an indirect free kick, you must always remember that another player must touch the ball after you before it can be ruled a goal. You don't know how many times goals have been called back on indirect free kicks because the originator forgot that someone else — a teammate or foe — had to touch the ball before it went into the net.

A player can find a better shooting angle on indirect kicks by playing the ball a couple of yards toward the middle of the field, where a teammate can shoot the ball immediately. Because the defending team can send a player toward the kicker, time is of the essence.

When he played with the New England Revolution and the U.S. National Team, Joe-Max Moore took many free kicks. Moore, who performs for Everton in the English Premiership, did not become proficient at free kicks overnight, but through years of practice.

"The most important thing to taking free kicks is the amount of practice and time you have to put into it. Find a way to get a wall, whether it is players or obstacles, so you can learn to bend the ball around and to get enough arc to beat the goalkeeper.

"The kick is learned through practice. You have to learn to hit the ball at a certain angle and put a top spin on the ball.

"When I was younger, I spent countless hours on my own practicing free kicks. I put tires up at the corners of the goal and aimed for them. I started at the penalty spot and kept backing up until I was shooting from 22–25 yards out."

Figure 9-1:
The free
kick.

Penalty kicks

Penalty kicks, also known as spot kicks, are the ultimate free kick. The referee awards this kick when a member of the attacking team commits a serious infraction in the penalty area (see Chapter 4), such as a tripping foul or a hand ball. In contrast to a quick free kick, however, the kicker is not allowed to shoot until the referee gives the signal to shoot by blowing his whistle. Any player on the team, and not just the player who was fouled, can take the penalty kick (see Figure 9-2).

While penalty kicks look like a way a player can pad his or her scoring totals, not every leading goal scorer takes them. Even the great Pelé did not particularly like attempting penalty kicks, especially in a close game. Some star players actually get nervous before taking the kicks and prefer not to attempt any.

Players need nerves of steel in this situation because they are one-on-one with the keeper. Other players may have a stronger or more accurate kick than the best goal scorer. Many teams use a player who is a reliable penalty kick taker, regardless of the position she plays and how many goals she has scored. Adding another goal on the scoreboard is more important than a player adding to her scoring totals.

Figure 9-2:
The penalty kick.

How great is the pressure of taking penalty kicks? When it came time to select the five American players for the penalty-kick tiebreaker for the championship game at the Women's World Cup in 1999, superstar Mia Hamm was willing to attempt a kick but did not want to take the fifth or last one due to the pressure. That responsibility went to Brandi Chastain, who converted her attempt to lift the U.S. to victory.

Players should pick a spot to shoot at, usually the lower or upper extreme corners, and not worry about the goalkeeper. Both teams are kept out of the penalty area, being forced to stand behind the penalty arc, which is 22 yards from the goal. After the shot is taken, players are advised to race in toward the goal in case the goalkeeper knocks the ball away, but gives up a rebound.

This type of kick is not practiced enough by teams — youth, amateur, and pros. Teams usually practice these kicks before a tournament, where penalty kicks are used to decide a match.

Eric Wynalda, the U.S. National Team's all-time leading scorer, had to do some quick thinking and changed his mind while attempting and converting a penalty kick against Haiti in the CONCACAF Gold Cup in February 2000. He was going to shoot to the goalkeeper's left, but the keeper was moving in that direction. Wynalda said he wouldn't recommend such a move for every player, but there is time for everything.

"I had made up my mind to go to the keeper's left," he said. "I got about maybe three feet from the ball — I actually had planted my left foot already. That drives coaches crazy and my teammates nuts to know that I did that.

"To change your mind, you have to have the confidence and instinct to say, 'You know what, I'm so close to the ball I'm about to shoot, I'm going this way.' I'm not looking at the ball. I'm looking somewhere in the middle. I was watching him moving. I have two options at that point. I try to stay with Plan A and try to put it little father into the (left) corner, but that's risky. Or just go with the instinct knowing that once a guy is going one way, he's not coming back the other way."

Corner kicks

A *corner kick* is awarded to the attacking team when the defending team is the last one to touch the ball before it goes over the goal line (and not in the goal). A corner kick is given after the goalkeeper tips a high shot over the crossbar or one of the defenders clears the ball out of bounds.

Corner kicks come in three varieties: inswinger, outswinger, and short ones. The names tell a lot about each play strategy.

✔ On an *inswinger,* the server drives the ball in the air to the near post to a taller player or one who is gifted in the air and can head the ball home around the goal box 6 yards out. (See Figure 9-3.)

✔ On an *outswinger,* the ball usually travels to a player, someone who has a good long-range shot, at the top or outside the penalty area. (See Figure 9-4.)

✔ On a *short corner kick,* the server shuffles off a short pass to a teammate. With the middle of the defense pulled from the middle of the area, that player has the option of taking an inswinger or outswinger. Or she can try to penetrate into the penalty area. If your team leads late in a match, you may want to attempt a short corner to retain possession and run the clock out.

A good server — someone who consistently places the ball on the money on an inswinger or outswinger — can mean the difference between an average team and a championship one. For example, Vancouver Whitecaps forward Alan Hinton was not a fabulous playmaker. But he collected 30 assists during the 1978 North American Soccer League season, mostly from corner kicks. (The Whitecaps, incidentally, reached the Soccer Bowl, the NASL's title game, that season, losing to the New York Cosmos.)

Yes, you need the great jumper or shooter, but you need someone to put the ball there first.

Figure 9-3:
The inswinger kick on a corner kick.

Figure 9-4:
The
outswinger
kick on a
corner kick.

Throw-ins

A throw-in (see Figure 9-5) is taken when a player on one of the teams sends the ball out of bounds over the touchline (sideline). The ball is awarded to the team that did not possess the ball. A player must throw the ball back in from out of bounds to resume play. (A throw-in is the only time a player is allowed to handle the ball.) Most throw-ins are short throws to teammates in midfield to maintain possession of the ball.

Kick-ins versus throw-ins

In recent years, there have been rumblings over the possibility of using kick-ins instead of throw-ins. The problem with that is that it would destroy the balance of a match because a player can kick a ball much farther than he can throw it, turning throw-ins from the midfield essentially into corner kicks. In 1994, the United Soccer Leagues experimented with that concept in one of its divisions, but it was quickly abolished for the 1995 season.

Figure 9-5:
A throw-in.

While not as dangerous as free or corner kicks, an accurate and long throw in the attacking third of the field can set up dangerous scoring opportunities and literally throw a kink or two into a team's defense because they can be used as corner kicks.

Since the mid-1980s, a number of American players have preferred to take a flip before they throw the ball into play. That is, they literally do a somersault just before they throw the ball into play. Nothing is illegal about this play, as long as the player is behind the line when he throws the ball. Yet, there is something unsettling about watching a player throw a ball in that way. Perhaps it is the possibility of the thrower botching the play and giving the ball to the opposition or the player unnecessarily injuring himself on one of soccer's most basic plays.

Defending Free Kicks

Knowing how to build a defensive wall of players on free kicks is essential for a team to be successful. The players stand shoulder to shoulder ready to block the kick or make it difficult for the shooter to put the ball over or around them. They don't have much time to build this wall, so many of the assignments are worked out in practice or in prematch strategy.

One blown assignment or crack in the wall may mean the difference to a shot bounding off a player or someone putting home the game-winning goal.

So many factors figure into building a wall. How many players do you use? Where are the other players positioned? If you are protecting a one-goal lead, do you bring back your entire team in the penalty area? What is the angle of the shooter and ball at the goal? Where is the kick being taken? What are the coach's tactics and strategy?

The number of players in the wall can vary from two to as many as six players. It doesn't matter what position they play, although the tallest players on the team usually make up the wall to make it more difficult for a player to shoot over the wall. A predesignated player, a wall captain, makes sure that the goalkeeper's line of vision is open and clear. (You'll know when a keeper is obstructed when he or she leaps for the ball one way and the ball travels into the opposite corner of the net.) Players aren't supposed to move or flinch, because that could give the shooter the opening he or she needs to score.

On some teams, the forwards get into the act, standing in front or in back of the wall to make sure that the goalkeeper does not have an obstructed view. Experienced goalkeepers may feel more comfortable in making sure that the wall is lined up correctly.

Some attacking teams place a player at the end of the wall, trying to open up space for the shooter. The moment the ball is struck, that player peels away, opening up another avenue toward the goal.

Many coaches want the walls as close to the ball as possible, leaving no gaps, so that when the shooter kicks the ball, it will likely ricochet off the wall. One player may be assigned to charge the shooter if he decides to pass the ball to a teammate.

If the free kick is more than 25 to 30 yards out, a team might place a two- or three-man wall in the penalty area.

Chicago Fire and U.S. National Team midfielder Chris Armas, shown in Figure 9-6, who has forged a reputation as one of the top defensive midfielders around, knows the value of stopping the opposition from scoring off free kicks.

"It could be the difference between winning and losing," he said. "Many goals are scored on set pieces (free kicks and corner kicks). It can be that crucial. So, why not do it the right way? You don't want to put your shortest guys in the wall. Sometimes my job is as a blocker at the end of the wall on an indirect kick.

Figure 9-6:
Chris
Armas, one
of the top
defensive
midfielders.

"A good wall will never give you 10 yards (as required by the laws of the game). You creep up a bit."

If a team takes too long to set up, the referee can award a yellow card to the last player in the wall for delay of game. If a team does not give the attacking side the allotted 10 yards after a foul, the last player in the wall could get carded for encroachment.

The United Soccer League has taken the 10-yard rule one step further. Actually, it's several steps further — to 15 yards — in an attempt to give the offensive team more room and a little more advantage. And if the defending team encroaches to 12 yards, at least the shooter still has at least that 10-yard gap.

If an indirect free kick is awarded in the penalty area, some teams will defend it by placing every player in front of the goal.

Remember, it's no disgrace for players to cover up their sensitive body parts with their hands on free kicks. Even the pros do it. The ball could strike you at a high velocity. It is, however, a crying shame if a player flinches and moves, and the ball goes into the net through that spot. The wall must hold together. That's why it is called a wall. No one moves. You must stand there and take it.

Defending penalty kicks

Only one player is allowed to defend a penalty kick — the goalkeeper. Keepers are at a distinct disadvantage during penalties, as 75 percent are usually converted. Saying that, keepers should look confident before, during, and after the kicks, which could very well give them a psychological advantage if they successfully defend them. Keepers also know that a quick penalty kick can't be taken, unlike free kicks, because the referee must blow his whistle before the kicker attempts his shot.

Some keepers play mind games with the opposition, taking their time getting into the net. I've seen other keepers go up to an opposing player before he took a kick and wish that player luck. Unnerved that the keeper made such an unorthodox move, the shooter then misses the ensuing shot.

Goalkeepers are now allowed to move from side to side before a penalty kick, giving them a better shot at making a save. Keepers, however, are not allowed to move forward before or during the kick. Tell that to U.S. Women's National Team goalkeeper Briana Scurry, who admitted she moved toward the Chinese player during her key penalty kick save in the tie-breaker at the championship match of the 1999 Women's World Cup. However, the referee did not notice, and the save was left to stand.

Penalty kicks are not automatic goals. They are much more difficult to convert than they look. During Copa America in 1999, Martin Palermo set an Argentine record by missing three — that's right — three penalty kicks in a game. His coach, Marcelo Bielsa, who had been red-carded by the time of the third attempt, tried to relay his order via mobile phone for Palermo not to take the kick, but apparently the message did not get through.

Defending corners

One way to defend corners is to load the penalty area up with as many defenders as possible, which should limit the attacking team's open space. The downside to this defense is blown assignments.

Defending teams need to remember to place a player at the near and far posts, just in case the goalkeeper comes out of the net and fails to secure the ball. Every other player should *pick,* or mark, an opposing player in the box to defend against when the corner kicks come in.

New England Revolution defender Mike Burns was nicknamed the "postman" for being stationed at the post on corner kicks either heading or knocking the ball out of harm's way. Burns saved a last-second shot in the U.S's surprising scoreless tie with Colombia in the 1995 Nike U.S. Open Cup. That reputation, however, was tarnished, when he failed to stop a three-yard shot by Andreas Moeller that someone got between him and the right post in the U.S.'s opening match of the 1998 World Cup. It was the first goal in Germany's 2-0 victory.

Having too many players in the box can ruin your chances for a counterattack because your key offensive players are bottled up in the defensive third of the field (30 to 40 yards in front of the goal). If you're in the final minutes of a match and the defending team leading, this rule doesn't apply.

Sometimes teams score off the opposition's corner kicks. France scored its third and final goal in the 1998 World Cup championship match off a counter from a Brazilian corner kick. During the 1999 Major League Soccer season, the Dallas Burn scored not once, but twice, off quick counters immediately off a pair of failed New York/New Jersey MetroStars' corner kicks. In fact, the Burn tallied twice in one game on 1-on-2 breaks as one player went against two defenders and the odds to find the back of the net. Oh yes, the Burn won that road match, 5-2.

U.S. Women's National Team midfielder Kristine Lilly realizes the importance of positioning better than anyone else. During extra time of the 1999 Women's World Cup title match, Lilly stood on the goal line to the left of goalkeeper Briana Scurry for a Chinese corner kick. Fan Yunjie unleashed a hard shot that appeared to was going to be a goal until Lilly headed the ball away.

"Every time there is a corner kick, I'm in that spot," Lilly said. "There is something to be said for being at the right place at the right time. A lot of times it isn't by chance, but rather by design. On the National Team, we practice defending against a number of set pieces such as corner kicks and free kicks. That's my job, to be standing on that spot on the line."

Understanding the Offensive Systems

A *system* or *system of play* is the way a team plays, whether it is one in which the team is attack-minded or one where it is defensive-minded going on attack and waiting to go on the counterattack. Depending on a team's strengths, weaknesses, injuries, suspensions, and confidence of a coach, team strategies may change from game to game. Many coaches and teams like to follow a single system in a game, while others will make adjustments at halftime.

How coaching affects the system

A soccer coach can be likened to a conductor. As with a fine symphony, most of a conductor's work should have been done in rehearsals. The same goes for a soccer coach, who should drill his playing system and strategy into the heads of his players during practice. It's up to the players to take that information into a game and make something useful out of it.

On game day, most of the coaching should be done before the match and at halftime. Coaches are allowed to shout instructions from the bench, although on many occasions they can't be heard over the noise of the crowd. However, if they repeatedly leave the bench and coaching box, coaches are supposed to receive a yellow card for repeated infractions of the rule, often leading to ejection.

At halftime, coaches usually can make one major tactical change and perhaps a couple of minor ones.

Every coach has his or her own ideas on how the game should be played. Some coaches like to deploy a no-holds barred type of attack and push as many players up front as forward as possible. Others like to play it conservatively and send only one or two attackers up and *pack in* the defense.

Most fans prefer to see a wide open attacking game, but tell that to a coach whose job is on the line.

Catenaccio: An ultra-conservative defense

The name Catennacio sends shivers into the minds and bodies of most soccer observers. *Catennacio* is Italian for the great chain, which is an ultra-conservative defense. Catenaccio was devised not to win games, but to avoid losing or losing by huge margins. Three defenders play man-to-man coverage with a fourth defender — a *libero* — who is free to patrol in back of the defense.

Triestina coach Nereo Rocco introduced Catenaccio in the late 1940s. Triestina struggled against the larger, wealthier clubs, but with Catenaccio, the team was more competitive in Italy's Serie A, that country's version of the First Division.

Inter coach Helenio Herrera perfected this system by using a quick counterattack to surprise opponents. Many of the Italian teams then copied and practiced his style. A number of Italian teams still play a form of it today, and it does creep up into the prematch tactics of an overmatched team trying to outwit or upset a favorite. Sometimes the ploy works, sometimes it doesn't.

Total soccer, or the Dutch Whirl

Contrary to popular belief, the *Dutch Whirl* did not have its origins in the Netherlands, but rather in Austria by journalist Willy Meisl in the 1950s. Meisl felt that every player should be able to play every position in a pinch.

In the early 1970s, Ajax, under coach Rinus Michels, perfected this concept with the marvelous Johan Cruyff orchestrating much of the attack from the midfield. Thus, *total soccer,* or total football, was born. That meant a defender could go up and join the attack without hestitation, while a forward could move back and play defense, if needed.

Michels, Cruyff, and a number of talented players brought this successful concept to the Dutch National Team, which still is regarded as the best team never to win a World Cup. The Dutch finished second to a pair of hosts in consecutive tournaments — Germany (1974) and Argentina (1978).

Long ball passing

The English perfected the long passing game because it was perfect for their climate. Many games are played in the mud, so it was easier to whack the ball down field and let a forward run onto it. In many cases, you can bypass moving the ball through the midfield by having a defender or midfielder send it directly to a tall target player up front.

Long ball passing is an unimaginative way to play the game because the options are very limited. If the defending team has a skilled, tall central defender, this type of strategy can get old very fast.

That said, this type of tactic often works when a team is trying to tie a game in the waning minutes, because it is the quickest way to move a ball upfield.

Short passing

The Brazilians perfected the short passing game, usually playing in a triangle of players who pass the ball to one another. Slowly, but surely, the players move up the field, and before you know it, they are in the attacking zone.

The advantages of such a system is that it allows the attacking team to play some defense when it has the ball. When you possess the ball, the other team cannot attack. It cuts down the number of shots taken by the defense and the number of dangerous shots as well. Former U.S. national coach Bora Milutinovic used this tactic — nicknamed "Bora Ball" by the media — during his tenure from 1991 to 1995.

The beauty of a short ball game is that a team can throw in a long pass once in a while to open up the defense. Brazil used this tactic in 1994 en route to the World Cup championship.

Choosing Your Formation

Formations are the way a team lines up its defense, midfield, and forward line at the beginning of the match. If you want to get technical, you could produce dozens of formations due to the mathematical possibilities and new ways coaches are trying to devise to play the game.

Soccer is a fluid game where a midfielder may become a forward for five or ten minutes and then return to his original position. Or, likewise, a forward can come back to defend.

When talking about formations, defenders are listed first and then midfielders and forward. For example, a 4-4-2 formation has four defenders, four midfielders, and two forwards. Goalkeepers are not counted because they are the one position that has not changed over the years.

Just remember, the best coaches aren't necessarily ones who devise the best formations, but rather are the ones who devise the best formation for their team to accentuate its strengths and to hide its weaknesses.

Youth soccer

In youth soccer, coaches should not introduce tactics until players have truly learned the game — usually around the age of 14. Players need time to develop, breathe, and have fun.

For the beginner, soccer starts out nearly the same. All the players run after the ball or the player with the ball, like bees after honey. Slowly, but surely, they learn to find their own space and spread out across the field.

The 4-4-2

England used the 4-4-2 formation (see Figure 9-7) en route to securing its first and only World Cup title in 1966. Again, another forward is moved into the midfield, putting a lot more pressure on the two players up front to score goals. Saying that, the 4-4-2 is one of the preferred formations of today's modern game. The theory in using another player in the midfield is that it will bottle up the opposition in the midfield before they can get to the attacking third.

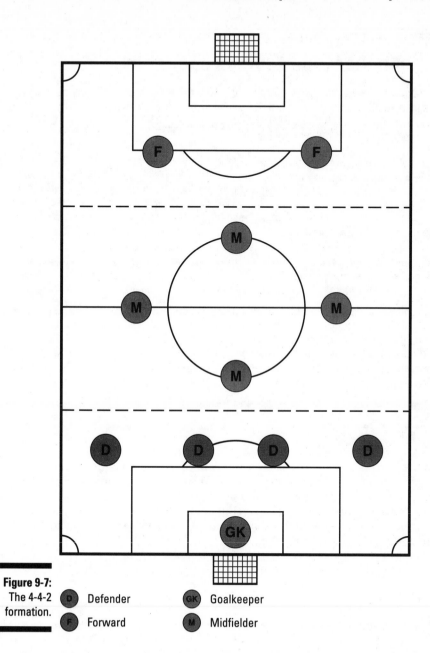

Figure 9-7:
The 4-4-2
formation.

D Defender   GK Goalkeeper

F Forward   M Midfielder

Soccer today versus soccer then

Unfortunately, the evolution of soccer systems has devolved from attacking concepts to defensive ones. It should not be at all surprising that soccer began as a total attacking game with only a couple of defenders in the back. In the past 100 years or so, there have been less and less forwards and more defenders and midfielders.

As a result, soccer has become more of a defensive game. Sure, players find ways to score goals, and once in a blue moon you hear about a professional player connecting for as many as five goals in a match. But if you compare the game in the 1950s and 1960s and even the 1980s to today's version, there is no comparison when it comes to attacking soccer.

In that era, players such as Ferenc Puskas, Alfredo DiStefano, Pelé, Johan Cruyff, and Franz Beckenbauer were among the giants of the game. They were allowed to really "play" the game and wound up known for their ability to give defenses headaches by either creating or scoring goals. Naming one player today who is close to them in talent and stature is difficult. Ronaldo of Brazil may be someday. But with the pressures of the modern game, the media, and his ailing knees — he says he plans to retire at the age of 30 — he may not reach that level.

This formation is a longshot to use consistently and successfully today because most coaches prefer to use four, five, or even six players in the midfield.

The 4-3-3

Many North American Soccer League teams used the 4-3-3 formation (see Figure 9-8) in the '70s, pulling one forward back into the midfield. Everything is relative. This formation, which utilized a sweeper (free safety), was considered more defensive than the 4-2-4. But compared to today's more cautious approach, the 4-3-3 would be considered an attacking formation in some quarters.

The 4-2-4

The 4-2-4 formation (see Figure 9-9) is the most offensive-minded in modern times. The 1958 world champions of Brazil, with 17-year-old Pelé, made this strategy famous and made it work. To take advantage of this formation, you must have talented and skillful midfielders and forwards to strike early and hold the ball for long periods of time because the pressure is on the midfield and defense big time when the opposition possesses the ball.

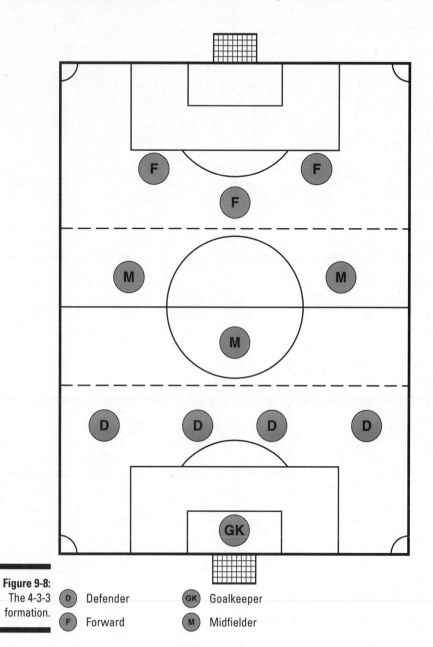

Figure 9-8:
The 4-3-3
formation.

D	Defender	GK	Goalkeeper
F	Forward	M	Midfielder

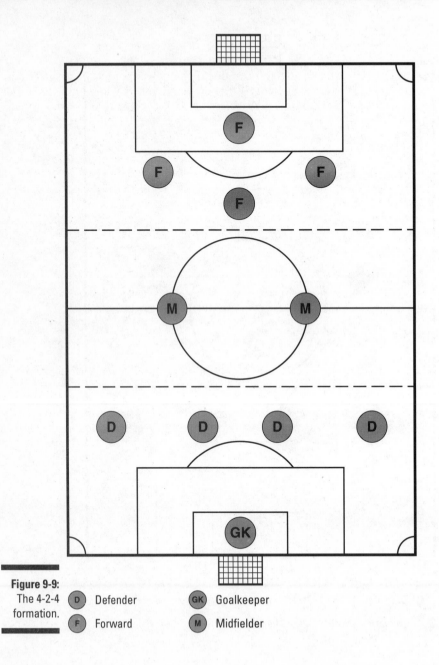

Figure 9-9:
The 4-2-4
formation.

D   Defender   GK   Goalkeeper

F   Forward   M   Midfielder

The 3-5-2

Today's game is won or lost in the midfield, which is why the 3-5-2 formation (see Figure 9-10) is popular. A team that doesn't have its midfield operating at peak efficiency will suffer in ball possession and scoring chances. So, many coaches like to use as many as five midfielders, although two outside midfielders may have more defensive responsibilities than their mates.

The 3-6-1

Many German teams utilize the 3-6-1 formation (see Figure 9-11) in road games as they try to clog the opposition up in the midfield, attempting to pull off a tie or a win.

This strategy may be dangerous. Former U.S. national coach Steve Sampson used this formation during the 1998 World Cup and failed miserably. After the team used primarily a 4-4-2 formation, Sampson deployed it some two months before France '98, and it backfired, producing just one goal in three games.

A coach should not change a team's formation drastically during a match, particularly for young or inexperienced teams who may get confused. If a team is trailing and trying to tie up the match, taking out a midfielder for a forward will work. If a team is leading, replacing a midfielder with a defender and/or a forward with a midfielder are also proper tactical moves.

Tackling: The Other Side of the Ball

Tackling can be called the antidribble, when an opponent tries to take the ball away. Tackling in soccer is not the same as tackling in football. You don't have to take down an opponent to separate him and the ball. In fact, tripping an opponent in an attempt while going after the ball is illegal. Players must combine skill, finesse, and timing to pull off the proper tackle. Again, these things come from experience.

Because they break up scoring opportunities, tackles are a necessary part of soccer. They don't have to be dirty or spectacular, only effective.

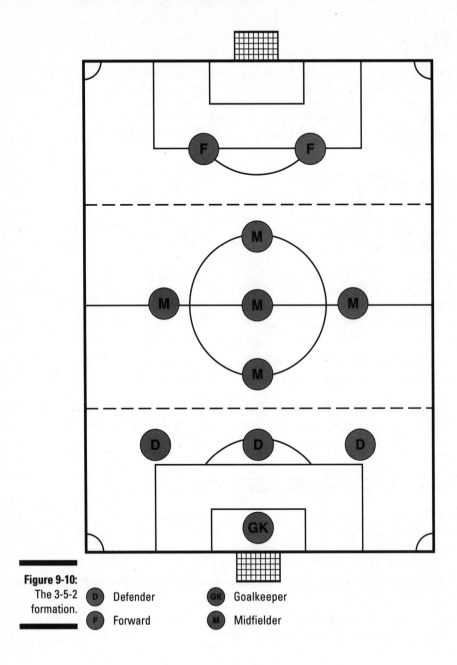

Figure 9-10:
The 3-5-2
formation.

D Defender   GK Goalkeeper

F Forward   M Midfielder

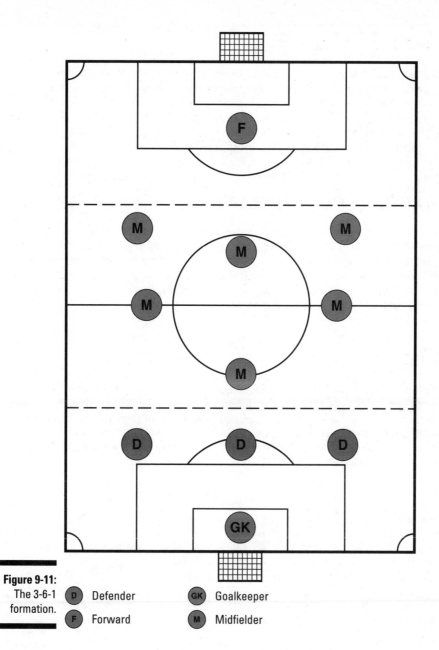

Figure 9-11:
The 3-6-1
formation.

D   Defender

F   Forward

GK   Goalkeeper

M   Midfielder

2-on-1 takeaways

Two-on-1 takeaways are also called *funnelings,* as two players go after the player with the ball. The defending players approach the attacker at an angle to limit his options. As they get closer, the defenders should shorten their strides with their knees bent and their weight on the balls of their feet. Players have to be concerned about overcommiting and allowing the attacker to push the ball into open space around the defender.

Marking the opponent

When a player *marks the opponent,* the defender should keep his weight evenly balanced with his eyes on the ball. He should bend slightly from the knees and the waist. If possible, the player should be angled slightly toward the attacker with one foot closer to encourage him to run in the least dangerous direction. The defender must worry about overcommiting or being so far away that no pressure is on the attacker.

Toe poke

Sooner or later, the attacking player will expose the ball to a defender by accident. That's the time for the defender to use a *toe poke,* shown in Figure 9-12. She should lock her ankle and then use the foot that is closer to the ball and knock the ball away from the attacker and hopefully to a teammate. The defender should be aware of deflecting the ball back to the attacking player. Timing is important as the ball leaves the attacking foot.

Block tackle

Sometimes a player wants to take more of a risk at winning the ball. Sometimes the *block tackle* is the most effective way of reaching that result. The defender should keep her supporting foot next to the ball while leaning forward from her shoulders, as shown in Figure 9-13. She should then lock the ankle of her tackling foot and drive through the ball just above its center.

Figure 9-12:
The toe
poke.

Figure 9-13:
The block
tackle.

Hook sliding tackle

The more spectacular looking tackles are, not surprisingly, the riskier ones. It takes experience and confidence to attempt a *hook sliding tackle,* which will bring a lot of oohs and ahhs from the spectators if done correctly. If it isn't done correctly or if he gets the player instead of the ball, the defender can look very foolish and also be penalized.

The defender should go for the ball with a slide when it is separated from the attacker. He should strike just about the middle of the ball with the instep of his upper foot and then swing the challenging foot in a slightly downward trajectory (the ankle should remained locked). The defender, with his body weight behind the ball, should wedge the ball against the attacker and the ground, as shown in Figure 9-14. The attacker should then fall over the ball.

Regardless if he gets the ball, the defender must recover quickly — to defend again or perhaps start a counterattack.

Conventional sliding tackle

As the attacking team gets closer to the goal, the defending side might take more risks with a more *conventional sliding tackle,* shown in Figure 9-15. As in the hook sliding tackle, failure can be costly — a foul, or worse, a goal-scoring opportunity.

The defender should always challenge from the side and not from behind. He should attempt this maneuver when the ball is separated from the attacker. His challenging leg should swing into the plane of the opponent and strike the near side of the ball. When the defender comes through from the left side, he should use his right foot. To avoid fouling his man, the defender should challenge with only one foot and make contact with the ball first.

Figure 9-14:
The hook
sliding
tackle.

Figure 9-15:
The sliding
tackle.

Again, regardless of whether he retains possession, the player must get up as quickly as he can to defend or move up field on attack.

A no-no: Tackling from behind

Timing is extremely important if you must tackle from behind. If you miss the ball and get the man, it can be and look like a vicious foul. Unless you want to find yourself on the sidelines in a hurry and the owner of the one of the worst reputations in the sport, you want to avoid tackling players from behind. Outside of a flagrant kick to a player who is on the ground, it is one of the crudest fouls and plays in the game.

First of all, it shows that your man has beaten you or you made a bad decision. Second, you should be red-carded immediately for this offense, although some referees incredibly have misinterpreted the move, somehow ignored it, or only awarded a yellow card.

This rule initially was enforced in 1998 in the matches preceding the World Cup. It caused a lot of confusion because it was implemented only months before the World Cup and virtually every player and referee had limited experience under the new rules. Sometimes it takes years to get rid of what has been ingrained in a player.

Jeff Agoos, a member of the U.S. National Team and Major League Soccer perennial power D.C. United, has made more than his share of tackles.

"If you do the tackle, you should time it well and you should get the ball," he said. "It's a sense of timing and a sense of the position. . . . The riskiest tackle is when you're on the ground and you've committed yourself on getting the ball. If you don't, you have to get up in a hurry."

Part III
Calling All Soccer Moms and Dads

The 5ᵗʰ Wave   By Rich Tennant

In this part . . .

*I*f you're a soccer Mom or Dad, then this part is especially for you. You find out how you can become involved with your child's soccer team and how to make sure that your child's experience is a safe and positive one.

Chapter 10

Coaching Youth Soccer

. . . .

In This Chapter

▶ Starting out as a coach

▶ Going back to "school"

▶ Running a successful team

▶ Tackling some difficult coaching issues

▶ Coping with soccer moms — and dads

▶ Volunteering: The other side of the game

. . . .

So, you're thinking about becoming a coach of a youth soccer team? It's not an easy decision because you need to consider many factors. Are you willing to learn a new subject? Are you willing to be patient, especially with young children? Will your work schedule permit you to run midweek practices? Will your spouse allow you to take the time to coach a team? Those are just a few of the questions you must ask yourself before undertaking such a challenge.

You may like coaching youth soccer and stay for years. Many parents continue to coach long after their sons and daughters have left the program and gone to college. Why? Because they have become students of the game. More likely than not, these coaches realize that the sport has many more levels than youth soccer, with college, pro, and international games as well.

Then again, you may hate coaching youth soccer. It's not the end of the world. Coaching isn't for everyone. In this chapter, I tell you how to make your coaching days — whether you love it or hate it — the most positive experience possible for you, your team, and their parents.

Taking Those First Important Steps

Parents become soccer coaches for some of the most logical and sometimes not-so-logical reasons. The most common reason is because one of your children plays the game, and you want to be around them. Sometimes no one else steps forward to coach the team, and you are thrown into the fray because the team is in danger of disbanding if a parent doesn't do something. Or perhaps you see a challenge of learning a new sport. Or maybe you played the game once many, many years ago, and you want to give something back.

Whatever the reason, coaching children in any sport is a serious responsibility. Anyone interested in learning the basics of the game, anyone on an ego trip, or anyone who is trying to relive those glorious athletic days of the past need not apply.

Unless you are a former college or pro player, few coaches start at a high level of youth soccer. Call it paying your dues or just learning the game.

American coaches who made their mark

A number of American soccer coaches have left their mark (and are still leaving it) on the sport:

✔ **Bruce Arena:** Presently the U.S. Men's National Team coach, Arena directed the University of Virginia to five NCAA Division I men's titles, from 1989 to 1995, and D.C. United to the first two Major Soccer League crowns.

✔ **Bob Bradley:** In only his first year as an MLS coach, Bradley directed the Chicago Fire to the ultimate double in American soccer: the league championship and the Lamar Hunt/U.S. Open Cup title. Bradley had been an assistant for Arena at Virginia, at D.C. United, and with the National Team.

✔ **Tony DiCicco:** Despite a lot of initial questions and skepticism, DiCicco (see figure) successfully replaced Anson Dorrance as U.S. Women's National Team coach in 1994. After stumbling to a disappointing third-place finish at the Women's World Cup in 1995, DiCicco led the American women to a gold medal at the 1996 Olympics and a title at the 1999 World Cup.

✔ **Anson Dorrance:** Dorrance is considered to be the father of American women's soccer, leading the University of North Carolina to

International Sports Images, Pam Whitesell

an amazing 15 NCAA Division I crowns in 18 seasons and guiding the U.S. Women's National Team to the very first World Cup title in 1991.

✔ **Buzz Lagos:** In a business where change is the only constant, Buzz Lagos has survived and thrived as coach of the Minnesota Thunder of the A-League with a winning record for ten years. After three failures in the championship game, Lagos and the Thunder finally grabbed the brass ring in 1999.

✔ **Ron Newman:** Newman, who retired as coach of the Kansas City Wizards in 1999, virtually did it all as a coach for 30 years, directing teams to championships in indoor and outdoor leagues. When Newman, a naturalized American citizen who was born in England, stepped down as coach of the Kansas City Wizards in 1999, he left with an overall coaching record of 753-296-27, the most wins of any soccer coach.

✔ **Sigi Schmid:** Schmid led UCLA to three men's Division I titles before taking the Los Angeles Galaxy to the final of the MLS Cup in his first pro season in 1999.

✔ **Jerry Yeagley:** The veteran and well-respected coach of four-time men's Division I champion Indiana led the Hoosiers to the 1999 crown, the team's second consecutive title.

Licensed to Coach

Say that you have decided to coach a team, and the only time you kicked a ball was during physical education classes, in a kickball game, or while making an error at second base during a baseball game.

What do you do? Learn — quickly.

Instructional books

If no coaching courses or schools are scheduled in your area, the fastest way to learn the basics — and I stress basics — of the game is reading about it in a book much like this one. It may not have all the answers. It might not teach you about why so many people around the world have such great passion for the game. But it will give you enough knowledge to stand on your two feet at practice.

And don't bring a book and read from it at practice. It will tell your pupils that you're learning the game as well, and that's not good for a teacher.

Coaching courses and schools

The most important thing is to learn the rules and basics. One way is to read (see preceding section). The next level is to be in a classroom, take notes, and observe.

Many leagues and state associations have coaching courses for beginning, intermediate, and advanced coaches. These courses, which are generally given once a week over several weeks, stress rules, trends, and tactics, with different emphasis at the three levels. Coaching schools are more intense than coaching courses because of the material covered over a shorter amount of time. Many are residential schools in which a coach attends between a week and ten days and take an intense look at soccer.

Coaching licenses

More and more leagues are demanding that coaches have some sort of coaching license, even if it is the most basic, a league or state license. These licenses are usually awarded after a coach passes a test or a series of tests at a coaching course or school.

Not surprisingly, the courses and tests become more difficult as the coach goes up the ladder.

The highest coaching licenses granted in this country are done through U.S. Soccer's National Coaching School, which offers a nine-day coaching course at several locations around the United States for A, B, or C licenses. The courses emphasize field instruction in technique, tactics, and fitness. The course also includes team management and sports psychology.

A national youth license recently was added for youth coaches. The course consists of four days of classroom and field instruction and one day of written and practical examinations. The course is age specific (Under-6 through Under-12), tackling topics as the playing and psychological aspects of the game.

The courses offered by the national coaching school are not a walk in the park. The first seven days focus on instruction, and the final two days on oral, written, and practical exams. An A license is valid for four years — coaches must participate in U.S. Soccer maintenance programs to keep their license current — while B and C licenses never expire.

You don't immediately go after an A license. You must work your way up the ladder, starting with a C license. Costs for taking these courses range between $525 and $850, depending on whether you're in a residency program or a commuter.

Getting a license doesn't mean you are necessarily a good coach. It means that you have learned the required material at that level. It's what you do in practice and on the sidelines during a game that counts. (See the section "Tips on Running a Successful Team," later in this chapter.)

Viewing games

All the theory in the world is useless unless you know how to use it. One way is to watch as many games as you can so that you can pick up the nuances of the game. (I warned you coaching soccer could get time consuming.) You can watch games on three levels:

- ✔ **Go to the videotape.** Hundreds upon hundreds of videotapes abound about the game. You can find out the rules from an instructional video (if you can't wait, you also can learn about the rules in this book in Chapter 4). Or you can watch some of the great goals and passes from another. Or, if you really have the time, you can watch highlights of some of the greatest matches ever played or the entire 90 minutes.

- ✔ **Watch TV.** Thanks to cable television and satellite technology, there has never been a better time to watch soccer on TV. (See Chapter 15 for more details on which networks to watch.) Depending on your cable system, you can usually catch several games a week from Europe, South America, or from the United States. While watching TV is not the same as witnessing the match in person, it does give you an idea of how the game is played at the highest level and educates you on the passions of the most passionate fans in the world.

- ✔ **Watch games live.** Actually, viewing games live is a two-pronged attack. If you are a beginning youth coach, you might want to watch games from your age group and other divisions as well, to understand what is expected of you. As you progress as a coach, you probably will want to seek out higher levels of competition to watch, whether it be college, amateur, or the pro ranks. In fact, if you're a player, it wouldn't be such a bad idea to watch games live as well. You might discover something about a favorite player, team, or hero in the process.

Tips on Running a Successful Team

What constitutes success? It's all relative. Success may be winning a championship. It can be being promoted to a higher division. Or it just might be winning your last game of the season for your only victory of the year.

Here are tips on how to enjoy the game. If you enjoy the game, there is a good chance your team will as well.

NSCAA: The largest coaches' club

The National Soccer Coaches Association of America, which boasts more than 14,600 members, is the largest single-sport coaching organization in the U.S., if not the world.

Members get an opportunity to attend clinics, coaching academics, and seminars to enhance their knowledge of the game, receive the *Soccer Journal,* which is published eight times a year, and get discounts on books, videotapes, and other soccer-related publications. Members also are eligible for $1 million in liability insurance, which covers coaches in virtually all soccer-related coaching activities.

The cornerstone of the organization is the annual convention, which is usually held in the middle of January, with usually more than 4,000 coaches attending. The convention includes clinics, seminars, and luncheons honoring regional and national coaches of the year and All-Americans at the youth, high school, and college levels (member coaches vote on them). It is also a time for old friendships to be renewed and friendships to begin anew. The 2000 convention was in Baltimore, while the 2001 event is scheduled for Indianapolis.

A regular annual membership is $60, while it's $40 for youth coaches, $80 for European coaches, and $90 for other foreign coaches.

For more information, contact the NSCAA at 1-800-458-0678.

Be prepared

Be prepared not only for practice but for the game as well. During the week, children have an hour or two hours at the most to kick the ball around. You don't want to let the children, and worse, their parents, know that you are disorganized or ill prepared. They will begin to wonder why they are wasting their time and good money on soccer. Besides, you don't want to waste your time as well.

You should have a good idea of what you want to accomplish at a practice, whether it is fitness drills, dribbling skills, or, for the older age groups, strategy in a key game. Obviously, surprises pop up once in a while, but it's better to have a game plan than not to have one.

For games, the coach should come ready with a starting lineup and who to substitute and when. For the younger age groups, a coach should strive to get as much playing time for every player, no matter how talented or poorly skilled a player is.

Just like the pros

Coaching at the youth level is different than the pros. Right? Not exactly. Los Angeles Galaxy coach Sigi Schmid, who has coached at the youth, high school, college, youth international, and professional levels, feels that coaches can incorporate many of the drills used in the pros with children.

"I believe you do to the same things with kids as you do with professional teams," he said. "I'll coach an Under-9 team the same way I could coach my pro team. There is a phase in practice where you can play the same way on both levels. Let's say it's a 5-on-5 passing drill. The main difference is the space between the players and the touch restrictions."

For example, a youth team may be allowed to touch the ball two or three times during a 5-on-5 drill, whereas a professional team would be restricted to one touch before a player would have to pass.

Keep it fun

Once practices and games become boring and tedious, players will look for excuses not to attend. That's the death knell of team. Besides, how can you expect bored players to perform well when the game is on the line?

For the younger age groups, you can keep practices fun by including new and different drills at each training session, by having the team select their favorite practice skills once in a while, or by letting them just play a game of soccer. (See Chapter 11 for more ideas on keeping practice fun.)

Keep it simple

Keeping it simple goes double, especially in the younger age groups. Unless you have a really gifted bunch of players, which is extremely rare, you should not teach tactics until a player is 12 years old. Players should be allowed to develop his or her skills up to age 12. In many respects, this bit of advice is related to keeping it fun (see preceding section).

Talk, don't yell

Yes, it can get frustrating that a player or teammates don't catch on to a particular skill or make a mistake during a game. But yelling is embarrassing to them and shows the team that you're losing your cool, and that's not cool to them. (Remember, these kids look up to you.)

Constructive criticism are the key words here. Take the player aside and explain the particular skill or drill again. If it is a game situation, explain to them how they made the mistake and, importantly, how to correct it. Always remember that it's a game.

If you are coaching teams eight and under, remember that children look up to you. At those ages, their minds are like sponges, and they will retain a tremendous amount of information. Whatever you do or say, you are setting an example.

Keep parents in line

Mothers and fathers screaming at the top of their lungs on the sidelines during a game look ridiculous and certainly do not foster the correct playing atmosphere for the children. Coaches have been known to get yellow cards — a caution — or, heaven forbid, a red card — an ejection — for being unable to keep their team's parents under control.

Some coaches make sure that the parents are on the other side of the field so that they cannot interfere with his or her decisions and the children's focus on the match. Some parents have been banned by their league and even by their own teams from watching their children play.

Know your limitations

It takes years to truly understand the intricacies of the sport. Every time you reach a new level, you encounter seemingly another set of important drills, regulations, or tactics to learn.

Recognize your limitations and make up for them. In fact, one coach I know realized his weaknesses. Instead of teaching his team a certain skill, he brought in a former professional player to show how it was done.

Tackling Difficult Issues

It's not always what happens between the lines on a soccer field. Sometimes the most difficult part of coaching occurs off of it.

Assistant coaches

Not every coach is cut out to be a head coach. If you don't have the background or the time to put into it and you're still interested in lending a hand, you may want to consider becoming an assistant coach. If you have aspirations to coach a team of your own someday, this is a great way to learn on the job. And you can learn — from the coach, players, and parents.

If assisting works for you, you may want to move on to a head coaching job. If not, well, there's certainly nothing wrong about being a lifelong assistant coach. It happens in other sports, such as football, baseball, and basketball. Besides, the most successful coaches on the most successful teams have excellent lieutenants, or in this case, assistant coaches.

Coaching your son or daughter

Welcome to the darned-if-you-do and darned-if-you-don't scenario of youth soccer. The advantages of coaching your child includes quality time with them. The disadvantages are players and parents who may accuse you of favoring your own child or who claim that you expect too much of your child and criticize her.

Unless your child is exceptionally gifted in the sport — then there will be little or no complaints from other players or parents — sometimes it is better if you don't coach your son or daughter. Before doing anything, you should talk to your child about it and see what he or she thinks about it. After all, youth soccer is about them, not necessarily you.

It takes a special parent to coach his or her own children. The best way to deal with it is to keep the communication lines open and let them know they will be treated like any other member of the team and receive no special favors. Sooner or later, problems may occur. Talk about any problems before they can get blown out of proportion.

Coaching the opposite sex

For years, men have coached female soccer teams. In the past decade or so, a growing number of women are directing boys' teams. As long as the coaches are qualified and are good teachers, coaching the opposite sex shouldn't be a problem. Some boys prefer a man guiding their team, as do girls with women.

Coaching boys versus girls

If you coach a boys team one season and a girls team the next, you may have to change your coaching style because there are important differences in attitude and behavior that go well beyond playing styles.

"Girls are more team-oriented and boys are more for themselves," said Bobby Howe, U.S. Soccer director of coaching education. "When you're working with males, you can be critical of them in a group. I don't think you can do that with females."

Coaching the same age groups

Some ambitious coaches wind up directing older age group teams because they have the competitive spirit. Others find a level with which they are content and comfortable and wind up coaching the same age group year after year. There is no shame to that. I knew of one such man who had coached beginning soccer for children (between the ages of four to eight years old) for eight years. I attended practices, which were geared to having fun and playing games. After one game, he asked me, a seasoned soccer writer, how he was doing. I replied that the children are having fun, and that was the main thing.

Using specialist trainers

One of the most controversial topics in youth soccer is the idea of bringing in specialist coaches to work or train a team. Unlike most coaches, who do it on a volunteer basis, trainers are paid by teams. They are supposed to raise the level of players and of the team, whether it be for league competition or the State Cup and beyond (see Chapter 17). Many leagues, clubs, teams, parents, and players see trainers as essential in the development of players, while others feel they are throwing their money away.

Playing up

Sometimes a youth team dominates its age group so much that it's no fun at all. In these rare instances, teams are given permission from their league to *play up* an age group. For example, a Girls Under-13 team that is undefeated and has outscored its competition 140-3 will be allowed to perform in the Under-15 league the next year (when the team should be playing an Under-14 schedule). Many of these talented teams hold their own. The ones that don't many times are brought back down to their age group the next season. You don't want to destroy the confidence of an exceptional team.

Moving up to travel teams

After coaching intramural or recreation teams for several years, you may want to "graduate" to the travel team program, as a youth player would. Life becomes a lot more competitive at that level. But you will know if you feel ready to teach intermediate and eventually, advanced players.

Coaching two teams at the same time

For those of you who have plenty of time or are really passionate about the sport, you may want to coach two teams at once. It's rare, but men and women have managed to pull it off. The key here is to be organized, making sure that practices and games don't conflict. Because your league does game scheduling and you don't, sooner or later you will have games at the same time at opposite ends of your town. That's why it's important to have a strong assistant coach.

Many high school coaches guide club teams in the spring and their school sides in the fall.

Tryouts

Tryouts are one of the most controversial and politically charged aspects of soccer, particularly at the Olympic Development Program (ODP) level.

Many leagues hold tryouts at the beginner stages to separate the players by skill so not that many mismatches occur in games.

The ODP program, which is run by each state association, is open to boys and girls age 12 and up. Many of these tryouts are by invitation only, usually for players who have played for their league select teams.

So much is at stake here besides pride. These ODP teams get higher levels of competition, travel throughout the United States and sometimes overseas, and the opportunity to be seen by many Division I coaches. Going to a Division I school on a full athletic scholarship can save a parent or student thousands of dollars.

The never-ending coaching carousel

To truly appreciate the pressures of coaching professionally, you have to remember the axiom that a coach is hired to be fired. It never was more true than in pro soccer, where coaches are here today and gone tomorrow.

Here are some of the most bizarre and unusual examples of coaching at the pro level:

✔ **The reign of terror.** That's what they call Jesus Gil's regime as president of Atletico Madrid in Spain. During his 12-year tenure as owner of the club, Gil has fired more than 30 coaches, sometimes employing four in a single season. A maximum of one coach a season would suffice.

✔ **He's in, he's out, he's in, he's out.** In Germany, in November 1987, Hamburg coach Josip Skoblar did not know if he was coming or going over a three-day span. After only 132 days as coach, Skoblar was fired by the club, which announced that Willie Reimann would take over. On November 10, however, Skoblar was back in charge because Reimann could not get out of his job as St. Pauli coach. A day later, Reimann was named coach, and Skoblar was sacked again.

✔ **Unbeaten and unemployed.** Despite his fourth-place team having an undefeated record of 2-0-4, Mario Beretta was fired as coach of Como of the Italian Third Division in October 1997. Club president Enrico Prezosi, obviously an impatient man, wanted to get promoted to the Second Division (the top two teams move up), and he felt the team had little time to lose, even though seven months were left in the season.

✔ **Is the third time a charm?** Former Brazilian World Cup captain and one-time New York Cosmos all-star defender Carlos Alberto returned to coach at Botafogo in Brazil for the third time in his career in 1999.

✔ **Before a ball was kicked.** A good five weeks prior to the start of the 1978 North American Soccer League season, well-traveled English coach Malcolm Allison had not signed a player for the expansion Memphis Rogues. His departure was mutually agreed upon.

✔ **In your own backyard.** In the States, the New York/New Jersey MetroStars have forged a reputation of having a never-ending revolving door for coaches. Entering its fifth MLS season in 2000, the MetroStars have employed six head coaches — the most by any of the 12 teams. Its list includes Eddie Firmani, Carlos Queiroz, Carlos Alberto Parreira, Alfonso Mondelo, Bora Milutinovic and Octavio Zambrano, who took over for 2000. Right behind the MetroStars is the New England Revolution, which has employed four coaches.

✔ **A two-timer.** Of course, sometimes the coach enjoys the last laugh. The late Alex Perolli, who coached for the San Antonio Thunder and Rochester Lancers in the old North American Soccer League, once coached two teams in the same city in the same league at the same time. Honest. Perolli managed to pull off this chicanery in the National Soccer League of Canada in 1968. He coached the White Eagles and the Greeks in Toronto.

"You shouldn't do that," Perolli said in an understatement. "The presidents of the teams were friends of mine. . . . I coached one team in the morning, and the other in the afternoon." But when these teams met on the playing field, Perolli sat in the stands with the two presidents. Fortunately, the game ended in a tie.

How controversial can ODP tryouts be? For example, some parents have claimed that the coaches who pick ODP players have made up their minds before the tryouts and usually choose players from last year's group, supposedly making it difficult for newcomers to break into the program. These charges are difficult to prove.

Soccer Moms and Dads

The term *Soccer Mom* became important during the 1996 presidential election as Clinton and Dole both went after that important part of the electorate. Of course, everyone knows that Soccer Moms have been around for years and always have been a vital part of soccer. That goes for Soccer Dads as well (but they haven't been thrown into the middle of a national election — yet).

Game conduct

By now you probably have heard about those "ugly" parents who scream and shout at sporting events, venting their anger at the world and their frustrations at their children, coach, or referee in trying to relive their youth through their children.

Shouting or even telling instructions to your children probably doesn't work. They probably know the game better than you. (That's why you're reading this book, right?) Second, you probably never played the game, so you may not know what you're talking about. And third, your child may not hear you through all the other commotion.

You should attend a game to enjoy it and be proud of your child's efforts, whether or not he scores a goal. If they look at you for encouragement, particularly in the early years, give them the thumbs up and smile. If your child sees you yelling at her all the time and is not enjoying it, then she probably isn't going to enjoy the game as well. Remember, it is their time in the sun, not yours.

Learn the game

To appreciate what's happening on the field and even practice and teach your children, parents can learn the game. You can bone up on the sport in many ways — by reading about it, taking a refereeing rules or coaching course, or watching games and videos. (See the section "Going Back to School," earlier in this chapter, for details.)

Quiet on the set, please

On Oct. 4, 1999, the Northern Ohio Girls Soccer League held "Silent Sunday," as parents were asked to not utter a word on the sidelines. The 200-team league decided to make a point about parents and coaches who occasionally displayed some obnoxious behavior. It was considered an overwhelming success because the only sounds on the fields came from the players and referees, and the players were said to enjoy the atmosphere tremendously.

It will be interesting to see whether other leagues will emulate the Northern Ohio Girls Soccer League.

The referee dilemma

The biggest crisis facing soccer these days is referees, or the lack thereof. Many game officials leave the game early because they are turned off by abusive behavior — verbal and physical — by coaches, players, and yes, parents. Is it worth putting one's health on the line for $25 or $50 a match? Besides, how would you like it if you were constantly harassed while you were trying to do your job?

Far too many incidents have been reported about referee assaults. Not only are leagues taking action, but some of these cases have entered the judicial system. Some parents and coaches have been banned from watching their children and team play. Some, believe it or not, have been prosecuted and jailed.

For a game, it's just not worth going to jail and being humiliated in front of your local and soccer communities. Yes, referees, especially young referees, make mistakes. But they are only human.

Volunteering: Something You Can Do Other than Coaching

Coaching isn't for everyone. Yet you still may want to participate in the your son's or daughter's team in a different way. Here are a few suggestions.

Orange cutting

Orange cutting? That's right. Some teams rotate the parents' responsibilities so that each week a different mom is in charge of bringing and quartering oranges for the halftime break or a dad's priority is to bring donuts for the postgame snack. For other parents, it may become a "full-time job," at least with the team.

Don't laugh. You will be greatly appreciated. Eating — at halftime and at the completion of games — can be one of a child's favorite parts of playing games. Besides, you never know what it may lead to from there. Peter Masotto, the president of Eastern New York Youth Soccer Association who coached the Massapequa Falcons to the Girls Under-19 national title in 1986, likes to remind people that he started out in soccer by cutting oranges for his daughter's team.

Field lining

Field lining is one of the most thankless tasks performed by members of a soccer club, but an obvious necessity. If the fields aren't lined for Saturday's or Sunday's game, you don't have a game. If you're into gardening or making sure that things are straight, field lining could be up your alley.

Refereeing

Refereeing? Yes, refereeing. There is a serious shortage of referees. Who knows? Your personality could fit the job. If you have a thick skin and want to give something back to the game (and earn some money on the side), refereeing could be a perfect job. Besides, it will give you a better appreciation of what game officials have to go through.

Administrator

Becoming president doesn't happen overnight. You can't walk into a soccer club and say, "Here I am. Make me the president." You have to pay your dues with perhaps one of the responsibilities earlier in this section. Or, you might have some interesting ideas for your club's monthly meetings. A board member might be impressed with your foresight and ask you to be on the tournament committee. Who knows? Eventually you might get nominated for a position on the board. Good, hard-working volunteers are difficult to find.

Be a supporter of your children

And if you don't have the time or these other tasks don't interest you, just be a big fan for your children. Make sure that they know when games and practices are and make sure that they arrive on time. They'll appreciate that more than anything else.

Chapter 11

Staying in Soccer Shape: Conditioning, Practice, and Diet

Due to the nature of the sport, soccer players must be among the fittest athletes in the world. Some players run as many as eight miles in a game, so a player must be in tip-top shape. If a player does not play up to her potential, she's wasting her time. And just as bad, she will become an early substitution. No player likes to be constantly replaced because she is not in shape. But you can have a fate worse than being subbed a lot — one where you don't play at all — if you're not in shape.

Keeping in Shape

Long gone are the days when professional players go to preseason training to get into shape. They have to be in excellent shape entering training because these teams get down to business very quickly. Jobs are on the line, and coaches want to see how well players perform as soon as possible. Formal preseason training isn't used to get fit, but rather to work on skills, dead-ball situations, and teamwork.

While not as demanding as the pros, youth and amateur soccer operates in the same way. Because of the limited amount of practices, sometimes only a fraction of that precious time can be devoted to fitness. Players are expected to be at a certain high fitness level entering the preseason.

If they're not fit, players pay big time with nausea, cramps, and soreness. The general rule for pro players is that for every week they take off from training, they will need two weeks to get back into shape.

Getting into Shape

It's this simple. If you are not 100 percent fit, it will become apparent on the field soon enough. There is no place to hide, and the opposition will exploit that weakness until your coach sits you down.

Running is the most important physical aspect of playing because you always have to use your legs. But you also need to have cardiovascular fitness, strength, abdominal strength, and flexibility.

Probably no one recognizes the importance of fitness more than U.S. Women's National Team midfielder Michelle Akers. For the past several years, Akers has been battling Chronic Fatigue Syndrome, which drains her of most of her strength. Despite this obstacle, Akers has excelled at her game by following a rigid fitness program and workout schedule. Akers offered these fitness tips for youth players.

"To play soccer at a competitive or even moderate level fitness is a given. If you don't do it, chances are good you won't play or the team won't succeed. However, when it comes to kids (12 and under), it's a whole 'nother thing. Sure, kids need to be in shape and able to play with out gasping for air, but they should not be put through the rigors that a higher level, more committed, older athlete has to endure.

"Fitness for young players should be minimal for many reasons. One, kids are out there to have fun, and if I'm not mistaken, most fitness is not 'fun.' Sure, eventually you learn to love it, but only after you've fallen in love with the game. It is that love that pulls and even motivates you to push further and faster, and fitness is seen as a tool or key to achieving a higher standard of play. As a kid , that love needs to be nurtured and grown until it's root runs deep and strong, so when it is time for fitness, they won't get turned off.

"Second, a kid's body just isn't ready for that kind of training. Holy cow. This a child, and there is no need for them to be training like Olympic athletes. Keep it in perspective and give them what they need, but don't treat them like adults.

"And lastly, kids, if you are reading this, yes, this even applies to those of you who want to be Olympics athletes one day. Train and practice hard, but adult fitness you don't need. All in good time. Trust me. There will be plenty of time to throw up or pass out later.

"So, what is acceptable? Well, it will vary with the age group and level of play, but I wouldn't do any fitness (maybe a lap or two) until the age of 10. Ball stuff is fine. And maybe throw in some situps and pushups as well, but that's about it. Just let them play. A good coach can structure practice so it is demanding enough (with out formalized fitness) to get the team in enough to play the required minutes of a match.

"At what age should fitness be added? At age 10 and 11, start to add a little running into the practice routine. A kid should be able to run a few laps without dying or getting turned off. If the kids are the 'serious' sort then, throw in a little more formalized stuff and see how they respond. Explain why it's necessary, the results, and the process (it gets easier the fitter you become) and get at it. However, the attitude of fitness is it must be fun. Don't make it a punishment and do not run them till they fall down. Keep it short, intense, and fun."

Running

Just keep reminding yourself legs are the ultimate tool of soccer, so you need to keep them in the best of shape. Each player in the pros seemingly is blessed with some sort of superior running skill, whether it's the ability to run like the wind or to pace one's self over 90 minutes.

When you're in the off season, any sort of running is good. The best way to keep in shape is by jogging for 45 minutes every day. You can break it up into a pair of 20-minute jogging sessions. It will always keep your heart rate at a healthy rate.

During the season, you need to run long and short distances. Long-distance running, which can be jogging or laps around the field, builds the base and endurance of an athlete. You also need to complete long and short sprints and to complete sudden stops, cuts, movements, turns, and action, which build power and explosiveness.

Coaches like to use wind sprints during practices. Some are called suicide drills — when players sprint 20 and 40 yards between cones. You may feel lousy doing these exercises, but you'll feel great during games, especially when you have the power and explosiveness to get a step on an opponent.

Quickness is the explosiveness a player has when he takes his first steps with the ball. The first three or four steps are very important because they can create vital space a player needs to get a step on the defender. Quickness, however, should not be confused with being fast. A player with average speed may be able to use his quickness to trap the ball or change direction to get a vital step or two on an opponent. You can be born with a certain amount of quickness. It also can be developed by doing wind sprints and suicide drills.

Aerobics

If you need to run at a high level, your lungs and heart must be in tip-top shape. Think of your lungs as the fuel (air) processor, which gives the pump (the heart) more power to give energy (blood) to the wheels (legs).

When you're not playing soccer, any type of sport is good to keep your body in shape and toned and your heart — the most important muscle in your body — pumping at a high rate.

Basketball is a perfect sport to play because it uses many of the same muscles as soccer. So are paddle ball and tennis because of the sudden movements that are needed. Many coaches don't want players to do these sort of activities during the soccer season.

Swimming is good as well, but you don't want to do it during the season because you use different muscles than the ones for soccer.

Despite the incredible advances of technology, heart surgery, and transplants, the heart is the ultimate pump. You are only given one, so you need to keep it at 100 percent efficiency not only as an athlete, but for a long, healthy life.

Weight training

Unlike football, baseball, or basketball, weight training, particularly of the upper body, isn't as vital to pro soccer because most of the power and strength comes from the legs. That doesn't mean that you should neglect the upper part of your body. Being in good physical shape is important. In soccer, however, the flexibility of a muscle is more important than the size of it. (See the section "Stretching those vital muscles," later in this chapter, for more on flexibility.)

In professional soccer, players use weight training perhaps once a week to keep their body toned or to recover from an injury. Repetition, which tones the muscle, is more important than the amount of weight used, which bulks up the muscle. This weight training is done in addition to the regular running drills and practices.

The stomach

Have you ever noticed a soccer player with a big belly? Probably not, because running keeps their abdominal (stomach) muscles in great shape.

Any type of sit-up or stomach crunches on a daily routine will certainly do the trick and keep those stomach muscles at 100 percent.

Stretching those vital muscles

If you want to avoid pulling muscles in practice and games, a good stretch of the key leg muscles is mandatory before a game. Stretching doesn't take very long — usually from 10 to 15 minutes — and these exercises are not complicated. Studies have shown that the more flexible players are, the less prone they are to injuries.

Each player should have his or her own stretching routine. Depending on the mass of the muscle, stretches can last a couple of stretches to doing it as many as ten times. The bigger the muscle, the more stretching it needs. Players who are long and wiry may not need to stretch as much as those who are smaller and stockier.

Try these stretches:

✔ **Quadriceps:** Sit on the ground. With one leg in front of you, place the other leg bent back on the side. To stretch, lean forward. For a deeper stretch, you can lean backward, as shown in Figure 11-1.

The other quadricep stretch is when you're on your side. Hold one ankle and pull it back while keeping the other leg parallel to the ground.

Figure 11-1:
Stretching
your
quadriceps.

- ✔ **Hamstring and lower calf:** Again, you're sitting on the ground. With one foot extended, extend your arm as far as you can to that leg while trying to keep your back straight, as shown in Figure 11-2.

- ✔ **Groin:** While you're still sitting on the ground, place the soles of both your feet together so that your knees are bent to the side. Then try to get the knees as close to the ground as possible while keeping your back straight and pushing your chest forward, as shown in Figure 11-3. Too many players miss games due to pulled groin muscles. This exercise decreases the chances of it occurring.

- ✔ **Lower back:** Lie down while you pull one or both knees toward your chest. You should keep your shoulders and head on the ground, as shown in Figure 11-4.

- ✔ **Calf muscle/Achilles tendon:** You will need a teammate or a wall for this stretch because you will be standing. Place one leg forward, bending it at the knee, as you push forward against your teammate or a wall. Keep your back foot flat on the ground. The forward leg stretches the Achilles tendon, while the straight back leg stretches the calf muscle, as shown in Figure 11-5. This stretch is a key for running long periods of time and in sprinting.

- ✔ **Hip flexor:** Get on one knee and then bend your rear leg so that the knee is near the ground while you extend the front leg and your hands forward toward your toes.

Figure 11-2:
Stretching your hamstring and lower calf.

Figure 11-3:
Stretching
your groin.

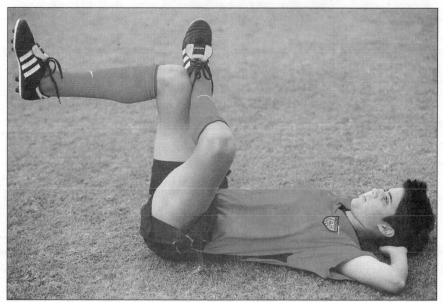

Figure 11-4:
Stretching
your lower
back.

Figure 11-5:
Stretching
your calves.

Cooling Down

Unfortunately, not enough emphasis has been put on cooling down after matches, especially after playing a strenuous game. Players who go from peak activity to doing nothing risk cramps because the muscles are fully extended.

Jogging is a good way to cool down. In addition, many prematch stretching exercises (see preceding section) and the simple shaking of the legs are perfect for postgame exercises.

Some pro teams perform a cool-down period for 30 to 45 minutes after games. It cuts down on the soreness the following day. A lot of lactic acid builds up in the muscles during strenuous activity, and the cooling down process relieves it.

Practice May Not Make Perfect, but It Makes a Better Player

In youth and amateur soccer, you may have only one organized team practice a week, so you need to practice on your own or with your friends. It doesn't have to be a formal one. Just kicking the ball around, dribbling, passing, and shooting will suffice. You cannot touch the ball enough. While dribbling, running, and passing, you will get exercise.

It's not such a bad idea to do some running and stretching before you stage informal practices.

In pro soccer, championships can be won or lost in the preseason. If preparation is done correctly, players and teams can avoid major muscle injuries during the regular season. Of course, no preseason regimen is foolproof. Accidents do occur, and so do injuries — major and minor ones — even to players who are in the best of shape.

Drills

In youth soccer, drills for the younger age groups usually consist of ones that enhance the players' skills and team work. Not surprisingly, as players get older, the drills change and can become a little more sophisticated as well. Here are some drills you should consider using in practice:

✔ **Shooting drills** are probably the most popular of all drills because players have an opportunity to shoot, everyone loves to score goals, and it sharpens their skills. You can vary the type of drills as well, from hitting a target in the corner of the net to placing your shot between the goalpost and a cone.

✔ Every team should take time attempting and **defending set pieces** — free kicks and corner kicks. Before you enter a game, you should know who will take your free kicks and corner kicks. You may even want to concoct an innovative play or two to take advantage of your players' skills. Defending these *dead-ball situations,* as they are also called, is vital as well. On free kicks, you want to know which players will line up in the wall and which players will be positioned near the net. That goes for corner kicks as well. It is important to know that a reliable player will cover the posts. Just remember: Converting and defending against set pieces could very well wind up as the difference between a win and a loss.

✔ If you're about to enter a knockout competition that requires some sort of tiebreaker after games that finish in a tie, it may be wise to have the players **practice penalty kicks** at the end of practices several days before you're first game. You don't know how many coaches have failed to advance in a competition without practicing penalties.

Scrimmages: The best part of practice

Practice should not be just about getting fit or dribbling the ball through cones. The best part of practice should be playing the game itself. Here are some of the most basic practice scrimmages:

✔ **Game scrimmage:** This scrimmage is the most popular scrimmage because it is played under game conditions with the coach usually acting as the referee. If you're fortunate enough to have 22 bodies at practice, you can play a full-sided game. But that's a rarity. So teams often wind up playing 8 versus 8 or 6 versus 6. There's certainly nothing wrong with that, especially when you get an opportunity to touch the ball more and participate more.

✔ **One-touch scrimmage:** This scrimmage forces players to literally think on their feet because they have to make a quick decision on what they're going to do with the ball before they even get it. A word to the wise: Young and beginning players should not participate in these type of scrimmages because their ability to dribble and other individual skills should be developed at the level they are currently.

The right time to spice up your practice

Say that you're a youth soccer player bored with just kicking the ball around with your friends or you're a coach who wants to add a little pizzazz to your practices.

Running around cones and passing the ball is only effective to a certain point. Sooner or later, you will want to make the practice a little (or a lot) more interesting. After all, youth soccer is supposed to be fun, not tedious. A bored player is an ineffective player.

Here are some ideas to try:

✔ **Small-sided games:** When in doubt, go back to the basics. Play 3 versus 3 or 5 versus 5 without a goalkeeper and using cones for smaller goals, not unlike what the youngest teams do at the intramural level. Due to the size of teams, you probably will need to have two or three games going on at the same time. But small-side games keep every player active and doing what she enjoys most about the game: kicking the ball and scoring goals.

✔ **Monkey in the middle:** This game is another basic, but effective, one that keeps the players active. You need a minimum of four players. The premise is simple: Three or more players have to keep the ball away from the fourth. While they are doing this game, the group in the circle are developing skills while playing in close quarters. The one in the middle is developing his defensive skills and ability to read where the opposition's pass is heading.

✔ **Heading volleyball:** The only drawback to this exercise, which should be used for players age 11 and up, is that you need some kind of a net or something to separate the sides. But this drill may improve the heading of your players. Treat it like a volleyball game and give points when a team is unable to head the ball over the net. Handling the ball is not allowed, unless it is for serving. Unlike volleyball, in which the taller players are sometimes at a greater advantage, the better skilled players with their heads could dominate.

You can do a variation of this drill in which only feet are involved.

✔ **Soccer baseball:** This game develops accuracy and power. Like heading volleyball, hands are not allowed. But unlike the other drill, everything is done with your feet. A minimum of five players a side is needed with an area big enough for a small baseball diamond. The object of the game is similar to that of baseball. The pitcher kicks the ball to the batter with his foot, and the batter "swings" with his foot as well. The obvious way to play it is as a regular baseball game. The fielders have to get the ball to the base before the batter or runner is retired.

One variation has the batter run around the bases after he has kicked the ball. The fielding team must pass the ball around the infield. If the batter beats the relay, his team gets a run. If the fielding team beats the batter, he is retired.

✔ **Soccer golf:** This exercise develops accuracy with short, medium, and long-range passing. Spread out cones throughout the field and have players kick the ball toward the cones. The one that has used the least amount of kicks to reach the cones is declared the winner.

✔ **Juggling contests:** The object is to juggle the ball with a foot, head, or chest for as long as possible. You can do this exercise individually or as a group. Juggling doesn't mean that you are a better player, but it certainly can develop your skills, especially when you are alone.

✔ **Hot potato:** This game is the musical chairs of soccer. You need at least four players to form a circle. The object of this game is to get rid of the ball as quickly as possible before the music — well, in this case, a clock or whistle — sounds. The player with the ball is eliminated. This goes on until you have a winner.

✔ **Walking only scrimmage:** This scrimmage develops the players' passing ability. Because it would take all day to bring the ball up the field by walking, players are encouraged to pass to move it up the field more quickly.

✔ **Score-off-a-head-shot scrimmage:** This scrimmage helps develop players' head shots in and around the goal. Both teams can bring the ball down field any way they so choose. The only goals that are counted are ones that are headed in.

Preseason practice for pros

Preseason practice probably is the most grueling and potentially the most boring part of practice. For the first five or six days of practice, professional players don't touch a ball as they are put through a series of running exercises designed to build up their aerobic base and extend their legs.

These running drills involve long sprints and short sprints, plus a change-of-direction drill, which is what a player does a lot in a game.

Besides, these practices get the players "hungry" for the ball.

Middle of the season practice

If a player isn't in shape by midseason, he is in big trouble.

If you're playing three games in eight days — Sunday, Wednesday, and Sunday again — there's no time for serious fitness practices. Players usually get a day after a game to rest physically and mentally. The next couple of days involve lighter preparation, physical and tactical, for the next opponent.

Some Food for Thought: Eating Right

I can't stress the need for good nutrition whether you are a player or not, but it is vital if you are an active athlete. You burn more calories and need more energy for practices and matches.

The Food Pyramid

Players, coaches, and parents should be familiar with the Food Pyramid well before they begin athletics.

The recommended diet for active soccer players should contain about 60 percent of the calories from carbohydrates, 15 percent from protein, and 25 percent from fat. Players should eat the most foods from the bottom of the Pyramid, gradually tapering off as you go up each level.

At the base are grains, such as cereals and breads, which include carbohydrates and vitamin B, which is used in energy production. Fruits and vegetables, which are also rich in carbohydrates and fiber, are at the next level. Then comes the dairy group (milk and cheese), which has calcium and protein. Next are meat, poultry, and fish, which furnish protein and a number of vital minerals. At the very top of the pyramid are the fats, oils, and sweets, which should be used sparingly. This group includes butter, soft drinks, salad dressing, and dessert.

What to eat before matches

Everyone has ideas on what to eat before a game. Generally, players should eat a meal three or four hours before the game for maximum energy and minimal digestive difficulty. Many players and coaches like foods that have lots of high carbohydrates, including pasta, cereals, bread, and vegetables.

In fact, many pro teams eat together — home and away — to make sure that players consume the proper nutrients before a game.

Stay away from fast foods and fatty foods. They are likely to remain in your digestive system longer than other foods. The last thing you need entering a big game is to be sluggish.

Liquid diets

Today, ads tells you that this nutritional drink will boost a player's energy levels. The sugar (glucose) from the drink helps the rate at which an athlete's body can absorb water. By getting fluid and glucose to the muscles, the player will have more energy to perform. All things being equal, most players prefer a sports drink that tastes good.

While studies vary on the value of sports drinks, the best drink in the world still is water. Players should get plenty of it — before, during, and after practices and games. Any coach who doesn't have water breaks, particularly on rather warm days, is negligent in his job.

Caffeine products such as soda, coffee, and tea should not be part of a young player's fluid intake because caffeine is dehydrating.

Some important tips about water

✔ Fluid intake varies per player. A 100-lb. boy or girl needs eight cups of water a day. If they reach 150 lbs., it changes a bit. A boy will require 13 cups, while a girl will need 12.

✔ Water intake will vary, depending on the weather. If you're playing in the middle of the day during the summer, you'll probably need more liquids than a cool night in September.

✔ Players should have water available even when it's cold out. You need water to replenish yourself.

✔ Always bring a bottle with you to games or practice. Do not assume that water will be available.

✔ You have two choices — bottled water or tap water. Pick the one that tastes best or is best for your budget. One isn't necessarily better than the other.

✔ Water has no calories, so drink away.

Chapter 12

Playing It Safe

· ·

In This Chapter

▶ Taking preventive measures

▶ Breaking the ice with ice

▶ Dealing with common injuries

▶ Coping with knee injuries

· ·

*L*ike it or not, injuries are part of the game — in all sports. Sometimes two players collide while pursuing the ball. Other times, a player pulls a muscle or turns an ankle when running. Most injuries are accidents, although players have been known from time to time to act maliciously with the intent to injure an opponent. If the referee sees this behavior, he should red-card the player immediately and write him up in the referee's postgame report.

In some soccer leagues in the world, the disciplinary committees have taken the eye-for-eye and tooth-for-a-tooth attitude. For example, if a player is to miss ten weeks with an injury, the player who caused the injury should miss ten weeks as well. This type of discipline may sound severe, but it could cut down the number of vicious tackles.

Helping Prevent Injuries

The best way to handle injuries is to be prepared for as many emergencies as possible and to do your homework. Follow these tips to decrease your chance of injury and to know how to handle them if they do occur:

✔ **Stay in shape:** A fit player can decrease her chances of getting injured. Of course, being in the best of shape doesn't stop every kind of injury. But being in shape is one less reason to pull a muscle or to take longer from coming back from an injury.

✔ **Get your preseason checkup:** Pro teams have preseason medical check-ups, and many older age youth teams do as well. Each coach should keep a list of the players who have allergies and the ones who have pre-existing medical conditions.

✔ **Don't forget to stretch:** If you want to avoid pulling muscles in practice and games, a good stretch of the key leg muscles is mandatory. Stretching doesn't take more than 10 to 15 minutes. Studies have shown that the more flexible players are, the less prone they are to injuries. (See Chapter 11 for some stretching exercises.)

✔ **Use the right equipment:** Don't laugh. Every precaution helps. Every player must wear shinguards, which protect a sensitive part of the body. Your soccer shoes should fit just right. Poor-fitting shoes can cause blisters and injuries. Soccer balls should not be over- or underinflated.

✔ **Have phone access:** In this age of high tech, at least one team should have a cellular phone in case of an emergency, on and off the field. If one isn't available, make sure that you know where the nearest phone booth is just in case a player needs further assistance after an injury. Also, parents should know the address of and directions to the field because many are in such out-of-the-way places.

✔ **Know your phone numbers:** The most important phone number to know is the closest hospital to the field you are playing. If you are on the road, remind yourself to research the nearest hospital. Assume that the home team doesn't have this type of information, although it should. Also, the coach should have home, work, paging, and cellular phone numbers for all players' parents and backup numbers for family and friends if the parents cannot be reached.

✔ **Have a First-Aid kit ready:** Every team should have some sort of a First-Aid kit to handle minor bumps, scrapes, and bruises. For the more serious injuries, you can still use a First Aid kit. But some players should be taken immediately to a doctor or hospital. At the very least, a kit should have plenty of sterile pads, gauze pads, bandages, scissors, towelettes, antiseptic, and disposal gloves.

✔ **Know CPR:** In a perfect world, everyone would know this important life-saving procedure. Every coach should have to take a CPR course. He or she probably will never have to use it, but the key word is *probably*. You never know when you will have to save a life on or off the field.

✔ **Check out the weather conditions:** Weather conditions can play a role in a player's health. While many pro teams play in all sort of conditions, from snow to high wind to high temperatures to torrential rainstorms, youth players should not be subjected to such severe weather. On an extremely hot day, a team and even individual players should have plenty of ice cold water. The last thing you want is a heat stroke.

✔ **Have plenty of water handy:** I cannot say enough about having cold water for replenishment, particularly on a hot and humid summer day.

✔ **Don't forget ice:** Someone, the coach, a designated parent or the home club, should have ice on hand in case of an injury.

✔ **Examine the field condition:** A player can sustain an injury — ankle, knee or other — from a field that has holes, divots, rocks, and even garbage on it. Before a home match, the players, coaches, and team officials should patrol the field to make sure that are no problem areas exist. In fact, away teams should examine the field during road games as well.

✔ **Make sure that a trainer, doctor, or nurse is available at camps and tournaments:** Even when you're not present, you can have influence. Always make sure that the camp and/or tournament your child or team attends has a trainer, doctor, or nurse. If not, attending the camp or tournament is not worth the risk of injury to your child.

Do not panic if your child is injured. Yes, it is a horrible time when your son or daughter is injured, but the last thing he or she needs is to see you upset because panic can set in.

Referees have been instructed not to touch a player who is seriously injured because many referee associations fear a lawsuit if a game official handles an injured player.

Treating Injuries: R.I.C.E.

On youth teams, make sure that someone — coach, parent, or team/club official — is in charge of bringing ice to games. More often than not, you may not need it, but it will be a godsend when you do.

Ice is used as a First-Aid treatment to decrease the swelling after a bruise, after pulling or straining a muscle, or after spraining or even breaking a bone.

The best way to remember ice's optimal use is by RICE:

R = Rest
I = Ice
C = Compress
E = Elevate

✔ **Rest** speaks for itself. The player doesn't move at all.

✔ **Ice** must be used properly. To stop or limit blood flow and pain, you should place crushed ice in a double plastic bag, a wet towel, or an ice bag. The ice pack should remain on the injury for 15 minutes of every waking hour for the first 24 to 72 hours, depending on the severity of the injury and how quickly the swelling abates. (See Figure 12-1.)

Figure 12-1:
Use crushed
ice to
reduce
swelling.

✔ You then need to **compress** the injury. After you finish with the ice, replace it with an elastic wrap. If you are wrapping an injured leg or arm, start at the place most distance from the heart and work your way toward the heart in a criss-cross fashion. Toes and fingers of the injured player should be slightly exposed so that you can watch for skin discolorations.

✔ You should then **elevate** the injured arm or leg above the heart level for the first 24 to 72 hours. You should go to a physician if swelling continues.

Handling Common Soccer Injuries

Like any sport, soccer players can be beset by any number of injuries, from broken legs to broken arms to separated and dislocated shoulders. These severe injuries, however, are quite rare in soccer. However, ankle sprains and groin pulls are more common. Because knee injuries can be so problematic and so common in soccer, I devote an entire section to it later in this chapter.

What if someone gets hurt?

When a player is injured at the lower age groups, the players have been taught to drop to the ground on one knee so that no one moves.

In the older age groups, the ball is immediately kicked out of bounds so that the team trainer or doctor can attend to the injured party.

Ankle sprains

Ankle sprains are perhaps the most frustrating of all injuries because they can happen to any player at any time if she turns the wrong way on the field (or even off of it). Ankle sprains, which are tears of the ligaments, are classified three ways.

✔ Very little swelling occurs in a *first-degree sprain,* and the player can return in two weeks.

✔ A *second-degree sprain* is much more serious because the ligaments are partially torn. A player can be sidelined from three to six weeks.

✔ The most severe is a *third-degree sprain,* which is an extreme tear of the liagments. Surgery is not normally required, but the injury can take from eight to 12 weeks to heal.

Groin pulls

Groin pulls are caused by the sudden overstretching of the leg and thigh and overstretched muscle fibers or tendons along the bony area of the pelvic area. Sometimes groin pulls occur in players who are out of shape. You can treat groin pulls with rest, physical therapy, anti-inflammatory drugs, and then even more rest.

If a player returns too soon and doesn't realize that the muscle hasn't healed properly, he can re-aggravate the injury.

Other common injuries

Soccer injuries aren't limited to sprains, pulls, and knee problems. Table 12-1 lists some other ailments you may encounter while enjoying the sport.

Table 12-1	Common Soccer Ailments	
Ailment	*Symptoms*	*Suggested Treatment*
Abrasion	Loss of skin surface	Cleanse with antiseptic and apply antibiotic ointment
Blister	Fluid buildup under the skin	Have it drained by a qualified person and clean the area

(continued)

Table 12-1 *(continued)*

Ailment	Symptoms	Suggested Treatment
Concussion	Severe blow to the head, which can cause dizziness, dull to severe headache, ringing in the ears, disorientation, and a possible loss of consciousness	Remove from contest and do not allow player to re-enter game even if he assures he is fine. Have the player see a doctor.
Contusion	A bruised muscle or tendon	RICE method
Cramps	Involuntary and painful contraction	Firm pressure on the muscle area combined with a gentle massage. Hydrate the player.
Heat exhaustion	Weakness/pale clammy skin, profuse perspiration, but normal body temperature, possible cramps, nausea, dizziness, vomiting, and fainting	Lie the player down with the feet slightly raised. Loosen clothing, apply wet cloths and fan player or remove to a cooler area. Provide water in small doses every hour. If the player vomits, discontinue fluids and take to a hospital.
Heat stroke	High temperature; red, dry and hot skin; rapid pulse; weakness (possible loss of consciousness); and little or no noticeable sweating	Remove clothing (without compromising privacy), sponge bare skin with cool water or place in a tub with cool water and bring to a cooler or air-conditioned area. Avoid stimulants and overcooling. Quickly get professional help.
Sprain	Injured ligament(s)	RICE method. If any doubt, seek professional help.
Strain	Torn muscle or tendon	RICE method. If any doubt, seek professional help.

Coping with Knee Injuries

Knee injuries can occur when a player has her leg fixed in the ground by the cleats of her soccer shoe and then is jolted by a sudden uncontrolled rotation of the body while she is passing, running, or colliding with another player.

Even though knee injuries can be serious, soccer has only one-fifth the number of knee problems as football.

Thanks to modern medical science and arthroscopic surgery, crippling knee injuries, for the most part, are things of the past. In fact, arthroscopic surgery has extended the careers of many talented players. For example, U.S. Women's National Team star Michelle Akers has endured 13 knee operations in her long career, and she still is an effective player.

While the treatment and care of these injuries has improved immensely over the past 20 years, you need to remember that players are only human and are susceptible to injury.

The knee

The knee is one of the most flexible joints in the human body as it can bend 150 degrees. You need that flexibility if you are to change direction quickly.

The knee has no muscles, but it has three bones — femur, tibia, and fibula — which are held together by ligaments. Knee injuries can occur in five places: ligaments, cartilage (called menisci), muscles surrounding the knee, kneecap (patella), and tendons. The most common injuries occur to four ligaments — anterior cruciate ligament, posterior ligament, medial collateral ligament, and lateral collateral ligament.

The three degrees of knee injuries

The degree of an injury is what tells you the amount of damage that has occurred. A first-degree injury is the least severe, while a third-degree injury is the most severe. If a player is not examined six to 12 hours after the injury, it is often difficult ascertain what degree of injury has occurred. The degree of injury determines the severity of the knee injury.

 ✔ **First degree:** This is a mild tear of the ligament, muscle, or tendon. It can be caused by a sudden twist or rapid movement, chronic overuse, or fatigue. Slight swelling occurs. The player has little or no limitations in his range of motion.

✔ **Second degree:** This is a moderate tear because there is a loss in function. The player feels a moderate amount of pain, swelling, and the loss of full range of motion of the joint. Other symptoms include a discoloration in the affected area and the possibility of a deformity.

✔ **Third degree:** This is worst type of tear, the complete rupture of a muscle, tendon, or ligament. Functional ability ceases to exist. Symptoms include discoloration, deformity, and possible joint discoloration. This injury often requires a brace, cast, or surgery.

Anterior cruciate ligament tear

The anterior cruciate ligament tear is the worst of all knee injuries.

The anterior cruciate ligament, or ACL, as it is commonly known, is a ligament within the knee joint that attaches from the posterior part of the femur to the anterior part of the tibia. Almost 60 percent of knee ligament injuries involve at least a partial injury to the ACL.

A player can injure his ACL by twisting or turning suddenly, getting kicked below the injury, hyperextending it, or quickly slowing down. A player may hear or feel a pop in his knee and feel as though the knee is going to give way.

If an ACL injury is suspected, you should assist the player off the field and have ice immediately applied to the injured area. Then wrap the injured knee in an elastic wrap. If reconstructive surgery is needed, the player will be sidelined for at least eight months.

U.S. National Team midfielder Tab Ramos tore his ACL when a Trinidad & Tobago player tackled him during a World Cup qualifier in November 1996. He was sidelined for eight months before returning to the New York/New Jersey MetroStars in July 1997. He made a full recovery and played at a high level until he re-injured the knee during a noncontact drill at a National Team practice in November 1997. Unfortunately, he has not made a full recovery since that injury.

Medial cruciate ligament tear

The medial cruciate ligament tear is the most common knee injury, comprising 90 percent of all knee-related injuries. The medial collateral ligament is a thick fan-shaped ligament that is located on the inside of the knee. It attaches from the femur to the tibia. It is the strongest ligament in the knee, yet it is one of the most commonly injured in sports.

Other tears

Other tears, which are not as common, include the posterior cruciate ligament and lateral collateral cruciate ligament. The posterior cruciate ligament is stronger and thicker than the ACL, so it is not torn as much. The lateral collateral ligament, which is smaller than the MCL, is rarely torn because the angle of force that would tear it is uncommon in sports.

Treatment for tears

In all cases regarding knee injuries, the player should be assisted off the field and immediately put ice to the injured area. Then you should wrap the knee in an elastic wrap and then see a physician.

Chapter 13

The Mental Game, Teamwork, and Winning

*W*hen a team is victorious in an important game, the players and coaches sometimes like to say that their team was "up for the game." What does that mean? Well, *up for the game* can have several meanings. Sometimes it is the will and desire of the players. Other times, it is how well a player or team is focused on a game. Sometimes it's being opportunistic and alert, taking advantage of the opposition's mistakes.

Setting Goals

Before a season, a coach and his team should make goals they want to reach. Goals can be simple ones. For younger youth teams, goals may include developing a skill or several skills over a series of games or over the season. For older age groups, goals may be qualifying for a state tournament or winning their club division. During the season, goals may change. A successful team may want to add winning a tournament or a cup competition if they're doing well. If things aren't going according to plan, the team may want to avoid relegation to a lower division.

In the pros, goals can include qualifying for the playoffs after a dismal season or reaching the championship game for a second consecutive year.

Understanding the Intangibles

You can measure a players' worth, skill, or productivity in many ways. How tall is she? How much does he weigh? How fast is she? How many goals and assists did he have in his last season, and so on?

But to measure the true worth of a player, you must go beyond the numbers. A good deal of it is through three intangibles — vision, heart, and guts.

If a player has all three plus talent, she can go a long way — perhaps as a star in college in a professional league or all the way to the National Team.

Vision

Vision is not about whether a player has 20-20 vision or wears glasses or contact lenses. It's about how he sees the game — for example, does he see a play or pass develop before it happens? Decisions have to be made quickly in soccer.

Former German international and New York Cosmos great Frank Beckenbauer had a great vision of the game. In only a fraction of a second, he could make a decision on what he would do with the ball, many times before he had received it from a teammate. His decision-making process included to whom and where he would pass, how he would pass it, and when he would pass it. Of course, Beckenbauer had another option as well — he could dribble the ball himself. (See Chapter 5 for more on dribbling the ball.)

Heart

When we say heart, we're not talking about whether a player has a healthy heart to pump blood to the legs, but rather whether she has what it takes to do the little extra things to win.

Can she play with a nagging injury or a little pain? Can she find a little extra when the game is tied late in a match? And can she find a way to win and bring out the best in a teammate?

Guts

Guts has nothing to do with the physical end — the stomach and a players' diet — although you may say having guts is whether a player can stomach the really tough parts of a game.

Can he avoid being intimidated by an opposing player? Is the player willing to put his body on the line to attempt a difficult tackle? Is the player willing to do the dirty work to help the team? Or is the player willing to take a little punishment from a defender while going for a loose ball? That's what having guts is all about, although pros use another term for that word. (But because this book is G-rated, we're not going to use that word.)

Developing a Passion for the Game

What separates the great players from the run-of-the-mill ones? Besides talent, passion for the game can be a determining factor. The more a player gets into the game, the more he learns about it and becomes a better player. In many instances, passion and talent go hand in hand. Translated: You've got to live the game!

Passionate players scour newspapers and the Internet to read about how their favorite teams and players are doing, not just in the United States, but worldwide as well. They subscribe to several soccer publications. They watch soccer videos. When they're not playing, they attend college and pro soccer games in their area or watch games on TV.

For some players, soccer becomes their lives. They either go on to become star college players or a professional in Major League Soccer, A-League, or D3 Pro League or a youth, high school, college, or pro coach.

Yes, youth coaches have gone on to coach pros. Al Pastore, who coached F.C. Westchester, a successful boys youth team in suburban New York City, went on to own and coach the Wilmington Hammerheads in North Carolina in the D3 Pro League.

For the beginner player, soccer videos should be limited to skills and instructional. After she has developed an understanding of the game, then she can go on to watch videos of historical games and the greatest goals.

Mental Preparation

Mental preparation for a game can take all sorts of avenues. In the pros, some players like quiet time. They prefer to lie down in and around their lockers, and some players actually sleep. Others are so keyed up that they don't talk to their teammates, while yet others joke around with their teammates.

Mentally preparing for a game doesn't have any set formula, and a player should establish a routine that he is comfortable with. The key is the player's focus on and preparation for the game. For the youth or amateur player, this may mean getting to the field at a certain time so that he can take his time preparing.

Besides being a marathon for the legs, soccer is a marathon for the mind as well. Players must be alert for 90 minutes. They should never, ever lose their concentration in a match. That little lapse may lead to a goal — the only goal in a game or the winning one.

It is a well-known fact that teams score goals and take advantage of players and teams who let down their guard at the beginnings and ends of halves and matches. Another time when a team or player can lose concentration is after their team scores a goal, especially after a celebration. They can become so keyed up or happy at that juncture that they actually lack focus and concentration to stop the opposition.

Thinking positive

If you think you can do it — beating a superior defender to score a goal or defeating a better team — you are halfway there. If you think you can't, you probably won't.

Before taking on China in the championship game of the 1999 Women's World Cup, former U.S. Women's National Team coach Tony DiCicco had a long list of negative things he wanted to go over with his team. But after talking to the team psychologist, he thought it was better to accentuate the positive and talk about the good things the players did and forget about the negative.

When he wanted to prepare his players for the 1996 Summer Olympics, DiCicco had the team imagine they were on the podium receiving their gold medals. DiCicco had the team close their eyes and imagine the incredible feeling and exaltation of being an Olympic champion. It worked. The U.S. won the gold.

Motivating yourself

Beyond an inspiring speech from the coach, every player should be able to get mentally prepared for a game. If a player can't become excited about a soccer game or any other sporting competition, then he must consider whether he should continue. Yes, everyone has down days, whether it is emotional or physical. But if a player can't get up for a match on a consistent basis, then something more serious is happening.

Motivating a team or player

Of course, coaches should not leave anything to chance. They should talk to their team about a game. The better the opponent, the more motivated and prepared the team should be. Coaches sometimes give their most important talks before their team plays an inferior team. They feel their team has to be reminded not to take the opposition too lightly or play down to them.

Most, if not all coaches today, have to be amateur psychologists in dealing with the different moods, personalities, and characters of players. What works with one team or player won't with another. The younger the team, the more likely the coach will take a more positive more approach. As players grow older into their teens, some players can be shouted or yelled at to get a point across or to take criticism. Others won't. By the time a player reaches the pro level, he should be able to motivate himself. However, by then, coaches aren't allowed to give a shout or yell when he feels a team needs a push or two.

Some players need to be coddled and not shouted at, while others thrive when a coach is on their backs. Some players, such as U.S. National Team and D.C. United defender Eddie Pope, who is one of the nicest guys in the sport, actually play better when they're angry.

How Sigi Schmid motivates his teams

Los Angeles Galaxy coach Sigi Schmid has a unique perspective of the game because he has guided teams at every level. He has coached every youth age category, from Under-9 to Under-19. He has coached in high school, college, and, of course, the pros. He also has coached internationally as an assistant with the U.S. National Team and most recently with the U.S. Under-20 National Team in the world championship in 1999.

"We've become a lot more self-centered society," he said. "When I would go into a kid's home to recruit him in the mid-80s, I talked about the team. Now, parents and players want to hear, 'I think you can be an All-American, player of the year.' The parents don't want to hear about you talking about the team. They want to know if their son can become the next Tiger Woods.

"I'm a team-oriented person. You have to take a look at the players' personality and character as much as talent. You have to be honest."

Living in Los Angeles, Schmid learned a lot from a pair of former basketball coaches in that area — UCLA's John Wooten and the Los Angeles Lakers' Pat Riley, who used the same unique psychology to get their message across to a pair of star players (Kareem Abdul-Jabbar and Magic Johnson).

"They were playing five-on-five in practice when Riley starts ripping into Magic," Schmid said. "The problem was that Kareem was dogging it. Riley knew that if he got on Kareem, he wouldn't take it."

So he picked on Johnson, who could take it, and the message would be passed on to Jabbar.

Remember, every coach has a different personality and philosophy that he brings to the table.

U.S. National Team coach Bruce Arena, shown in Figure 13-1, likes to add sarcasm to his practices to motivate players. It might work with John Harkes, whom he knows very well because he coached him at the University of Virginia and D.C. United in Major League Soccer. It might not work with a player he isn't familiar with personally.

Figure 13-1:
U.S.
National
Team coach
Bruce
Arena
knows how
to motivate
players.

If a coach makes every game a big game, the team could burn out or have difficulty preparing for a real big game, whether it is in a Cup competition or for a league championship. The players will tune out the coach and not listen to him because the players are hearing the same old stuff.

Leadership Roles for Players

Leadership doesn't always have to come from the coach. It can come from the players as well, whether it is a team captain or a natural leader who is not a captain.

Team captain

In many respects, the team captain is an extension of the coach. Many coaches like to pick their team captains, although at the professional level in Europe or South America, the team may vote on it. Teams can have a captain or cocaptains. Many high school and college teams like to have tricaptains — three veteran or senior players. It depends on what the coach is comfortable with.

Team captains have varying responsibilities. They are expected to lead the team in pregame drills. They also should be the only player allowed to talk with the referee after a controversial call without getting a yellow card (outside of dissent).

The success of the U.S. in the Women's World Cup in 1999 certainly was helped by the fact that the team had cocaptains who complemented each other quite well. Carla Overbeck was an experienced defender who organized the team on the field, while popular midfielder Julie Foudy acted as the team's voice when the game was over.

Captains' responsibilities change from level to level, according to Schmid.

"In Europe, it's more important (having captains). They negotiate the bonus structure with the team.

"As a college coach, I was the one who picked the team captain. I didn't want it to become a popularity contest.

"When I came in with the Galaxy, Robin Fraser was captain. I saw no reason to change. When he was injured, I picked Mauricio Cienfuegos. When both weren't there, I chose Cobi (Jones) as captain."

Team leaders

You don't have to be a captain to be a team leader, whether it's in the locker room or on the field. Some players are natural leaders and can have an effect on their team, whether it is by giving an impassioned speech before a game or at halftime or even by leading by example. If a star player is willing to do the dirty work in practice or during a game, there is a good chance the rest of the team will fall into line.

Veteran players have been known to take young players under their wing to show them the ropes, especially in college and the pros.

Tony DiCicco, who directed the U.S. Women's National Team to an Olympic gold medal and a world championship, realized the success of the team had a lot to do with attitude.

"You have to create a culture in the team. The coach can't do it alone. If you're going to create a mentality, the culture must come from within a team. That means within the leaders of the team. Some leaders are incredibly positive, and in our case, we had wonderful leadership. Carla Overbeck is one of our fittest players, if not our fittest player. She is our No. 1 leader. Julie Foudy — one of our fittest players. Kristine Lilly, one of our fittest players and one of our leaders. Mia Hamm, one of our leaders. Michelle Akers. All these players pride themselves on fitness. They pride themselves on training very hard every day in practice.

"A new player comes into the team. If they don't buy into this culture, it may happen that they don't make it. They just might fall out of the team. If you don't buy into this culture the team created, it won't work out for you. It's discipline on the field and off the field."

Schmid realizes how important it is to get his message out to key players, who could relay it to the rest of the team.

"At UCLA, I always established a group of four to six players who were sort of my core group," he said. "I would tell them what system we were playing and explained why. If you convince your core group, then it would be easier for the rest of the team. After I told the team, a player might ask another, 'Why are we playing it? It's stupid' One of my core players would say, 'I think it's a good idea.'"

Part IV
A Spectator's Guide

The 5th Wave   By Rich Tennant

WESTVIEW HIGH SCHOOL
SOCCER LEAGUE
VICTORY DINNER

Lucky Goalie—
gets to use
his hands.

In this part . . .

*1*f you can't get enough of soccer, make sure that you check out this part. You find specific tips for viewing soccer games, as well as TV shows, Web sites, and reading material you can review for maximum spectator enjoyment.

Chapter 14

Follow the Bouncing Ball

● ●

In This Chapter

▶ Knowing what to watch for at your first soccer game

▶ Keeping your eye on the goalkeeper

▶ Watching for opportunities after goals

▶ Understanding substitutions

▶ Watching soccer on TV

● ●

*Y*ou don't have to be an X's and O's person or take countless coaching courses to truly understand and enjoy the game of soccer. Here are some tips and pointers that will make your stay at the game, whether it be youth, college, pro, or international, that much more enlightening.

Some Quick Pointers to Get You Started

Here are some quick tips that will help you enjoy watching a soccer game even more.

✔ **Always be prepared.** If you're going to a day game, you may wind up sitting in the sun. So, sunblock isn't a bad idea. If it looks like it will rain, an umbrella will do just fine. Yes, you can even bring food into some stadiums (please check beforehand so you aren't disappointed), and many pro teams encourage tailgate parties before games.

✔ **Don't whistle an unhappy tune.** In Europe, South America, and most of the rest of the soccer-playing world, whistling during a game signifies disenchantment with the play on the field. So, watch when and where you whistle, unless you really, really mean it.

✔ **Color your world.** If you're going to a U.S. National team match, you might want to show some patriotism and support by wearing the home team's colors. You can do this for your club, high school, college, or pro team, too. Word of advice: Don't show up wearing the opposition's colors. It's not politically correct or good for your health.

✔ **Don't sit on your hands.** The biggest criticism made toward American soccer fans is that they don't know how to cheer or what to cheer for at a professional game. Make some constructive noise once in a while and not just on goals. (Root, root, root for the home team doesn't only apply to baseball, you know.) There are many fine plays and passes in the game that should be complimented. Many ardent spectators of pro teams have chants and songs for their heroes. You may want to join in on a few or make some up yourself.

✔ **Get plugged-in.** If your local college or pro team broadcasts the game on radio, you may want to consider taking a radio to the game. You may be able to find out some pointers about the game and something new about your heroes.

✔ **Go to the videotape.** If the game you are attending is being televised, you may want to tape it because there may be a memorable goal scored. Or, if you are a coach, taped plays could become a valuable vehicle in learning about and teaching the game. (For more on coaching soccer, see Chapter 10.)

✔ **Ask for signs of the times.** Unlike their counterparts in baseball, many pro and semi-pro soccer players love to sign autographs. And, they do it for free! It's great for the kids, who get an opportunity to meet their heroes — up close and personal. It's also an inexpensive souvenir. So, don't forget to bring your autograph book, or at least paper and pen.

The Formation

While not etched in stone, how a team lines up can tell you how they may play during a game. If a team deploys a 5-4-1 formation (that's five defenders, four midfielders and one forward), you probably should be prepared for that squad to play a more defensive game. If it uses a 4-2-4, expect it to attack a lot. (See Chapter 9 for more on plays and strategies.)

Figuring out a team's formation at the opening kickoff is difficult. It usually takes a good five to ten minutes before you figure out who is playing where. Count the players lining up immediately in front of the goalkeeper to determine who is playing defense. It's sometimes not as easy for midfielders and forwards because their positions can be a lot more fluid. Keep in mind, though, that not all formations are etched in stone. Players will wander from midfield to forward and overlap from defense into the attack. Other factors influencing formations are field conditions and dimensions and the opposing team's strengths and weaknesses. Also, teams may change their formations and tactics at halftime to counter the opponent. And as the game progresses, a team with the lead will drop back and become more defensive. A team trailing will become more offensive.

Another key to watching a game is if the defense can keep its shape; that is, defenders are in the area of the field they patrol. Depending on the formation, teams use from three to five defenders. Attacking sides will try to stretch the defense to get players out of position so that they can find a hole where forward or midfielder can put through a devastating pass or take a dangerous shot. The likelihood of this happening at the opening whistle isn't great, as it takes several minutes for teams to probe each other's defense. Keeping shape is also the way a team as a whole maintains the distance between all its lines — defense through offense, which allows it to close gaps. You may notice the right fullback is caught up field or standing too close to the middle, giving the opposing left wing an opportunity to run toward the corner unmarked for several seconds. In soccer, seconds is all it takes for an advantage.

The Beginnings and Endings

Here's an important tip: Be especially focused at the beginning and end of the half and game, because players score many key goals during the opening and closing five minutes. Teams sometimes slack off and lose concentration during those periods — it's only seconds before half, and you're ready for your halftime break. Opportunistic sides will take advantage. So, you may not want to leave too early to beat the concession stand rush.

Teams have won titles by scoring early and late. Just ask the Minnesota Thunder, which scored with two minutes remaining in the first half and in the opening minute of the second half of its 2-1 victory over the Rochester Raging Rhinos in the 1999 A-League championship game.

Goalkeeper Watch

Because goalkeepers can use their hands, spectators may identify with them more. Many times you can gauge how goalkeepers will perform from their early moves or lack thereof. Does the keeper hesitate just a split second before going out for a *cross* — a long pass from either the right of left side? Does he come off his goal line? How quick is his reaction time? They may not have any problems now, but that slight period of indecision could spell trouble or doom for the team later in the match, especially if the defense loses confidence in a shaky goalkeeper.

The Importance of That First Strike

How important is it for a team to score first? Check out Major League Soccer's 1999 regular-season record book. Teams that scored first went on to win 77 percent of the time. When they have the lead at halftime, it went up to 83 percent. The MLS figures are not an aberration. In the World Cup, that first-goal strike means teams win 77 percent of the time.

When a team scores first, it can relax just a bit and begin to dictate a match. As the opposition gets more antsy and starts to push up, the team with the lead starts to counterattack with the potential to add to its total. It doesn't happen that way all the time, but it is a familiar scenario. Sure, there are comebacks and great rallies by teams, but they aren't as plentiful as you may think. There are many occasions that teams work their tails off just to pull even. But they don't have enough energy to take the lead. They either wind up in a draw or fall behind again.

When Opportunity Knocks

It is rare that a soccer team will completely dominate a match from the opening kickoff to the final whistle. There is usually a push and pull to the game, meaning that both sides will have opportunities to score. On many occasions, teams can keep ball possession for a good portion of 10 to 15 minute spans, control the action, and dictate the pace of the game before the opposition can recover and start an offensive of its own. During these long periods of possession, the attacking team must score because serious scoring opportunities can be few and precious.

Warning about Two-Goal Leads

There is an old soccer cliché that rings so true: The most dangerous lead in the world is a two-goal lead. You can't count the times it has happened when a team with a supposedly insurmountable two-goal lead loses its advantage with lackadaisical play. It can happen in a flash. The opposition scores, which cuts the lead to one goal. That team gains confidence, realizing that a one-goal deficit is certainly not impossible to overcome.

Even some three-goal leads are not safe. Just ask the Brazilian Women's National Team. They enjoyed a 3-0 lead over Nigeria at the 1999 Women's World Cup, but the Africans rallied to force extra time. The Brazilians were spared further embarrassment by winning the game in extra time.

A Warning after Scoring a Goal

A team is most vulnerable after it has scored a goal. Depending on the situation, the players are happy, sometimes giddy. This could be a perfect opportunity for the opposition to launch a quick strike and score a goal of its own to stem the momentum. This has happened countless times in the past, and even though players and teams have been told to be on their guard, it will happen many times in the future.

Every Team Needs a "10"

Most successful teams have a No. 10, a playmaking midfielder who will create goal-scoring opportunities or someone who will control the pace of the game or dribble the ball up field in tight situations late in matches. He is the go-to player. When in doubt, give him the ball. Think of him as a point guard in basketball. In the original numbering system when starters were given numbers (from No. 1 to the goalkeeper to No. 11 to the last forward), the No. 10 position usually went to the playmaker or schemer. Pelé, incidentally, wore No. 10. It shouldn't be surprising that the most successful Major League Soccer teams have had dominant No. 10's. D.C. United has ridden the legs and brains of Bolivian Marco Etcheverry to a pair of titles. Former Polish international Peter Nowak was the midfield mastermind of the expansion Chicago Fire's 1999 championship. And the Los Angeles Galaxy has enjoyed its run of success behind El Salvadoran Mauricio Cienfuegos.

The "Other" Midfielder

It's not always glory. Sometimes it's guts. Take a look at the defensive midfielders. Is he doing his job, which is taking on the No. 10 of the opposition, winning balls (by intercepting passes and rarely giving them away) and helping the defense? A good defensive midfielder does all of this and gets involved in the attack as well. One key is a speedy transition game. After winning a ball, a defensive midfielder will quickly move the ball forward to an attacking player in an attempt to catch the opposition off-guard just for a couple of seconds to create a scoring advantage.

Some Offside Remarks

One of the most controversial calls in soccer is offside (see Chapter 4). The assistant referee — the linesman — must make a bang-bang call in a matter of seconds. There is no luxury of instant replay.

Record-setting offsides

In Major League Soccer's inaugural season in 1996, Tampa Bay Mutiny striker Roy Lassiter was called offside a league-record 70 times in 30 games, nearly as many times as D.C. United was (89) during its 32-game schedule. In fact, Lassiter was offside 26 more times than Kansas City Wiz forward Digital Takawira (44 times in 28 matches).

There are two basic reasons why a team is being called offside many times. (One former American Soccer League player, Pat Fidelia of the Carolina Lightnin', was called for the infraction 19 times in one match in the early '80s.) One, the attacking team's timing is off, or it is more than a bit anxious going after the ball or a player is not aware of his position on the field. Or two, the defending team is playing an offside trap, when its entire defense lines up in a straight line across the length of the field, stepping up before the ball is kicked, trying to pull a forward offside. Using the trap frequently is considered a lazy way to play defense. Sooner or later for a team that lives and dies by the offside trap, the player will be ruled onside, and the goalkeeper will find himself in a difficult one-on-one situation.

The Witching Hour

Players make mistakes all the time, but tired players make more mistakes in vulnerable places on the field. Major breakdowns on defense usually don't happen until the second half. While there certainly is no line of demarcation and it varies from player to player, it seems that players start losing their fitness after about 60 minutes. In a 90-minute game, that's 15 minutes into the second half. It's then when you see more passes going awry and intercepted and more yellow and red cards awarded by the referee.

When the Goalkeeper Tires

Even though goalkeepers don't run for 90 minutes as their teammates do, they still can get tired after having an active day, catching crosses or making saves. Sometimes you can tell a goalkeeper is tiring when he or she boots a punt or goal kick out of bounds late in a match, compared to earlier when they would have kicked it into the middle. Also, having little or no work can lead to lapses in concentration or mental fatigue.

Look Toward the Bench Once in a While

During a lull in action and especially in the second half, look toward the team benches. You may see the coach standing up and shouting instructions to the players or you may see potential substitutes warming up, giving you an early indication of some potential changes in the next several minutes.

Substitution Strategy

Even before a coach makes a substitution decision, you can have a pretty good inkling of who may enter the match. If a team is winning, it is a good bet a midfielder will replace a forward, or a defender will take over for a midfielder or forward to fortify the back. If a team needs to push forward, a midfielder is likely to come in for a defender, or a forward for a midfielder or defender.

Substitution rules vary depending on the level of play. Youth and high school games, for example, generally have free substitutions. College matches have open substitutions in the first half, but once you are replaced in the second half, you cannot return to action. Major League Soccer teams are allowed three substitutions, plus one for the goalkeeper in case he is injured. In the pros, once you're out, you cannot come back in.

Toward the Final Whistle

As the final whistle approaches, notice that the team with the lead isn't in a hurry to get the ball into the play. Defenders will kick the ball into the stands, which is legal. Other players will take their time setting up free kicks as will goalkeepers, taking a couple of extra seconds to get to the ball. Every second is precious. An alert referee will notice all the time wasted and add it into the stoppage time at the end of the game. (See the sidebar and Chapter 4 for more on stoppage time.)

And If You Have to Watch It on TV

Well, if you can't actually go to the game and you have to watch it on TV, it's certainly not the end of the world. But quite frankly, there is nothing like being there live. You can see off-the-ball runs, who is marking who, and which player is warming up. And, being able to see the whole field allows you to see the tactical movement of a team.

The mystery of stoppage time

It depends on which level you are watching, but not every game ends exactly at 70, 80, or 90 minutes. The official watch is the referee's. In virtually all professional and international matches, there is something called *stoppage time* added to the end of each half. It can range from one minute to four minutes, depending on how much time was taken to care for injuries, altercations, fights, substitutions, or arguments from the bench. The fourth official usually holds a sign with a number on it to tell the spectators and players how much time has been added on.

Stoppage also gives soccer something other timed sports don't have — an aura or mystery when you don't know when the game will end. In some quarters, stoppage time also is known as added time or injury time. Injury time is the time it takes to aid an injured player or get him off the field.

But there certainly is an upside to watching the game on TV. You don't have to battle the elements, instead settling in your den or on your living room couch. In most if not all matches, a clock usually appears in the upper left-hand corner of your screen. You see graphics, and, of course, the all-important replay, which is not always available at all stadiums on the scoreboard.

And, while there is continuous play for 45 minutes in each half, you still can run to a familiar (and clean) bathroom without waiting too long in line. And the refreshments can be more plentiful and less expensive at home, too.

Chapter 15

Soccer — from TV to Online

*T*here has never been a better time to be a soccer fan in this country. You can find out information about your favorite teams, players, and sport in so many ways, some of which are a bit untraditional. In this chapter, we tell you how to find out everything you want to know about your favorite players, teams, and leagues.

Soccer Web Sites

The Internet was made for soccer, which lacks coverage and attention in the local newspapers and television on many occasions. There are hundreds, perhaps thousands, of soccer Web sites out in cyberspace for virtually every interest, team, and even players, domestically and worldwide. To get started, I share with you some of my favorite sites.

The official ones

If you're new to soccer, you might as well start with the official Web sites. Here are several to peruse at your leisure:

✔ **U.S. Soccer:** The official Web site of U.S. Soccer includes all the latest news of its 11 National Teams, including biographies of every men's and women's player in the player pool. You can also find the latest rosters, press releases, and information on past tournaments. The site is being redesigned and expanded in 2000.

us-soccer.com

If you need to get more specific about youth or amateur soccer, just type in `usysa.com` (youth) or `usasa.com` (amateurs).

✔ **Major League Soccer:** This site has a full array of news and information — the latest team and player statistics, archives, and a scoreboard that is updated at intervals on game day.

```
mlsnet.com
```

✔ **The United Soccer Leagues:** The umbrella organization for soccer's minor-league system has information on all five of its leagues (A-League, D3 Pro League, Premier Soccer League, W-League, and Super Y-League), as well as a page for each of its more than 130 teams.

```
unitedsoccerleagues.com
```

✔ **Confederation of North, Central America, and Caribbean Association Football (CONCACAF):** This organization, which supervises soccer in North and Central America and the Caribbean, has news, tournament schedules, and qualifying updates for the region to which the United States belongs.

```
footballconfederation.com
```

✔ **Federation Internationale de Football Association (FIFA):** The site of the sport's world governing body deals mostly with all of the major international soccer tournaments, including the World Cup and Women's World Cup, and all of the different confederations. (For more on these two events, see Chapter 20.)

```
fifa.com
```

MLS team sites

Each of the 12 MLS teams has its own Web site, which gives fans up-to-the-minute information on injuries, player biographies, and statistics. Some sites even have a player diary. If you can't get enough of your team, this is the place to be.

✔ **Chicago Fire:** `chicago-fire.com`

✔ **Columbus Crew:** `thecrew.com`

✔ **Dallas Burn:** `burnsoccer.com`

✔ **D.C. United:** `dcunited.com`

✔ **Kansas City Wizards:** `kcwizards.com`

- ✔ **Los Angeles Galaxy:** `lagalaxy.com`
- ✔ **Miami Fusion:** `miamifusion.com`
- ✔ **New England Revolution:** `nerevolution.com`
- ✔ **NY/NJ MetroStars:** `metrostars.com`
- ✔ **San Jose Clash:** `clash.com`
- ✔ **Tampa Bay Mutiny:** `tampabaymutiny.com`

Web sites with an edge

You can find soccer news, features, and opinions on a daily basis at several sites.

If you need details about a game, event, or major tournament, you can surf to `CNNSI.com`, `Sportsline.com`, `Espn.com`, `foxsports.com`, or `sportingnews.com`. Not only do these sites give you the basic information, but they have columnists to comment on the events of the week and analyze the top matches.

Several other Web sites are informative as well, including `internetsoccer.com`, `goalnetwork.com`, and `soccertimes.com`, which all cover the full gamut of the sport domestically, and `collegesoccer.com`, which covers the college game, `soccergamenight.com`, which has same-day reports on every pro team in the U.S., and `soccerTV.com`, which has detailed television listings on virtually every network and cable concern.

If you want to enjoy a fan-run site, try Sam's Army at `Sams-army.com`, which is the address of U.S. Soccer's official fan club.

And that's just the tip of the proverbial iceberg. Just type soccer in your search engine, and you'll be surfing the Web for days, if not weeks.

Broadcast TV and Radio

Thanks to cable TV, you can find more soccer telecast than before, although certain channels or stations might not be available in all areas. You can also watch regional and local broadcasts of MLS and A-League games. And radio broadcasts of games are becoming more and more popular on the Internet. You should check the Internet sites of pro teams for more information (see preceding section).

ESPN and ABC

MLS and U.S. Soccer both have significant contracts with ESPN and ABC to show league and National Team games on a regular basis. Not all the games are televised on the weekend; some MLS matches are shown on Thursday on either ESPN or ESPN2. ESPN has an MLS shootout package on satellite, although that name might be changed in the wake of the league eliminating the shootout for the 2000 season. ESPN2 also has a weekly, one-hour highlight show for the 2000 season, scheduled for Monday nights. ABC will broadcast MLS games on the weekend and the MLS Cup and home matches for the Men's or Women's National Teams. Road matches are a rarity. ESPN also televises the European Champions League on various Wednesdays from September through May. Some cable companies have ESPN Extra, which televises international matches on a pay-per-game basis.

Fox

If you're into the international game, you can live by these networks. Fox Sports World, which also is available in Spanish, shows the English Premiership League, German Bundesliga, Argentine First Division soccer (see Chapter 16), and Asian highlights, plus a number of highlight shows. Fox Sports Net televises Premiership highlights and the A-League.

The Hispanic Market (Univision, Galavision, and Telemundo)

Whether or not you can understand Spanish, Univision, Galavision, and Telemundo are another option. Sunday afternoons wouldn't be the same without a doubleheader on Univision or Galavision, which includes a Mexican First Division match and then a highlight show later that night. World Cup ratings on Univision traditionally go through the roof. Starting with the 2000 season, Telemundo will show MLS matches, some of the most important Latin matches, especially the Mexican First Division, and a Sunday night highlight show. Even if you can't speak the language, you still can enjoy the game by viewing it. Besides, a "Gooooaal!" is universal.

RAI

Every Sunday morning from late August to early May, fans can catch the top Italian League games and some of the leading players in the world on RAI on cable. Availability depends on your cable system and whether you have a UHF station in your area that carries it.

Soccer in Print

If you're a bit old-fashioned and don't use the Internet for information about your favorite sport, then you're probably interested in newspapers, magazines, and books. I also list telephone numbers of the leading soccer publications in the United States at the end of each item.

Magazines

If you're a soccer fanatic, you'll want to check out *Soccer America*. This weekly publication has been around and kicking since 1972 and is considered the bible of the sport in the U.S. The publication has analyzed everything from U.S. National Teams and MLS teams to soccer leagues around the world with features and interviews with key players and officials. Phone: 510-528-5000.

Among other magazines that are published monthly or bimonthly:

- *Freekick,* the official program of MLS, is available at all league games and has features and news about the top players and teams in the MLS. Phone: 212-697-1460.

- *Soccer Digest* covers the professional, college, and National Team end of the game in a digest format. Phone: 1-857-332-2255.

- *Soccer Junior* has found its own niche writing for the ever-burgeoning youth market with stories, features, and cartoons oriented toward the younger crowd. Phone: 203-259-5766.

- *World Soccer,* which is published in England, offers a comprehensive look at the international game, with news, feature reports, and commentary by some of the top soccer writers in the world. Phone: 01444-445555.

In addition, many state and regional publications cover the youth and amateur game. (See Appendix B for addresses and phone numbers of state associations.)

Newspapers

Finding soccer coverage in your local newspapers isn't always easy. It may depend on what pro teams you have, how they fare in the standings, how many people attend games, and whether the sports editor likes the sport. In Columbus, Ohio, for example, the Columbus Crew is covered home and away on a regular basis and gets prominent mention in the sports section. (No other major league team is in the city, although Ohio State football and, on occasion, basketball come close.) In New York City, however, which has two baseball teams, two football teams, two basketball teams, and three hockey teams, soccer is not a major priority and sometimes can be difficult or impossible to find.

USA Today usually has some sort of story about soccer on a daily basis. And don't forget about your weekly community newspapers. Many of them not only have scores about youth games, but write-ups of games as well.

Books

For years, it seemed all that was available at bookstores for soccer fans were coaching books, like the most recent bible of coaching, *Soccer: How to Play the Game* (Universe), edited by U.S. Soccer director of coaching Bobby Howe and written by Dan Herbst. As the game has grown in the past decade, so has the variety of titles.

Recommended here are a pair by veteran and noted writer Paul Gardner — *The Simplest Game* (Macmillan), a book for the intermediate and advanced fan, which explains the logic and passion of the game, and *SoccerTalk* (Masters Press), a compilation of his best columns over the past 30 years.

For the first time, biographies have hit the bookshelf. Check out *John Harkes: Captain for Life* (Sleeping Bear Press), a sometimes controversial look into why he was left off the 1998 U.S. World Cup team, written with Denise Kiernan. And don't forget *Go for the Goal,* the autobiography of Mia Hamm, arguably the best women's player in the world, written with the help of Aaron Heifetz.

Writer-player Dave Ungrady talks about his trials and tribulations of playing for the D3 Pro League's Northern Virginia Royals in *Unlucky* (Sports Press International).

Lauren Gregg, former assistant coach of the U.S. Women's National Team, along with Tim Nash, recently penned *The Champion Within: Training For Excellence* (JTC Sports, Inc.), which includes insights about skills, conditioning, and tactics and insights into the triumphant U.S. Women's National Team.

World Cups have been covered extensively — Michael Lewis has authored a pair of books (1994 and 1998) *About World Cup Soccer* (Moyer Bell), which is about the men's side, while *Women's Soccer the Game and the World Cup* (Universe) was edited by Jim Trecker.

For the more advanced reader, *Rothman's Football Guide* (Headline Book Publishing), which has been published since 1969, has a ton of facts and figures about not only the English game, but the international end as well. *Soccer In The Sun And Shadow* (Verso) by Uruguayan Eduardo Galeano eloquently captures the vibrant spirit and passion of the South American game in intriguing vignettes about the players, games, and World Cups.

While they are not literary pursuits, MLS and U.S. Soccer publish and sell media guides on an annual basis with tons of facts and information about players and teams.

You may want to visit your local bookstore to see what's in the sports section. You might be pleasantly surprised thanks to the proliferation of soccer books. You also can browse for soccer books and videos online as well at Reedswain (reedswain.com) and Soccer Learning Systems (soccervideos.com). In England, check out Sportspages (sportspages.com), a well-known sports bookstore based in London, and Sports Books Ltd. (sportsbooks.com), a mail-order service. There is also amazon.com. Happy reading!

The National Soccer Hall of Fame

Situated in Oneonta, N.Y., the National Soccer Hall of Fame and museum has artifacts and great memorabilia from the game's past (the world's oldest soccer ball, from 1855), plus biographical data on all of the 220 Hall of Fame members. Established in 1979, the modern hall and museum had its grand opening in a modern, state-of-the-art facility on the Wright National Soccer Complex in central New York on June 12, 1999.

The new hall houses trophies, special exhibits (the great players, teams, and leagues), and interactive exhibits for fans as well, including computer stations, a video wall, and games. The complex includes several soccer fields for games and tournaments. (The New York State high school soccer tournament has been played there on several occasions.) There also are plans for a grand-stand stadium, an indoor arena, and a place for extended stays for players.

This shrine to the history of the American game is located only 28 miles from the Baseball Hall of Fame in Cooperstown, so a family can make it a long weekend or part of a memorable week's vacation. You can call 607-432-3351 or visit its Web site at soccerhall.com.

Chapter 16

Soccer or Futbol — a Worldwide Phenomenon

● ●

In This Chapter

▶ Examining why soccer is so popular

▶ Understanding the American connection

▶ Determining the best leagues in the world

▶ Finding out about promotion and relegation

▶ Understanding the youth system

▶ Trading and dealing players

▶ Determining the best dozen club teams

▶ Celebrating the best stadiums in the world

▶ Putting up with hooligans

● ●

*I*n this chapter, I examine the rest of the world's passionate love affair with the game. What makes soccer — *futbol* in Spanish, *calcio* in Italian, and *football* in England — so popular? There are many reasons why.

This chapter also explains the promotion and relegation system, the transfer and free agent systems, and the highly sophisticated youth system, where professional teams scout players for their teams.

Why Is Soccer So Popular?

Why is soccer so popular in the rest of the world? It's all about passion. In many instances, it is the only or major sport in a particular country. The fans, mostly male, grow up following one team from the time they can walk and talk until they die. More than one fan has had his ashes scattered on the field in which he literally spent his Saturday or Sunday afternoons for most of his life.

These fans go to great lengths to support their club and National Team — literally flying, busing, or driving from hundreds to thousands of miles. Some of this undying devotion has cost fans their lives in a number of well-documented stadium disasters (see last section of this chapter).

So, it should be little surprise that virtually every Saturday or Sunday, fans will wear the colors of their team, take a short trip to a neighboring town to cheer on their heroes, or huddle in front of a TV or radio to check out the action or scores. In fact, in many English towns and cities, a special edition of the local newspaper devoted to the games of the day, usually called the *green sheets,* is published and distributed barely hours after the 40-something professional games are completed.

If you ever attend a game in a foreign country, be forewarned that you better be aware of the colors for the home and visiting teams. If you wear the wrong colors, you could be in for a long game, taking verbal abuse, and in some stadiums, even some physical abuse as well. It may be best if you wear a neutral color, such as beige. (See the section "The Great Clubs of the World," later in this chapter.)

The American Connection

To fully understand soccer, the American soccer fan needs to understand and embrace international soccer because it is connected to the American game as well. Every four years the World Cup is held, and the United States has reached the last three competitions. In between those Cups, the U.S. National Team plays exhibition games, which are called *friendlies,* in preparation for the top competitions of the world.

A *friendly* or an international friendly is soccer's version of an exhibition game. It is not an actual competition, such as the World Cup, Women's World Cup, or European Championship. Ironically, some of those so-called friendlies have become fierce battles, with fouls and yellow and red cards punctuating the match.

Many American players travel across the Atlantic to hone their skills (or to earn more money) with First Division clubs. In the early 1990s, England was the place to play (their English team is in parentheses) as New England Revolution midfielder John Harkes (Sheffield Wednesday, Derby County), U.S. National Team goalkeeper Kasey Keller (Millwall, Leicester City), and New York/New Jersey MetroStars goalkeeper Mike Ammann (Charlton) were among the pioneers who took a gamble overseas. Lately, Germany has grabbed up the top American talent, with as many as nine current U.S. players playing in Deutschland. Former Kansas City Wizards and U.S. National Team defender Alexi Lalas, who retired from pro soccer after the 1999 season, played for Padova in Italy's Serie A (First Division) from 1994–1996.

The American foreign legion

Among the U.S. National Team players now performing in the German Bundesliga (First Division) are former Tampa Bay Mutiny defender Frankie Hejduk (Bayer Leverkusen), midfielder Jovan Kirovski (Borussia Dortmund, and Fortuna Cologne of the Second Division) and former D.C. United midfielder Tony Sanneh (Hertha Berlin). Former University of Virginia star midfielder Claudi Reyna stars for Rangers in Glasgow, Scotland, after a stint with Wolfsburg in Germany. Former New England Revolution midfielder-forward Joe-Max Moore joined Everton in the English Premiership in December, 1999. Goalkeeper Kasey Keller is a key performer for Rayo Vallecano in the Spanish First Division, while his national backup, Brad Friedel, has sat the bench for Liverpool (England).

The Best Leagues in the World

Do you want to start an argument among soccer fans from different countries? Just ask them what is the best First Division soccer league in the world.

In the United States, the organizer of a team is known as the coach. That's not necessarily the case elsewhere in the world. In many countries such as England, the coach is known as the manager, the man who not only makes player deals, but decides which players to play in a match and what tactical approach to take. In those countries, a coach usually is one who trains the teams. Not to confuse matters more, but in Germany, the coach is known as the team trainer. That is not to be confused with an athletic trainer, who rubs sore muscles and makes sure that players are in the best shape possible. In Spain and Italy, the head coach is known as "Mister"and is addressed as such.

Italy

The Italians will boast of their Serie A, which traditionally attracts the best players in the world. Serie A also has forged a reputation as being the best defensive league in the world. The Italian League also has some of the best South American players.

Juventus, A.C. Milan, and Inter Milan have been the dominant clubs in the past decade. The leading players include Inter Milan forward Christian Vieri, Juventus forward Alessandro Del Piero, and A.C. Milan defender Paolo Maldini. The foreign contingent includes Inter forwards Ronaldo (Brazil) and Ivan Zamarano (Chile), Fiorentina forward Gabriel Batistuta (Argentina), Juventus midfielder Zinedine Zidane (France), who scored two goals in the 1998 World Cup final, and Lazio defender Sinisa Mihajlovic (Yugoslavia). And that's only the proverbial tip of the iceberg of international stars.

Spain

Of course, Spain will place its claim to the best soccer league in the world, as it plays a more open, attacking style than the Italian league. Real Madrid, which struggled through the early portion of the 1999–2000 season, and Barcelona have dominated Spanish soccer for almost the last century. Occasionally, a team such as Deportivo Coruna sneaks in to win the First Division crown.

Raul, a scoring terror for Real Madrid, is considered one of the best Spanish players today. Barcelona midfielder Rivaldo (Brazil), Real Madrid forward Nicolas Anelka (France), Barcelona forward Patrick Kluivert (Netherlands), who has underachieved after a promising start, Real Madrid defender Roberto Carlos (Brazil), and Barcelona defender Frank DeBoer (Netherlands) are among the top internationals playing in Spain.

England

In recent years, the English Premiership, thanks to a multi $100 million deal on the SkySports satellite network fueled by Australian media magnate Rupert Murdoch's SkySports TV empire, has siphoned away some pretty impressive talent from Italy. The English Premiership, long known for its boring, long-ball style of play, has changed its tune and style, thanks to the tremendous influx of foreign players. In fact, to play in England these days, a player must be a member of his country's National Team and participate in 75 percent of those matches.

Manchester United is perennially among the top teams, although Arsenal and Liverpool and have won or made serious runs for the title in recent years. Manchester United midfielder David Beckham and Liverpool forward Michael Owen are among the top players. Internationally, Arsenal forwards Davor Suker (Croatia) and Dennis Bergkamp (Netherlands) and Chelsea defender Marcel Desailly (France) have stood out.

Germany

While it has produced some of the best players in the world, the German Bundesliga cannot be placed in the same class as the aforementioned leagues, but it certainly has produced players who have gone on to star in Italy and England. The German National Team has aged considerably in the past decade, without many new stars coming up through the ranks to take the place of team captain and defender Lothar Matthaeus, for example.

Netherlands

You can place the Dutch Honor Division at the same level as Germany. For a country the size of the Netherlands (15 million), the Dutch produce some of the most talented players in the world. The best Dutch players go on to greater fame and fortune because other European clubs can offer more money. Many, however, return home for the waning years of their career. The next star expected to leave is PSV Eindhoven scoring terror Ruud van Nistelrooy, who had 22 goals midway through the 1999–2000 season.

Argentina and Brazil

In South America, the title for the best league is a two-horse race between Argentina and Brazil. Many of South America's top players have opted to play in the Argentine or Brazilian First Division if they don't go to Europe. Ironically, Brazil, which is known for producing some of the world's best players, is considered to have the most physical and arguably violent league in the world because of vicious fouls and tackles. The Argentine league can be physical as well, but it is a highly competitive league.

The rest of Europe and the world

France got a boost of respectability after it captured the World Cup in 1998, although many of its top players perform abroad. The quality of the Portuguese First Division can run hot or cold because its many clubs can't keep up with some of the larger clubs in the world. Scotland is considered a proving ground for players because its top players perform in England.

Several countries in Eastern Europe — Yugoslavia, Croatia, Romania, Bulgaria, Poland, and Russia — have produced excellent players. But again, the best ones play somewhere else on the continent.

Compared to the rest of the world, club soccer in Asia, Africa, North America, and Oceania, which includes Australia and New Zealand, is not taken as seriously because many of their top players perform in Europe.

What's in a name?

If you were a Brazilian TV announcer, what do you think would be easier to say?

Goal by Edson Arantes do Nascimento or goal by Pelé? Pelé, of course.

Brazilian names can be long and cumbersome because of the tradition of putting mother's maiden names and the names of other family members in it, so fans, media, and players have been known to shorten those names with a nickname.

The full name of Barcelona midfielder Rivaldo, the 1999 FIFA player of the year, is Victor Borba Ferreira Rivaldo.

Ronaldo's given name is Nazario de Lima Ronaldo. While performing for Brazil at the 1996 Olympics, he was known as Ronaldinho, although he has gone back to his original nickname. It's for the best and less confusing because since then, another player who goes by the nickname of Ronaldinho has emerged on the soccer scene.

Saying that, just how did Pelé get his nickname? It isn't a play on any of his names. Actually, his friends gave him that nickname when he was 12 years old. The meaning is unknown, although a volcano on the big island of Hawaii is named Pelé.

Pelé admitted he did not take to his newfound nickname very quickly as he constantly got into fights about it. Today, his name is associated with greatness and class.

The Great Clubs of the World

Every country in the world has at least one special or great club. It would be impossible to list every pro soccer club in the world, even in the leading countries. But to truly understand the scope of the sport, here are a dozen clubs that have withstood the test of time and moved to the top of the heap not only in their country, but in the world as well.

A.C. Milan

A.C. Milan, which was relegated to the Second Division in 1980 after a bribery scandal, was saved from backruptcy in 1986 by Italian media magnate Silvio Berlusconi, who invested $36 million and turned around the fortunes of the team dramatically. The club purchased the contracts of defender Frank Rijkaard, midfielder Ruud Gullit, and striker Marco Van Basten of the Netherlands. The club went on to win the European Cup three times (1989, 1990, and 1994).

Milan, which played in the shadow of Inter until after World War II, enjoyed its first resurgence behind the attacking Swedish trio of Gunnar Gren, Gunnar

Nordahl, and Niels Liedholm in the 1950s. In later years, Milan has been dominated by talented foreigners. Besides the aforementioned Dutch masters,
Liberian forward George Weah and Yugoslavian midfielder Dejan Savicevic
have helped Milan attain its lofty status. Team colors: Red and black striped
shirts and white shorts.

Ajax

Formed as a club in 1900, Ajax's greatest days incredibly did not start until
1971. Under the leadership of coach Rinus Michels and midfielder Johan
Cruyff, Ajax used the "Total Soccer" concept — in which every player could
play every position — and turned the club into a winning force. Ajax (pronounced *I-yax*) has captured 26 Dutch titles and the European Cup four times,
including three times in a row (1971–1973).

Ajax, called "the nursery of Europe," because so many players have gone on
to bigger clubs on the continent, has defined youth soccer (see sidebar "Ajax:
The nursery of Europe," later in this chapter). Besides the marvelous Johan
Cruyff, Marco Van Basten, Frank Rijkaard, and Clarence Seedorf have forged
their reputations with the Amsterdam, Netherlands-based team. Team colors:
Red and white broad striped shirt and white shorts.

Barcelona

Barcelona, considered the second best club in Spain to Real Madrid, has the
most loyal following in the world. The Barcas, as they are called, have more
than 110,000 club members, making it the largest club on the planet.

Despite that fantastic support, Barcelona still many times has to take a backseat in Spain to Real Madrid. Yes, the Barcas have won 15 league titles and 24
Spanish cups, but the ultimate continental club championship — the
European Cup — had eluded Barcelona until former star Johan Cruyff guided
the club to the title in 1992.

Some of the world's greatest players have performed at Nou Camp Stadium.
Ronaldo (Brazil), Ronald Koeman (Netherlands), Hristo Stoitchkov
(Bulgaria), Diego Maradona (Argentina), Rivaldo (Brazil), and Michael
Laudrup (Denmark) have performed for Barcelona. Team colors: Blue and
red striped shirts with black shorts.

Bayern Munich

The German Bundesliga club celebrates its 100th anniversary in 2000 as Germany's most glamorous team, although it truly did not come into its own until the 1960s. Since then, the best German players have starred for Bayern, including Franz Beckenbauer, now the club president, Karl-Heinz Rummenigge, Gerd Mueller, Paul Breitner, and, most recently, Lothar Matthaeus. Bayern has won 16 Bundesliga titles, dropping a heart-breaking 2-1 loss to Manchester United in the European Cup championship game. Team colors: Red jerseys and red shorts.

Boca Juniors

The most popular club in Argentina, Boca Juniors has captured the First Division title 19 times, Copa Libertadores twice (1977 and 1978), and the World Club Championship once (1977). A number of big names have played for Boca, including Diego Maradona, who had a pair of tenures with the club at the beginning and end of his sometimes glorious, sometimes controversial career. Team colors: Dark blue shirts and gold shorts.

D.C. United

D.C. United is by far the best of the MLS, winning three MLS titles in its first four years in the league. The team beat Vasco for the InterAmerican Cup in 1998 and routinely competes in international club tournament as the U.S. representative.

Juventus

Juventus, nicknamed "The Old Lady," is known as the New York Yankees of Italy, having earned 24 First Division titles. Juve, which the team is nicknamed, solidified its reputation during the 1930s, when it won five consecutive championships. The Turin-based club also has captured two European Cups (1985 and 1996) and ten Italian Cup crowns.

The team has produced many great players who have gone on to club, international and World Cup fame, including Paolo Rossi, who went from pariah to hero in the 1982 World Cup after a two-year ban for his involvement in a betting scandal, and defender Marco Tardelli, and, more recently, 1994 World Cup hero Roberto Baggio and Gianluca Vialli. Team colors: Black and white striped shirts with white shorts.

Manchester United

Manchester United has celebrated three major eras in England:

- ✔ The Busby Babes era of manager Matt Bubys through the Munich plane crash of 1958

- ✔ The rebuilding of the team, which culminated in winning the European Cup in 1968

- ✔ The modern era under recently knighted Sir Alex Ferguson, the untiring manager of what is considered the best known soccer club in the world (fan clubs are in several countries, including the U.S.)

United, or ManU as it known to its supporters, completed a remarkable year in 1999, becoming the first English team to win the treble. Those three major titles include the European Cup (European Champions League title), English Premiership crown, and the English Football Association Cup title. United capped off the year by besting Palmeiras (Brazil), 1-0, in the Intercontinental Cup (also known as the Toyota Cup) in Tokyo in December. In fact, United is so loaded with talent that it can literally field two full competitive starting lineups, except for perhaps goalkeeper. Dwight Yorke of Trinidad & Tobago is a key goal scorer, although midfielder Roy Keane of Ireland is the backbone of the team. Team colors: Red jerseys and white shorts.

Olympique Marseille

If Paris is considered the capital of France, Marseille must be considered the capital of football. The fans are absolutely crazy about their team in the south of France. Olympique Marseille's ardent supporters fill the Velodrome for every match.

Marseille has enjoyed great success in recent years. The club captured the French First Division title from 1989–1993 and became the first French team to capture the European Champion Cup, in 1993. A bribery scandal, however, marred that triumph, as the team was forced to relinquish its French First Division crown and accept a demotion into the Second Division. Marseille was quickly promoted to the First Division, thanks to a successful Second Division season. Team colors: All white.

Rangers

No team has dominated its league like the Rangers of Glasgow. The club has captured 47 Scottish Premiership crowns, including a run of an incredible nine in a row from 1989 to 1997, and 27 Scottish Cups and 19 league cups.

Rangers, on the other hand, have not fared as well in the European club competitions (they captured the European Champions Cup in 1972) because they perform in a league that is not nearly as competitive as its counterparts in Italy, Spain, England, and Germany. Rangers, which had used only Protestant players, did make history in 1989 when it signed Mo Johnston, a Catholic and a one-time member of archrival Celtic. Needless to say, this move did not sit well with some supporters, but Rangers kept on winning. They're known in the soccer world as Rangers, not "the Rangers." Team colors: Blue jerseys and white shorts.

Real Madrid

The trophy room at Santiago Berbeneau Stadium overflows with more than 5,000 trophies commemorating the incredible success of Real Madrid. The most important ones are the 28 League Cup, 17 Spanish Cup, seven European Cup trophies, and two intercontinental cups. (Real won the first five championships from 1956–1960.) Real forged a new path in European and international success in the late 1950s.

Some of the world's greatest players have worn the famous white uniform of Real, including Alfredo DiStefano (Argentina, but eventually became a Spanish citizen), Ferenc Puskas (Hungary), Raymond Kopa (France), Didi (Brazil), Hugo Sanchez (Mexico), Spain's Emilio Butragueno, and most recently scoring star Raul. Team colors: All white.

River Plate

While Boca Juniors may be the most popular team in Argentina, River Plate is the most successful. The Buenos Aires-based team has won 26 league championships, the most in the country. Great success means great players, and the list seemingly goes on and on — Mario Kempes and Daniel Passarella from the 1978 World Cup champion team, Oscar Ruggeri and Nery Pumpido from the 1986 championship side, and of course, the great Alfredo DiStefano, before he went to Real Madrid. Team colors: White and red sash on the shirts and black shorts.

Vasco da Gama

Compared to the rest of the clubs that we list in this section, Vasco da Gama was a late entry into the professional scene, entering the top Brazilian division in 1923. Vasco won the title that year and hasn't stopped since, taking home 17 Rio League trophies and five Brazilian championships.

Vasco's support has come from Rio de Janerio's Portuguese population. Eight players from the club played for the 1950 Brazilian team that finished second in the World Cup. The club has been known for its offensive stars, such as Leonidas (1938 World Cup), Ademir (1950 World Cup), and Romario (the MVP of the 1994 World Cup), who have led the way. Team colors: All white with a black sash.

And that's not to forget . . .

You probably can make a pretty convincing list of the teams that we left out: Anderlecht (Belgium), Arsenal (England), Benfica (Portugal), Borussia Dortmund (Germany), Celtic (Scotland), Dynamo Kiev (Ukraine), Flamengo (Brazil), Inter (Italy), Liverpool (England), Nacional (Uruguay), Penarol (Uruguay), PSV Eindhoven (Netherlands), Red Star Belgrade (Yugoslavia), Sporting Lisbon (Portugal), and Steaua Bucharest (Romania).

A Number of Leagues of Their Own

In contrast to men's club soccer around the world, women's soccer isn't nearly as popular or profitable.

Many countries, including England, Italy, Sweden, Norway, and Japan, have top flight amateur or semi-pro clubs. A number of American players have performed overseas, including Michelle Akers, who has played in Sweden, and Shannon MacMillan, who played in Japan.

Many of those foreign clubs and players have fought for recognition as women's international soccer has had to overcome old world thinking that a woman's place was somewhere else other than on a soccer field. They have also had to overcome prejudices in many, if not most, countries. While growing up in England, Kelly Smith, who eventually led all college players in goal scoring while earning All-American honors at Seton Hall University, played on boys teams because there were few or no girls teams. A number of rival teams refused to play her team because she was on it.

Several members of the Brazilian Women's National Team, which finished third at the 1999 world championships, claim that the greatest obstacle in their home country is the men's game. They say men's pro leagues and team refuse to fund and actually try to hinder the growth of the women's game.

U.S. Soccer plans to start a women's professional league in eight to ten cities following the 2000 Summer Olympics in 2001. The league plans to sign U.S. Women's National Team players and the best players in the world.

Derbies: When Archrivals Collide

Americans call them rivalries. Overseas, they are called *derbies* (pronounced *darbies*). Among the most enduring overseas rivalries:

- **Tottenham versus Arsenal:** Whether the games are played at Tottenham's White Hart Lane or Arsenal's Highbury, it is certain that both grounds in north London will be packed for the most intense rivalry in English soccer.

- **A.C. Milan versus Inter Milan:** Playing at the same stadium, this one's a natural. A.C. Milan fans boast of their 15 league titles, while Inter supporters stand behind their 13 championships.

- **Barcelona versus Real Madrid:** It's not just about the two best clubs in the history of Spanish soccer. This derby pits two distinctively different cities. Real represents the traditional culture of Spain, while Barcelona is situated in Catalonian region, which has a strong separatist movement that desires independence from Spain.

- **Rangers versus Celtic:** It's more than just a soccer game in Glasgow, Scotland. It's literally a religion in a rivalry that is called the "Old Firm." Rangers' supporters are predominantly Protestant, while Celtic's are Catholic. Even though they play each other four times a season during the course of the 12-team Scottish Premier League, supporters of each side rarely get tired of this confrontation of the perennial Glasgow powers.

- **Boca Juniors versus River Plate:** The very first professional match in 1931 between these two Buenos Aires rivals set stage for some unforgettable Argentine First Division clashes. River Plate walked off the field in protest after Boca scored the tying goal after a controversial penalty kick. Boca was awarded the victory.

- **Vasco da Gama versus Flamengo:** Traditionally, the games between these two Rio de Janeiro rivals are played at Maracana Stadium. Through the years, these confrontations have become more physical.

- **And the list goes on and on:** In Germany, Bayern Munich and Munich 1860 have an ongoing rivalry between the haves and have-nots of the Bundesliga. The same can be said between Manchester United and Manchester City in England, although United and Liverpool, two leading clubs, have a healthy rivalry as well. Lisbon rivals Benfica and Sporting Lisbon have played many memorable matches in the Portuguese First Division, as have Ajax and Rotterdam in the Dutch league. In Uruguay, Penarol and Nacional have bumped heads on numerous occasions.

The Old Firm rivalry

When he joined Rangers in Scotland in 1999, American midfielder Claudio Reyna was introduced to one of the fiercest rivalries on this planet — The Old Firm rivalry — which is also known as Rangers versus Celtic.

Even though Rangers and Celtic play each other a minimum of four times a season, each game is played as though it is the team's last.

"I've never seen anything like it in the world," Reyna said. "It's amazing the way such a small city has two massive clubs. It still surprises me to this day. I've been there for a while. Every time you play that game, it's an incredible game. It means so much to the fans. Every time we step onto the field to play them, they want nothing but a victory, whether it is home or away.

"It's a game played at an almost ridiculous pace for 90 minutes. Every tackle is like it better be you're last tackle. That is what the fans expect. You feel that when you come out of the tunnel,

the fans are right on you. And they push you to play that way. It's a fun game to play. I always look forward to it. It's the biggest game in Scotland. I think players on both sides always look forward to that fixture."

In fact, Celtic fans invaded the field in Reyna's first derby in 1999.

"It was a bit surprising," he said. "I was more concentrated on the result for us. That was the championship game. That's what I was more interested in. I never knew if anything like that happened before. It was amazing the way the tension from the field boiled over onto the fans. The Celtic fans got upset because we beat them there. The referee made some decisions that they didn't like. It was a terrible scene. The fans got on the field as things got out of hand. It was a sad day for Scottish soccer. That game is watched around the world and they gave it bad press."

Moving Up and Down: Promotion and Relegation

Most countries have as many as four professional divisions. In fact, the face of each league changes every year due to a promotion and relegation system based on a team's final league record. For example, the top few teams in the Second Division will move up to the First Division, while the bottom two teams in the First Division will drop into the Second Division. This scenario is followed in the lower divisions as well. In some of those leagues, the last-place team of the bottom professional division will drop out and be replaced by a semipro or amateur team.

These club cups runneth over and over

It seems that soccer has more cup competitions in the world than any other sport in the world. Here are some of the best-known ones:

✓ **European Cup:** The European Champions League, whose teams vie for the European Cup every May, is the most important club competition in the world. The tournament is open to selected league champions, second-place teams from selected countries, and countries that have qualified through play-in games. The league, which is played once a month on Tuesdays and Wednesdays, begins in September of each year with 32 teams (eight groups of four teams each). This competition is not to be confused with the European Championship, a competition that is held once every four years for National Teams, and not club teams.

✓ **European Football Union (UEFA) Cup:** Just as the European Cup is the equivalent to the NCAA basketball tournament, the UEFA Cup is more similar to basketball's National Invitational Tournament, in which teams that finish between second and fifth place in their respective leagues are invited to play. Also, with the demise of the European Winners Cup, Cup winners also are eligible to play. The title also is decided in May.

✓ **Liberatores Cup:** This competition is the South American version of the European Championships league.

✓ **Intercontinental Cup (Toyota Cup):** The winner of the European and South American club competitions meet in a one-game playoff in Tokyo every December. The victor is declared club champion of the world, although that might change, if FIFA has its way.

✓ **FIFA World Club Championship:** This tournament, which was played for the first time in Brazil in January 2000, brought together the top clubs teams from all of FIFA's six confederations. With club and country schedules already packed, it is not known if this Cup will be played again. One possibility has it becoming a preseason tournament in August.

✓ **CONCACAF Club Championship:** It has the same task as the European Championship League: to determine the champion of its continental confederation. In this case, it's the Confederation of North, Central American and Caribbean Association Football in a five-day tournament. It was played as a single-elimination competition in Las Vegas in 1999 with Necaxa of Mexico emerging as champion. There are also continental club competitions in Asia, Africa, and Oceania.

✓ **Football Association Cups:** Virtually every country, including the United States, has a nationwide tournament in which every team — pro, semipro, or amateur — is eligible to compete in season-long, single-elimination playoffs. That means lower division teams can upset the favored First Division clubs. The F.A. Cup in England, which has been alive and kicking since 1872, is the best-known of these tournaments. In the U.S., it's called the Lamar Hunt U.S. Open Cup (named after the soccer pioneer and owner of the Columbus Crew and Kansas City Wizards). These are not to be confused with the various league cups, which are open to every professional team in a country.

Although the United States has four distinct leagues and levels of play, there is no forced promotion or relegation . . . yet. The last-place team in Major League Soccer will remain in the league, as will the A-League champion. However, there can be movement between leagues in the United Soccer Leagues (A-League, D3 Pro League and Premier Developmental Soccer League) if a team has the financial means and resources (higher player salaries and more travel costs) to remain in a higher, more competitive league.

Transfers: Another Way of Saying Trades

In the United States, moving one player from one club to another is a *trade*. In Europe, South America, and a good portion of the rest of the world, they are called *transfers*. That's when one player is essentially sold from one team to another. There are some interesting differences to when a player is sold from one baseball or basketball team in the U.S. In a transfer system, players and their agents usually receive 10 percent of the price paid between two teams. So, if a player is transferred for $1 million, he should be able to pocket $100,000 before his agents'commission. Transfer fees can range from a free one, in which no money is exchanged, into the tens of millions of dollars.

So, a player on the way up who moves around every two or three years will not only receive a salary increase, but will get some substantial transfer bonuses as well. On the other hand, a journeyman player — an average player, who is transferred for low sums of money, won't get rich.

Free transfers are deals where a player is allowed to move from one club to another without any money being spent. For example, A.C. Milan of the Italian First Division allowed World Cup midfielder Roberto Donadoni a free transfer to Major League Soccer, which owns all its player contracts in contrast to the rest of the world. MLS allocated Donadoni to the New York/New Jersey MetroStars in 1996. When Donadoni wanted to return to Milan after the 1997 season, MLS — his contract was owned by the league — gave Donadoni a free transfer back to Italy.

You also have *loans* — not in money, but in players. For example, say that a player for Manchester United in the Englishship Premiership is not playing too much. The club can loan him to a team in a lower division. Sometimes the player impresses the coach or manager, and he signs with his new club. Many times he returns to his former club.

Trades — when players are dealt for players — are rare, but they do happen every so often.

In 1995, a startling and momentous decision by the European Court of Human Rights forever changed the way players move around in Europe when an obscure lower division player in Belgium, Jean-Marc Bosman, contested his transfer from his club, Liege, and won his case for freedom of contract. Now, players become *free agents* — they are able to move to another team without a transfer fee — at the end of their contracts, denying clubs huge transfer fees. To combat this, clubs are now signing players to longer contracts, adding exorbitant buyout clauses.

Now, players are allowed to move for huge sums of money, thanks to the multimillion dollars that television offers many teams from satellite TV revenue because of the ever-growing interest in the international aspect of the sport.

The transfer record was set in June 1999 when Inter Milan dealt for Italian international forward Christian Vieri from Lazio for $49.5 million. Lazio, however, offered Barcelona of Spain $64.5 million for Brazilian international midfielder Rivaldo, the 1999 European Player of the Year, in December 1999.

When will all this spending end? The sky is the limit, as are the dollars generated by satellite TV.

Youth Soccer: It's a Whole Different World

Because soccer is considered such an important part of life in many countries, youth soccer is under greater scrutiny and more emphasis in Europe and South America. Players are routinely signed to pro contracts as teenagers. Some, such as Michael Owen of England who starred in the 1998 World Cup at the age of 18, stand out early. Others take a few years, and yet another group never makes it as a pro at all.

In a number of European countries, youth soccer is not as organized as in the United States. Instead of having players perform on 11-man teams at an early age, they are allowed to play in 8-man versus 8-man teams until they reach 14. The advantages of that philosophy is that the player gets an opportunity to touch and kick the ball more in a game, which hastens the development of his skills. The more times you kick the ball properly, the better you become.

At the age of 14, players begin to play full-sided matches and learn about tactics. Regardless of how much knowledge a player has of different systems of play, proper positioning and the like, if he doesn't have the basic skills, he is essentially useless.

Ajax: The nursery of Europe

Ajax is the model for youth and professional soccer success in the Netherlands and for many parts of the world. The Amsterdam-based club has won 27 Dutch titles, including four European Cups, and has been the core of a successful National Team that has seen a pair of second-place finishes at the World Cup (1974 and 1978). The Dutch finished fourth at the 1998 World Cup.

At the Ajax museum at The Arena, the team's state-of-the-art, 21st century playing facility that includes a grass field under a retractable roof, a saying proudly hangs on the wall of one of its exhibits: "De Kweekvijver van Europa." Translated, it means "The nursery of Europe."

Many of Ajax's top players "graduate" to bigger and wealthier clubs within the continent.

Unlike other teams in Europe and South America, where a team's playing philosophy and system changes from one coach to another, Ajax follows only one. The club has been following its unique system since the '70s, when coach Rinus Michels introduced his system of "Total Football," in which each player could play any position in a pinch. Ajax's current philosophy is more one of attacking soccer.

The scouting process begins in the Amsterdam area and takes a year. Scouts — the club has five full-time and 20 part-time scouts — scour the city, looking for the best youth players, beginning as early as age six. About 4,000 boys will be invited to *talent days,* or tryouts. Perhaps a lucky handful will be asked to join the club. The team will scout four players who can play attacking soccer for the left side. The best player will be a forward, the second one a midfielder, the third on defense, and the fourth best will be on the bench.

The fortunate ones become Ajax players and eat, live, and breathe soccer from the Under-8 division all the way to U-18. A total of 160 youngsters are involved. They go to a special school at the club's youth complex in the morning and practice in the afternoon. They also do their homework in the afternoon so that they can return home without any outside pressures. The best players are asked to sign a professional contract at the age of 16.

According to Hans Westerhof, head of the Ajax youth department, the club spends $2.5 million a year on youth development. Over ten years, Ajax has gotten back $100 million after it has sold players to other clubs and teams, so the investment is viable.

Although it has changed a bit in South America in recent years, soccer still is a way out of poverty and the inner-city ghetto, not unlike basketball in the United States. Many players develop their skills just by playing for a couple of hours every day with their friends in the streets, with little or no coaching or adult supervision. In some places, the story of Pelé and his friends kicking around rolled up newspapers or old, tattered clothing as a ball still isn't that far-fetched.

The real untapped soccer market is considered to be in Africa. Approximately 600 players are performing in European leagues, although many soccer observers feel that they have only skimmed the surface of a seemingly endless pool of talent in a continent that includes 750 million people.

Stadiums: Soccer's Great 'Cathedrals'

They are the true monuments of the game — these great stadiums in which the best soccer players in the world perform. Some have weathered the test of time. Others are dinosaurs waiting for renovation. Others are a modern tribute to the technology of the 20th and 21st centuries.

Each stadium, whether it be a First Division club or a struggling Fourth Division side, has its individual uniqueness. Here are several stadiums that either sparkled more than most or are drenched in history, in order of significance and importance.

Wembley

FIFA president Sepp Blatter called Wembley, located to the north of London, "the cathedral of soccer." With its two majestic twin towers, the 80,000-seat *ground* — that's soccer talk for stadium — has been the cornerstone of English soccer since it was built in 1923. Wembley has hosted every F.A. Cup final since then, virtually every important match involving the English National Team, the 1966 World Cup championship match, and the 1996 European Championship final.

Wembley, which is the centerpiece of England's bid for the 2006 World Cup, will be out of commission for several years because the stadium is being rebuilt for $760 million after the government determined it will be used only for soccer and rugby and not track and field in the Olympics. The seating capacity will be increased to 90,000, but the twin towers will be removed.

Maracana Stadium

The size of Maracana Stadium is so deceptive that the first time you stand inside this circular structure, you can't believe that it actually once held 235,000 people. Maracana was built in Rio de Janeiro in 1950, the only time Brazil hosted the World Cup. For the final match, a Cup-record 199,500 watched Uruguay defeat Brazil, 2-1. Today, Maracana holds 120,000, which was cut back due to security and safety reasons. Still, that should be big and imposing enough.

Giuseppe Meazza Stadium

It's also known as San Siro, home to two of the best clubs in the history of Italian soccer — A.C. Milan and Inter Milan. That means the field is being used at least once a week, and that means the field takes a pounding. Built in

1926, the stadium added a roof before the 1990 World Cup, giving the impression of an enclosed stadium. Named after former Italian star Giuseppe Meazza, one of two players who performed for Italy's world champion teams (1934 and 1938), most of the stadium's 83,000 seats are usually filled, unless those teams are going through a rare slump. The opening game of the 1990 World Cup was held at Meazza.

Nou Camp Stadium

Home to perennial Spanish power Barcelona, Nou Camp hosted the 1982 World Cup opener and the 1992 Olympic gold-medal match. At a capacity of 115,000, Nou Camp is the largest stadium in Europe. Every time Barcelona performs at Nou Camp, a sellout and an electric atmosphere of its own is ensured because the club has 110,000 members and season ticket holders, making it the largest club in the world.

Santiago Bernabeu Stadium

The ground is named after Santiago Bernabeu, who was an attorney, team captain, club secretary, coach, and president of Real Madrid and who helped turn the Spanish club into a super power. After the Spanish civil war of the 1930s badly damaged the old stadium, Bernabeu felt a new, super stadium was needed. Bernabeau, which was build in 1947 and seats 105,000, was the venue for the 1982 World Cup final.

Estadio Guillermo Canedo

Estadio Guillermo Canedo might be its official name (named after Canedo, who died in 1997 after he was Mexico's top soccer official for two decades and a FIFA vice president), but in many corners of the planet, it is still known as Azteca Stadium. The stadium, which seats 111,000 and can be extremely intimidating to visiting teams because the passionate and noisy crowds are only 30 feet away from the action, has seen better days. Azteca holds the distinction of being the only stadium to host two World Cup finals (1970 and 1986) and an Olympic final (1968) as well.

Estadio da Luz

Estadio da Luz, translated, means Stadium of Light. It would be appropriate to say the stadium takes its name from its lights, rather than from the nearby Lisbon district of Luz. Still, the home of Portuguese power Benfica is an imposing structure that once seated 130,000, which made it the largest stadium in Europe. The capacity of the stadium was reduced to 92,000 after the standing sections were eliminated, because of many crowd disasters throughout the world. A statue of Eusebio, erected in 1992, stands at the entrance of the stadium, honoring the former Benfica scoring star.

Amsterdam Arena and Gelredome

The Arena and the Gelredome are used as a double entry because they are both housed in the Netherlands and demonstrate the triumph of modern technology. When the United States announced that it would hold the 1994 World Cup games under a dome on real grass, the rest of the world laughed. Ajax of the Netherlands listened, and in 1996, the Arena, the first grass field under a retractable dome (51,260 capacity), was built.

Vitesse Arnhem, an up-and-coming Dutch club, has done Ajax one better with a domed stadium named the Gelredome (26,600) that allows for the field to be moved outside and the soccer club to hold concerts, conventions, or other big events without damaging the turf. And for the 2002 World Cup, the Sapporo Dome in Sapporo, Japan, which is to scheduled be finished in 2001, takes high-tech one step further. Not only will the field be movable, but it can be turned in any direction. The dome, nicknamed Hiroba (which means plaza in Japanese), will hold at least 40,000 spectators.

What's next on the drawing board? A double-decker soccer stadium with two fields under a dome? Don't laugh; it could be a reality by the end of the 21st century the way technology has progressed.

And one unique favorite

I'm talking about Griffin Park, home of Brentford in the English Second Division — A Second Division stadium that seats but 12,750 spectators? Yes, it is a favorite of mine because of what's outside the ground — four pubs (eating and drinking establishments), one on each corner of the stadium, where fans can gather before and after matches. That gives it a distinct flavor. Now, don't get me wrong. I don't condone drinking, but a little uniqueness and atmosphere go a long way.

And that's not to forget . . .

Virtually every country has one unique centerpiece of a stadium. You can't list them all, but here are some other impressive structures:

- ✔ Centenario Stadium in Montevideo, Uruguay (76,000), site of the first World Cup final in 1930

- ✔ Hampden Park in Glasgow, Scotland (50,000)

- ✔ Monumental Stadium in Buenos Aires, Argentina (76,000)

- ✔ Olympia-stadion — also known as Olympic Stadium — in Munich, Germany (74,000)

- ✔ Parc des Prince in Paris, France (48,700)

- ✔ Rose Bowl in Pasadena, California (102,000), the site of the 1984 Olympic gold-medal, 1994 World Cup final, and 1999 Women's World Cup

- ✔ The new Le Stade de France (80,000), site of the 1998 World Cup final

Hooligans: Soccer's Dark Side

The darkest side of soccer are so-called fans who are destructive in nature and will do anything to disrupt a soccer game or event. You may have heard many stories about them — they are called *hooligans*.

Like it or not, English fans are the most notorious of the lot. They gained international headlines in the 1980s with several unfortunate incidents, the biggest of which when fans of Liverpool went after their Juventus counter-parts at the European Cup title match at Heysel Stadium in Brussels, Belgium in 1985. A charge by Liverpool fans at the Juventus supporters resulted in a wall collapsing and the deaths of 39 Italians. That resulted in a five-year ban of all British teams from European club competitions, which restarted the development of the game in England.

Many hooligans are not soccer fans at all, but rather right-wing radicals who travel around looking for an excuse to make trouble and a statement for their cause. Some, called *skinheads,* are easy to spot because of their bald heads and belligerent demeanor. Some are not.

Some fans have been known to protest controversial calls and riot after matches, especially after they thought the referee stole the game from their team by calling or not calling for a penalty kick, for example.

Fans in Germany and Netherlands have been known to be destructive in recent years as well. But they are not as well known because they have not made as many blaring international headlines, and few, or no people, have died during incidents.

Incidents have died down some in recent years, although there was a marked increase in fan unrest as 1999 drew to a close. Local police and even sometimes the military have become involved in policing the fans before, during, and after matches. Many stadiums in Europe and South America have surveillance cameras to weed out the troublemakers, but a lot of the trouble occurs outside the stadiums, when these so-called fans drink and loiter around in public places such as the downtown or beachfront of a city.

Some disturbances and tragedies even occur away from the field. About two weeks after he had inadvertently scored for the U.S. in a 2-1 loss in the 1994 World Cup, Colombian defender Andres Escobar was shot dead by disgruntled bettors outside a nightclub in his native Medellin.

If you ever encounter a fan disturbance, walk, walk fast — or even run — the other way.

Part V

From Saturday Soccer to the World Stage

The 5th Wave   By Rich Tennant

In this part . . .

Soccer has something for everyone, whether you're age 5 or over 40. In this part, you find out about the different levels of soccer, including youth soccer, amateur soccer, pro soccer, and international soccer.

Chapter 17

Where It All Begins — Youth Soccer

*T*he best thing about soccer is that there is something for everyone. No matter what type of player you are, you should always be able to find a level to play at. This chapter examines the various levels of the game for youth players, both on and off the field.

The Youth Soccer Boom

You may not see it quite yet, but a quiet revolution is occurring at the youth sports level. Once occupying the bottom of the totem pole of school sports, soccer is not only tolerated or accepted today, it has become a welcome part of the sports scene.

If you ever have the time, take a look at recess at a grade school. Don't be surprised if you see boys and girls together, virtually everyone from the same class, kicking at and running after a ball. This wasn't the case for kids who grew up in the '60s and '70s.

Some issues to consider

From time to time, parents will wrestle with some key issues.

✔ **When should my child should start soccer?** That answer varies from parent to parent and child to child. Some children start as young as four. Other youths don't join until their friends do. Players have been known to start the sport as late as age 10. The main consideration is making sure that the child has fun at playing the game.

✔ **Should my daughter play with boys?** The answer is yes — up to a certain age. Most girls can certainly hold their own until puberty sets in between the ages of 12 to 14. Physical differences, for the most part, preclude girls from playing many contact and physical team sports with both sexes, although there are exceptions to every rule.

✔ **When should my child change teams?** Sometimes things don't work out for a player on a particular team, whether you have a problem with the coach or a talented player not getting enough playing time. If these problems cannot be resolved, it may be time to switch teams. But a word to the wise: Don't become a parent who has his son or daughter switch teams every year because they don't like this about the team or that about the coach. Reputations are forged very quickly in youth soccer and are difficult to live down.

In fact, some of those children don't play on organized soccer teams or in leagues at all. Soccer has become one of the "in" things to do and is an important part of the sports culture of the current generation, as is basketball. Whether that translates into bigger crowds at professional games in the years to come remains to be seen.

Unless you have been living in a cave, you should already know that youth soccer has taken off dramatically in the last generation or so. Since 1980, the numbers have quadrupled from a total of 888,705 playing soccer to an astounding 3.5 million with the three major organizations — U.S. Youth Soccer Association, American Youth Soccer Organization, and Soccer for American Youth. (See the section "Beyond the USYSA," later in this chapter, for more on these organizations.)

In 1998, 2.8 million children played under the USYSA roof, another 625,000 under AYSO rules, and 78,646 for SAY, according to figures released by the Soccer Industry Council of America (SICA). SICA, which is based in North Palm Beach, Florida, is one of 12 committees under the Sporting Goods Manufacturers of America. (SICA represents manufacturers of soccer uniforms, cleats, balls, and other game-related items.)

The 1994 World Cup, which was hosted by the United States, gave youth soccer a much needed boost. For example, USYSA participation had increased by about a healthy 100,000 per year. Thanks to the World Cup, the increase has been about 200,000 a year since.

The effect of the 1999 Women's World Cup is yet to be seen, although officials won't be surprised if female participation rises dramatically in the next several years.

The Youth Soccer Pecking Order

Most parents and children only know soccer through their own youth team or club. But a long ladder reaches to the very top of youth soccer in this country. See Figure 17-1.

The umbrella organization for a good portion of youth soccer in the United States is the U.S. Youth Soccer Association, which is also known as U.S. Youth Soccer. It encompasses 55 associations in all 50 states and 3.5 million children between the ages of four and 19. The USYSA organizes the national tournaments and is affiliated with U.S. Soccer. Its offices are located in Richardson, Texas.

The four regions

The USYSA is broken into four regions.

- **Region I:** East (from Maine to Virginia)
- **Region II:** Midwest (from Ohio and Kentucky to and including North and South Dakota, Kansas, and Nebraska in the west)
- **Region III:** South (from the Carolinas and Tennessee, Arkansas, and Oklahoma south)
- **Region IV:** West (from Montana, Colorado, Wyoming, and New Mexico to the West Coast)

The 55 state associations

There are 55 state associations and 50 states in the union. Each state has an association that relegates the sport in its area. Because of a state's sheer size in territory and population, two state associations are needed in California, Texas, Ohio, Pennsylvania, and New York.

Hundreds of leagues

Each state association has several leagues, sometimes as many as a dozen, which administer clubs, teams, and players. Depending on the rules, regulations, and by-laws of a particular state, a league can be defined as having four clubs or 100 clubs. There is more than a good chance there is a league in your area. Clubs without a league may be affiliated directly to a state association. To find out the nearest league in your area, please see Appendix B for the addresses, phone numbers and e-mails of the various state associations.

Beyond the USYSA

The USYSA isn't the only organization that promotes youth soccer in the United States. A pair of organizations — AYSO and SAY — also do as well.

✔ **AYSO:** The American Youth Soccer Organization, which was founded in 1964, has more than 625,000 children playing in the United States and Russia. It has been guided by the philosophy of "Everyone Plays" on recreational teams. According to AYSO rules, every player has to play at least half of every game. Teams also are balanced to assure competitive play. Its headquarters is in Hawthorne, California.

✔ **SAY:** Soccer Association for Youth, which was established in 1967, has grown to 78,646 children participating in what the organization calls a competitive recreational program. SAY was formed with the idea that any child could learn and play soccer. Its headquarters is in Cincinnati.

Hundreds of leagues, some ethnic, others in small towns or operated by churches or local youth organizations, have yet to affiliate with either USYSA, AYSO, and SAY. So, there is still incredible potential for growth. It is estimated that thousands of children are playing in such leagues.

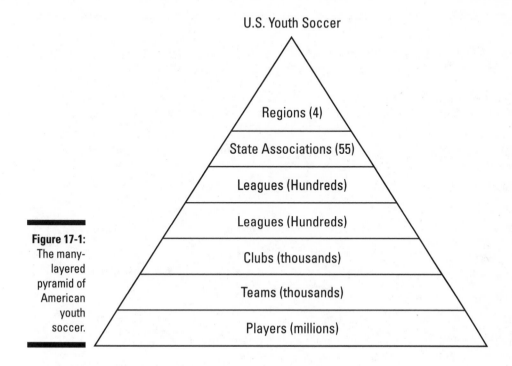

U.S. Youth Soccer

Regions (4)

State Associations (55)

Leagues (Hundreds)

Leagues (Hundreds)

Clubs (thousands)

Teams (thousands)

Players (millions)

Figure 17-1:
The many-
layered
pyramid of
American
youth
soccer.

The Different Club Levels

You need to remember the distinction between a team, club, and a league. A team plays in a *league*. A *team* is made up of players and usually belongs to a club. A *club* usually has several teams from the same town or geographical area at different age groups for both boys and girls, usually from Under-10 to Under-19. These teams from the same club rarely, if ever, play against each other in league competition, although larger clubs have been known to host two travel teams in the same age group.

Recreation

Recreational soccer is the most basic of the four levels. The age groups for boys and girls start at four and run through 14, although some leagues have recreational programs for youths as high as the 16-year-old age group. While many clubs sponsor recreational or in-house programs, churches, YMCAs, police athletic leagues, or public schools operate them as well.

Field size and game length grow as your child grows

You should not be surprised that the size of the field and length of the game increases with each age group. The older a child becomes, the more stamina he or she has to run in a larger field and the bigger the ball they can handle. Here is a quick reference chart, as recommended by the USYSA:

Age	Field Dimensions	Players Per Team	Ball Size	Game Length
Under-6	25 x 20 yards	3	No. 3	32 minutes
Under-8	50 x 30 yards	4	No. 3	48 minutes
Under-10	70 X 50 yards	8	No. 4	50 minutes
Under-12	100 X 50 yards	11	No. 4	60 minutes
Under-14	100 X 50 yards	11	No. 5	70 minutes
Under-16	100 X 50 yards	11	No. 5	80 minutes
Under-19	100 X 50 yards	11	No. 5	90 minutes

Note: The field dimensions are the minimum required. Goalkeepers are not used at the Under-6 and Under-8 age groups, and a keeper is optional at Under-10.

These leagues do not require much traveling and usually are held on fields at neighborhood schools.

Between the ages of four and 10, a child is expected to have fun, so while learning the game is important, it is not mandatory to teach children tactics at this level.

At the younger levels, it is common for teams to play 3 versus 3 or 5 versus 5 on smaller fields. This allows more participation by the players (the more you touch the ball, the more comfortable you get with it) and, of course, cuts down on the running.

Many, if not all, recreational leagues do not keep score of the matches. Most beginners don't know or care what the score is, as long as they have fun. I have put this "litmus" test to several children by asking several children what the final score of their games were. They did not know it.

Saying that, a number of leagues have special tournaments for the best players and teams in the older age groups — the American Cup.

Travel

As a child gets older, he may become more proficient in the sport and want to move on to the next level. This level is called travel because some — and sometimes a lot — of travel is involved. Travel teams, which usually are made up of players from the same town, community or geographical area, start for boys and girls at the age of 10 and run through Under-19 teams, which is when they go to college. If players don't attend college and still want to play the game, they can play amateur adult soccer (see Chapter 18).

Premier

For the talented player, a new level has seen the light of day since the mid-1980s — premier teams. These teams are made up of only the best players from a particular age group. Premier teams are not to be confused with league select or state Olympic Development Program teams (see the "Challenges for the Gifted Player" section later in this chapter) because they can come from various leagues.

Some of these premier teams play games in their home league on a Saturday and perform in the premier league on Sunday. In fact, many states operate such a league already.

Challenges for the Gifted Player

If a player is truly gifted with talent and ability beyond that of players in his or her age group, he or she can go places, in four distinctly different levels.

League select

The first level is the *league select team* for the top players in a particular age group. This team practices at least once a week, usually on an off-day from its club team practice. This team plays in some of the more important tournaments, usually out of state.

State Olympic Development Program

Every state association has an Olympic Development Program. This program doesn't have anything directly to do with the Olympics, although players could eventually wind up on the Olympic soccer team. (The program was formed many years ago as the Junior Olympic Developmental Program with the ultimate goal of making the Olympic team.)

Its program is similar to that of league select, except that the teams play a higher level of competition and may go to more difficult tournaments and even overseas tourneys as well. Tryouts for ODP can be controversial and sometimes politically charged because sometimes making the team can mean the difference of gaining an athletic scholarship from a Division I school.

At these tryouts, players are rated by area coaches in four areas — technique, tactics, fitness, athletic ability, and attitude.

The program is important because it is the first step of the identification of the best players, which culminates with the National Team.

Regional teams

Each state sends its boys and girls ODP teams to regional camp, which identifies the top players in each age group. The various state teams play against one another, and the regional coaches choose whom they consider the best players for the regional team.

National Teams

If a regional player is exceptional, he or she may be picked for a national youth team. The regional teams usually meet over a long holiday weekend in a warm climate such as Florida, where they compete in a series of matches. The best players are selected to the National Team of that particular age group — Under-14 through Under-20.

National Cup Championships

Every summer the top club teams in the country vie for National Cup titles in four age groups for boys and girls — through a series of cups and tournaments. It starts at the state level with, well, a state cup. That tournament usually runs over the course of several months and is usually a single-elimination competition. The Under-12 through Under-19 age groups qualify for the four regional tournaments, which usually are held at the end of June or beginning of July.

For the ages

Here's a quick reference chart for the various age groups for the 2000 state, regional, and national cups:

- U-10 — born Aug. 1, 1990, and later

- U-11 — born Aug. 1, 1989, and later

- U-12 — born Aug. 1, 1988, and later

- U-13 — born Aug. 1, 1987, and later

- U-14 — born Aug. 1, 1986, and later

- U-15 — born Aug. 1, 1985, and later

- U-16 — born Aug. 1, 1984, and later

- U-17 — born Aug. 1, 1983, and later

- U-18 — born Aug. 1, 1982, and later

- U-19 — born Aug. 1, 1981, and later

In this aspect the United States differs from the rest of the world, which uses the calendar as age group guidelines.

The winners from the four regional competitions at the Under-16 through Under-19 age groups qualify for the nationals. This is a round-robin competition in which every team plays each other at least once. The top two teams then face off for the national title. It used to be a single-elimination tournament, but youth officials thought it was unfair for a team to travel so far and play one meaningful game and then be eliminated.

The 2000 USYSA nationals are to be held at Disney's Wide World of Sports in Orlando, Florida. The 2001 and 2002 competitions are set for Mitchel Athletic Complex in Uniondale, New York, in suburban New York City.

Each of the eight age groups have a cup named after a late soccer player, coach, or administrator. For the boys, there's the D.J. Niotis Cup (Under-16), Don Greer Cup (Under-17), Andy Stone Cup (Under-18), and James P. McGuire Cup (Under-19). For the girls, there's the Patricia Louise Masotto Cup (Under-16), Laura Moynihan Cup (Under-17), Frank Kelly Cup (Under-18), and J. Ross Stewart Cup (Under-19).

High School Soccer

While high school soccer is not affiliated with U.S. Soccer or USYSA, it is still a part of youth soccer because it encompasses the Under-13 to Under-19 age groups.

In fact, its participation rates have climbed considerably over the past 20 years. More than a half million boys and girls participated in high school soccer in 1998, according to the National Federation of State High School Association and SICA. A total of 309,484 boys played the sport, and 246,687 girls did as well.

In 1998, soccer moved past baseball into fourth place among high school sports, trailing only basketball, football, and track. It is also the fastest growing sport among girls, and again, the effects of the 1999 World Cup won't be known for several years.

Some soccer purists have leveled the same criticism at high school soccer as they have at the college game — that the season is too short. A typical season is about 15 games before county, regional, and state playoffs. Most fall seasons run from the beginning of September to the end of October with local and state tournaments to follow. Some warm weather states hold their seasons in the winter, while others use the spring.

Other critics bring up the fact there is too much free substitution in the game, hurting an opportunity for the player to test his stamina or pace himself. Because it is a public school and open to everyone, coaches try to get as many players into the game.

Why kids quit soccer

Many players quit the game at the age of 13 or 14.

The reasons?

✔ **Burnout:** Burnout can come in so many different forms. Sometimes it is a child playing too much soccer. If your child plays for a club team and a select or ODP team (see the sections earlier in this chapter), that means she is playing games at least once a week and practicing at least twice. That's four of the seven days devoted to soccer. Sometimes parents push their children so much that the game isn't fun anymore. Sometimes the game is more important to the parents than to the child.

✔ **Other interests:** Sometimes in the natural progression, children lose interest simply because they find other interests and other sports or hobbies they may excel at.

✔ **The opposite sex:** In their teenage years, boys and girls discover the opposite sex. While this cycle is not always interrelated, getting a job to pay for dates and a new car has interfered with players pursuing soccer at a serious level. Giving the sport up is not an easy decision to make. If a player is that talented, he or she could get a scholarship — a free ride — to college.

In fact, some high school coaches have used, and some critics claim abused, the rules for their own purposes. Coaches have been known to have specialty teams, not unlike football. That's when a taller group of players, for example, replace smaller teammates on corner kicks, when height can be used as a great advantage in front of the goal. The problem with this is that some of the taller players never became soccer players, rather "corner kick specialists." They never had an opportunity to play a full game. Fortunately, these abuses have decreased significantly in recent years.

At one time, college and pro coaches and the media had a serious concern about the quality of some of the coaches because many were "recruited" teachers who didn't know the sport. If they did not coach the team, there might not be a team. The quality of coaches has improved considerably over the years, with many becoming students of the game.

At many schools, junior high or middle school players who are gifted are allowed to play with the varsity as eighth-graders.

Soccer in the Inner City

For the most part, youth soccer is a suburban sport. Fueled by Pelé's entry to the New York Cosmos in 1975, the sport has grown by leaps and bounds since then.

A number of urban soccer leagues have been alive and kicking for years — the Cosmopolitan Junior Soccer League has been serving New York City children since 1935. But many cities do not have proactive soccer programs and leagues.

A number of organizations have attempted to bridge the gap in the inner city. The best known is Soccer in the Streets, a nonprofit agency that was formed by Carolyn McKenzie in 1989 and that develops soccer for children in low-income neighborhoods and public housing in the inner city. The organization's motto is "Let's kick drugs and crime out of our communities." For more information, call (770) 477-0354.

When Travel Teams Really Have to Travel

What's the best thing about youth soccer? Well, outside of winning championships and trophies, it's the traveling. On a travel team, you get an opportunity to see your local area, county, or if there are not enough teams around, your state. Teams are allowed to use *guest players* — players from another team in the state — in tournaments as long as the player has permission from his or her club and state association.

The biggest tournaments in the United States are usually held in the summer or over long holiday weekends, such as Memorial Day, Columbus Day Weekend, Easter, Thanksgiving, and even Christmas.

Many travel teams play in tournaments in their geographical area. If these teams are really good, they venture out of their area and participate in more competitive events, such as regional and national tournaments. The more gifted players get an opportunity to test their abilities in some of the top tournaments in the United States and in Europe.

Some intriguing U.S. tournaments

Not surprisingly, the best and most prestigious tournaments are the most difficult to enter. The Dallas Cup, which is held Easter week (with the championship games culminating on Easter Sunday), has stringent requirements. It takes only the elite of the elite boys teams because of the extremely difficult level of competition, which includes teams from some of the top international clubs, such as Real Madrid (Spain), Manchester United (England), Ajax (Netherlands), and A.C. Milan (Italy), plus the world-famous Tahuichi Soccer Academy in Bolivia.

The WAGS tournament, which stands for Washington Area Girls Soccer in the Washington, D.C., area, is considered the premier tournament for girls because many college coaches scout players. Like the Dallas Cup, WAGS also has some tough prequisites because it takes on only elite teams.

The USA Cup is the largest youth tournament in the U.S. as teams cover the fields at the National Sports Center in Blaine, Minnesota, every July. The Potomac Cup, another capital-area competition, is held on Memorial Day weekend and also attracts many coaches from leading Division I colleges.

The best in Europe

Across the Atlantic, many countries offer opportunities to play against some of the best youth teams in the world. The Gothia Cup (Sweden), Dana Cup, (Denmark) and Haarlem Cup (Netherlands) are regarded as three of the top summer international tournaments.

How to Be a Happy Camper

A player should not go into a camp thinking that he will become a better player overnight. He should consider working on or improving one skill.

Trying to find the right soccer camp for a player can entail a lot of hard work. But if you ask the right questions and do the correct research, a player will definitely enjoy a week or two of their summer vacation.

So, what do you look for in a soccer camp?

Well, it all depends on what you want. Do you want to travel far? Do you want to stay close to home? Do you want a recreational camp? Do you want a specialty camp — for example, for goalkeepers?

Some players and parents want day camps. Others want overnight or residential camps. Still others — select players, for example — may opt for the advanced session camps.

After you've answered those questions, the best thing to do is to gather as much information as you can.

After you have read the brochures and whittled down your choices to a precious few and you still are undecided, don't be afraid to ask questions and compare and contrast. You're not charged when you ask questions (and if you don't, you might be paying more later), no matter whether you're asking the camp director, a friend or teammate who attended the camp, or another parent. Word of mouth can be a powerful tool. If you don't know, how else are you going to find out?

Here's a quick, but effective, checklist of factors to consider when choosing a soccer camp:

- ✔ **Camp director:** A camp director does not have to be a famous player or well-known coach — current or former — but he or she must have an outgoing personality and be a coach or have some kind of education background. You also need to make sure that the director attends and participates in the camp sessions and is not a figurehead who shows up only when the campers arrive and leave. The camp staff also should have some kind of educational background: instructor, teacher, or coach, too. A good camp has a mixture of experienced coaches and college-age players on staff. The campers may look up to the older staff members, but may relate better to the younger ones.

- ✔ **Experience:** The number of years a camp has been around can be a determining factor. Those camps with solid reputations should have quite a few references, especially for the campers who keep coming back.

- ✔ **Facilities:** The campground should be one of high quality. And because it is a summer soccer camp, make sure that there are contigency plans for rain and thunderstorms. Is there a gymnasium for indoor activities in an emergency? Is there a TV with a VCR so players can learn about the game? There is nothing worse than bored campers having nothing to do, sitting around in the gymnasium or worse, in their dorm rooms all day while it pours outside.

- **Ratio:** A sound ratio should be one full-time staff member to ten campers so that the kids have an opportunity to work in small groups and get an education. Obviously, the smaller the group, the better. Be wary of camps that have 20-1 ratios. It may be a baby-sitting service rather than a soccer camp.

- **Focus:** Look at what the camp has to offer. Does the progression from hour to hour and day to day make sense? Is there enough activity and rest in between? Is it a soccer-only camp, or is soccer just one of several activities? Some camps may offer other activities such as swimming and other sporting pursuits. Does your son or daughter want a soccer-only environment, or does he or she want a variety of choices?

- **Specialty camps:** More camps are specializing in positions (goalkeepers and strikers) and in advanced tactics. For example, if you are an aspiring high school goalkeeper, you may want to attend a keeper's camp instead of a general one. If your child is a competitive player and wants to play in high school, you probably would be interested in a camp that focuses on techniques and tactics. If he or she is part of the Olympic Development Program pool and is heading for college, find a camp that is designed for the elite player.

- **Skill levels:** How are the skill levels and age classification broken up? Players should be grouped according to age and ability. Pairing an advanced 15-year-old select player with a 10-year-old intramural player is nothing short of ridiculous.

- **Medical care:** A registered nurse or an athletic trainer should be on staff and on call at all times for the safety of all campers. There should be no exceptions.

- **Hidden costs:** Make sure that everything is spelled out in the brochure so that you won't have any surprises come July and August. Some camps require that a player brings his or her own balls. Many give out shirts, souvenirs, and awards. Others have souvenir stands.

- **Food:** Find out what the week's menu is. It should be varied and nutritional. If it's hot dogs for lunch everyday, then the camp is heading for trouble. A fast-food diet and soccer do not mix.

You may have a few more questions of your own to ask before making that final decision.

More than Just Kicking a Ball Around

If you thought that youth soccer was just running around after a ball in the great outdoors, guess again. The following sections show you what some state associations and leagues offer their players.

Indoor soccer

You can kick the ball in the great indoors in cold-weather regions during the winter months. While many purists feel that indoor soccer is an entirely different game than the outdoor version, this might be the only way a player can stay fit — physically and mentally. With the success of the Major Indoor Soccer League in the 1980s and the National Professional Soccer League in the 1990s to the present, most major metropolitan areas have an indoor facility where camps and different league games are held year-round.

Conventions

Some leagues or state associations hold conventions, usually in the winter or right before the spring season kicks off. The activities can include coaching clinics and college fairs (when you're looking for a college) to special seminars on First Aid.

Scholarships

Due to the rising costs of college and clubs, players can take advantage of the special scholarships for the exceptional player or student-athlete that leagues and state associations award. These scholarships can range from $500 to $2,000.

Sportsmanship awards

Some leagues hand out sportsmanship awards to the best-behaved teams. The conduct of these teams are graded by local referees, and a final score for the season is determined. In some leagues, these honors are more valued than winning a division title.

Recruitment of high school seniors

Many leagues sponsor a special event to showcase the top high school seniors in their area, usually on Thanksgiving weekend. Given that many colleges don't have tremendous recruiting budgets as in football or basketball, this event gives coaches an opportunity to scout and assess the best talent in one place.

Everyone can play

When I say youth soccer is for everyone, I'm not joking. Even players with disabilities can get into the act and play the world's most popular sport.

A number of youth leagues have established a Special Children's program, which allows youths with disabilities or impairments to play soccer.

The Long Island Junior Soccer League established the first Special Children's program through the Huntington Boys Club in 1981. It has blossomed to nine clubs and 225 players whose limitations range from learning disabilities, autism, Down's Syndrome, behavioral problems, mental retardation, cerebral dysfunction, and epilepsy.

These players play once a week in the spring and fall. At the end of the spring season, all the players, parents, and families get together for a big tournament and barbeque at the league's soccer park. Every player receives an award at the program's awards dinner in December.

The USYSA also has created The Outreach Program for Soccer (TOPS), which gives every player with a disability an opportunity to play the sport. TOPS is open to youths between the ages of 6 and 19 and include children who have leg, visual, and hearing impairments and varying degrees of mental retardation.

Chapter 18

Amateur Soccer: They Don't All Play for Pay

Not everybody plays for pay. Some players like to play soccer just for fun on the weekend. Sunday is usually the day for recreational adult leagues, as former youth, high school, and college stars are allowed to have another day or two in the sun, and one-time pros still are given an opportunity to kick the ball around as well.

Amateur leagues have been the backbone of U.S. soccer since the turn of the 20th century, but recently they haven't gotten much publicity because of other high-profile soccer events at the international, professional, college, and high school levels.

Many National Team and pro players have passed through these leagues, including New England Revolution and former U.S. National Team captain John Harkes, Kansas City Wizards goalkeeper Tony Meola, and New York/New Jersey MetroStars midfielder Tab Ramos.

The Top Areas and Leagues

In many respects, amateur soccer is not all that unlike professional soccer. Many leagues are set up in four divisions — by team ability — and they play for local or area championships and even national titles, such as the Lamar

Hunt U.S. Open Cup. In fact, many of the players who perform in Major League Soccer and the A-League have played in one amateur league or another before turning pro.

It should come as no surprise that the best amateur soccer is played in metropolitan areas with large population bases.

Men's teams and leagues from New York, Chicago, Los Angeles, and Washington, D.C., perennially have captured amateur titles. During the 1940s, 1950s, and even 1960s, thousands of people would line fields to watch their favorite teams battle one another or, occasionally, a team from Europe or South America.

Today, although crowds are not so high, the quality of soccer can be.

The New York metropolitan area has a huge population base with several quality leagues. At one time, the Northeastern Super Soccer League (now, that's a mouthful!) was arguably the best amateur/semipro league in the country, as it brought together champions and top teams from New York, New Jersey, Connecticut, and Pennsylvania. In recent years, however, the quality of the teams has gone down.

When amateurs and pros can meet

No other sport in the United States can boast a competition like the Lamar Hunt U.S. Open Cup, which is literally open to every adult men's soccer team, from amateur to semi-pro to professional.

The competition, named after Lamar Hunt, owner of the Columbus Crew and Kansas City Wizards (both Major League Soccer) in 1999, has been around and kicking since 1914.

The likelihood of pitting a top amateur club in the final against a Major League Soccer team isn't that great, but every year there seems to be a host of upsets. In 1997, the San Francisco Seals of the D3 Pro League, the Third Division of the U.S. pro soccer pecking order, turned giant killers. The Seals knocked off several A-League and MLS teams before meeting its match against D.C. United in the semifinals.

That's what makes the competition so intriguing — the possibility of an upset by a lower team, not unlike the granddaddy of all cup competitions, the English Football Association Cup.

In fact, a player and a general manager in MLS treasure memories of winning U.S. Open Cup medals.

"That season would have been a disappointment if we hadn't won the championship," said Tampa Bay Mutiny general manager Bill Manning, a member of the Brooklyn Italians, the 1991 Cup winners. "We focused the entire season around it."

New York/New Jersey MetroStars defender Mark Semioli fondly remembered his experience with the 1994 champions, the Greek Americans.

"We won a cup that have might have been the biggest trophy in American soccer that year," he said. "We had such a camaraderie on that team. We were on the same page, and we had respect for each other. . . . We were not making any money with that team. We wanted to be national champions.

"I still cherish that more than anything. I still have that medal. I keep it along with my championship ring (1991 A-League champions, the San Francisco Bay Blackhawks). It really defines why we play soccer. It wasn't for the money. It was a continuation of the way we grew up. It was a real special moment. I don't think that the Open Cup will be that way again."

The Cup certainly has had its moments over the past decade:

✔ In 1989 and 1990, former North American Soccer League goalkeeper Dragan Radovich lost twice in the final minutes with two teams. He was in the nets for the H.R.C. Kickers' 2-1 victory over Greek-American Atlas (New York City) and then endured another defeat to the Chicago Eagles, 2-1, while playing with the Italians a year later. The 1990 defeat was most painful, as Radovich bobbled a shot into the goal with 30 seconds remaining.

✔ In 1991, the third time was the charm for Radovich, who registered a shutout for the Italians. Brooklyn defeated the Richardson Rockets (Texas), 1-0, on a goal by former Nigerian youth international Ernest Inneh. The Italians played most of the match a player down after Manning was red-carded for a controversial professional foul. Manning was escorted from the Brooklyn College stadium, but managed to watch the rest of the game from his car in the parking lot.

✔ From 1992–94, club teams enjoyed a last hurrah in the competition. In 1992, the San Jose Oaks started a three-year championship run by San Francisco Major Division League teams, defeating Vasco da Gama (Conn.), 2-1. The next year, C.D. Mexico rolled to a 5-0 victory over the German Hungarians (Pa.). C.D. Mexico overcame a pregame headache that saw them and the Hungarians wearing similar-colored green jerseys. Mexico donned makeshift white shirts with numbers made from black magic markers. In 1994, in a rare meeting of former U.S. National Team coaches, the Greek Americans defeated Bavarian-Leinenkugel (Milwaukee), 3-0. The Greek Americans were guided by current San Jose Earthquakes coach Lothar Osiander, former coach of the U.S. National and Olympic teams. Bavarian was directed by Kansas City Wizards coach Bob Gansler, who guided the U.S. in the 1990 World Cup.

✔ In 1995, the Richmond Kickers capped an amazing run for USISL (now D3 Pro League) teams by capturing the Cup. USISL teams surprised A-League teams in three quarter-finals before the Kickers defeated the El Paso Patriots in the final in a shootout, 4-2, after playing to a 1-1 draw in regulation.

✔ Since 1996, MLS teams have dominated the Cup. In that year, D.C. United completed a double, winning the MLS title and the Open Cup championship, 3-0 over the expansion Rochester Raging Rhinos of the A-League. Raul Diaz Arce, Eddie Pope, and Jaime Moreno scored in that match. In 1997, the Dallas Burn salvaged a medicore season by winning the Cup, surviving a penalty-kick tiebreaker, 5-3, after playing to a scoreless tie against MLS champion United. In 1998, the expansion Chicago Fire duplicated United's 1996 feat by capturing the double, stopping the Columbus Crew in overtime in the the finale, 2-1, on a goal by Frank Klopas. And in 1999, Rochester finally completed its quest, stopping the Colorado Rapids in the championship game, 2-0.

San Francisco Major Division League can make an argument in staking a claim to the best league. In the mid-1990s, Bay Area Soccer League teams captured the U.S. Open Cup three years running — San Jose Oaks (1992), C.D. Mexico (1993), and the Greek Americans (1994).

The nation's oldest surviving league is the Cosmopolitan Soccer League, which has been alive and kicking since 1923. CSL has teams in four men's divisions and two Over-30 divisions from New York, New Jersey, and Connecticut.

At one time, teams from New England, New York, Philadelphia, and St. Louis dominated the American soccer world, due in part (except for St. Louis) to their large ethnic base. But since the incredible growth of the game at all levels since 1975, the best teams and players can come from any state in the union.

In fact, many of the best players are coming from the Sunbelt and California because the mild climate affords players more quality time to play and practice outdoors.

Before the United Soccer Leagues, the minor league system of soccer, expanded dramatically in the mid-1990s, amateur leagues literally had the best soccer in town. When a chance at a pro career, and perhaps a lucrative one, beckoned, many of these teams lost their best players to the USL.

A number of amateur leagues needed time to "reload," to find top talent to replenish what they had lost. It remains to be seen whether these teams and leagues will rediscover their past glory days, but amateur soccer will always remain a vital link between the youth and professional ranks.

Amateur Soccer from Top to Bottom

Like its youth and pro counterparts, amateur soccer has a certain pecking order and several levels of play.

U.S. Amateur Soccer Association

The U.S. Amateur Soccer Association (USASA), which is at the top of the pyramid, coordinates all activities, programs, and national tournaments.

According to the Soccer Industry Council of America, more than 250,000 players over the age of 19 play in a team or league affiliated with the USASA and U.S. Soccer Federation.

The four regions

For soccer purposes, the United States is split into four regions — Region I, which is the Northeast (from Maine to Virginia); Region II — Midwest (from Ohio and Kentucky to and including North and South Dakota, Kansas, and Nebraska in the west; Region III — South (from the Carolinas and Tennessee, Arkansas, and Oklahoma south); and Region IV — West (from Montana, Colorado, Wyoming, and New Mexico to the West Coast).

The regional chairmen and committees organize soccer in their areas.

The 55 state associations

There are 55 state associations and 50 states in the union. Each state has an association that regulates the sport in its area. Because of a state's sheer size in territory or population, two state associations are needed in California, Texas, Ohio, Pennsylvania, and New York. (See Appendix B for contact information.)

Some associations are more active than others because of the size of state. Some states have one person as the president, vice president, secretary, and treasurer. Other states have more officers and volunteers than they know what to do with.

Affiliated and non-affiliated leagues

To be eligible for playing insurance and have an opportunity to play in national tournaments, every player, team, club, and league must belong to the USASA and U.S. Soccer.

Hundreds of unaffiliated ethnic leagues are in metropolitan areas (Hispanic, Caribbean, and European leagues, for example). These leagues are not affiliated for various reasons. Some are not familiar with U.S. Soccer and what it can offer, while others have no desire to join.

Since 1990, U.S. Soccer has made great strides in bringing all these leagues under its umbrella. It still is a work in progress.

Leagues for Everyone

Depending on your level of play and age, the amateur league seems to have just about something for everyone — men and women.

Sunday recreational leagues

These leagues are for players who want to play more for the fun of it and then hang out with the guys over beers at a local pub afterwards. Those leagues usually are one of the lower divisions of an established league or one based on skill.

Leagues for the more serious player

Other leagues are usually reserved for the former player who isn't afraid to get his nose, face and uniform dirty. Many former high school, college, and pro players usually dominate this level. In fact, some clubs and teams pay their players from $100 to as much as $500 a game, under the table in cash. That's when you know things are serious; because if a "paid" team doesn't win or take home the league title, payments might wind up being a little "late" after a loss or tie, or the club management will put a lot of heat on the players.

Some of those leagues have reserve teams for their First and Second Division teams. And some leagues have as many as four divisions, depending on the ability and success of the team.

State select teams

For the best players, state select Under-23 teams exist. These teams, which can have teenage players if they're good enough, compete in regional competition for the right to play in the Donnelly Cup, usually over Thanksgiving weekend in Florida. (The Cup is named after the late George Donnelly, a member of the National Soccer Hall of Fame and a well-known soccer administrator.)

Over-30 and beyond

For those masochists out there who want to continue playing past college and amateur ball and wake up aching Monday mornings (and sometimes Tuesday mornings as well), there are Over-30 teams and leagues. While the skill level of the players may still be quite high and the playing experience second to none, the legs, in terms of speed and endurance, are usually the first to go.

As baby boomers grow in age, the number of leagues for older players increase. In the past several years, leagues for players Over-40 and even Over-50 have sprouted up. Are Over-60 leagues not far behind?

A word to the wise: If you have not played soccer in a while or participated in a stressful activity, get a full medical check up before playing.

The ultimate soccer moms

With more and more of the youth players getting older, women's soccer leagues have popped up all over the country. Some are open to females of all ages, while others are Over-30 leagues, because the huge disparity of ages.

Many of these players played in youth leagues, high school, or college, although an expanding group of players decided to play after watching their children perform, giving a new meaning to the term "Soccer Mom." These teams can compete in the U.S. Women's Amateur Cup, a national competition for the best teams in the country, if they so choose. The Amateur Cup starts at the local level, and as a team progresses it will play against teams from its region (East, Midwest, West and South) before reaching the national Final Four.

Co-ed teams

Yes, there is co-ed soccer available for those who like to play the sport with the opposite sex. You usually have special rules for this game, such as the ratio of men to women allowed on a team and allowing a man to come only within a certain amount of yards of a female opponent.

In fact, the USASA has started a national Co-ed Cup. The first tournament was won by the Mall Rats, a team from the Metropolitan D.C.-Virginia Soccer Association in September 1999. The Mall Rats defeated Lempira (Louisiana), 3-0, in League City, Texas. In the Over-30 Division, the Plaza Delphinus (Austin, Texas) beat the Express (Texas South), 5-0.

For more information

For more information on where to find the right league for you, consult Appendix B in the back of the book for your amateur state association contact information.

Counting the numbers

If you want to get technical, the 250,000 or so men and women who play amateur soccer is just a drop in the bucket compared to what is happening with youth soccer.

According to the Soccer Industry Council of America (SICA), more than 18.2 million Americans played soccer at least once in 1999. That might include a mother or a father kicking a soccer ball around with their son or daughter. Moreover, 8.9 million Americans played 25 or more days a year — those who participate in an organized league, according to SICA's 1999 survey.

Here are some more interesting figures from that survey:

✔ A total of 10.6 million males play soccer as do 7.4 million females. (It will be interesting to see how that latter total rises in light of the U.S. Women's National Team capturing the 1999 Women's World Cup.)

✔ California has the most participants — 2.1 million, followed by New York (1.3 million) and Texas (1.2 million).

✔ The top soccer market in the United States is New York/New Jersey/Connecticut/Pennsylvania area at 1.1 million, followed by Los Angeles/Riverside County/Orange County (1 million) and Washington, D.C./Baltimore (453,000).

✔ Utah leads the way in participation rates by the states at 17.3 participants per 100 people. Next are Rhode Island (16.7) and Kansas (14.1).

SICA, which is based in North Palm Beach, Florida, is one of 12 committees under the Sporting Goods Manufacturers of America. SICA represents manufacturers of soccer uniforms, cleats, balls, and other game-related items.

The Growth of Soccer Clubs

For many years, particularly in the Northeast, ethnic soccer clubs dominated the scene. A player could start out as a youth player and play his entire career with one club, from youth to the adult side and eventually the Over-30 team.

Many of those teams would have at least one field — or even a small stadium on which to play — with a clubhouse and locker room.

In some places, the ethnic scene is dying out as more and more people move to the suburbs and rural areas. However, as the old clubs die out, new ones are being born.

All those cups runneth over and over

In some respects, U.S. soccer is right in line with its overseas counterparts, especially with the various cup competitions. Here are the major annual cup competitions that are open to amateur and semipro teams:

✔ **U.S. Open Cup:** This competition, officially called the Lamar Hunt U.S. Open Cup, is open to any club affiliated to U.S. Soccer in this country. For amateur teams, the qualifying process is more drawn out than for its professional counterparts because the teams must start with their state and then regional qualifying before reaching the latter rounds. Due to the development of the United Soccer Leagues, the A-League, and Major League Soccer, the last amateur team to win the Open Cup was Greek-American of San Francisco in 1995. The competition dates back to 1914 (the Brooklyn Field Club defeated the Brooklyn Celtics), making it the oldest cup event in the U.S.

✔ **Men's Amateur Cup:** Any amateur team is eligible to compete, and the teams go through a similar qualifying process through state and regional competition before the final is held in mid-summer. It is unadvisable for a team to vie for both the Open and Amateur Cups because many of the qualifying matches are played on the same dates. Besides, many teams like to focus on one

cup at a time. The Kutis Soccer Club, which is sponsored by a St. Louis funeral home, has won the most Cups with seven (six consecutive times from 1956 to 1961 and 1971).

✔ **Men's Over-30 Cup:** This competition, which was started in 1983, has a similar set up to the Amateur Cup. There is also a Men's Under-23 Cup.

✔ **Women's Cups:** The Women's Amateur Cup kicked off in 1980, while the Over-30 Cup was added in 1986, a Women's Open Cup and an Under-23 Cup joined the list in 1996. Some of these teams now sport members of the U.S. Women's National Team and W-League teams from the USL umbrella of leagues.

✔ **Women's Over-30 Cup:** While the competition is not as difficult as the men's, the quality of play in this event will continue to grow as more players from the soccer boom of the 1970s and 1980s continue to play the game.

✔ **State Cups:** Many state associations have cup competitions for men and women that are separate from the national events. In fact, some states have broken down their cup competition by the division a team plays. In other words, all First Division teams will vie for one cup, while Second and Third Division teams will battle for another.

Today, a modern soccer club includes several layers, where a player can literally play his or her entire soccer career. It starts, of course, with the youth, where the players can play just for fun at a young age (from four to nine). These players can develop into a travel team player (from ages 10 to 19), and during high school or after college, a senior, or adult team (from teenager to whenever a player runs out of steam or energy in his legs) before joining the Over-30 team. In fact, some clubs have women's teams as well.

A clubhouse or locker room is considered a bonus. The key thing is playing the game.

College Soccer

Well, college soccer is considered amateur, even though the best Division I men and women in the National Collegiate Athletic Association are compensated through scholarships. College soccer has been a springboard for many players to play in Major League Soccer and on the U.S. National Team. It also has been a proving ground for many members of the U.S. Women's National Team. (For more on the National Team, see Chapter 20.)

In fact, the growth of women's soccer has exceeded the men's by a considerable amount, thanks to Title IX. That rule, implemented in 1972, mandated that women should have an equal number of athletic programs to that of men in college.

Since 1981, the number of women's soccer teams has increased tenfold. Only 77 schools had women's programs then, compared to 790 in 1999, according to the Soccer Industry Council of America. There were 521 men's programs in 1981 and 719 in 1999.

The three NCAA divisions are determined by financial commitment and what level of competition the school wants to play. At the Division I and II levels, schools are allowed to give out athletic scholarships (the better players usually wind up at Division I schools), while Division III colleges are not allowed to award athletic scholarships. Financial aid is okay, however, at all three levels.

NCAA Division I

Division I is the cream of the crop of college soccer for both men and women. Schools are allowed 9.9 scholarships per season, so that makes it a coach's challenge on how to divvy up some of the money.

Indiana, which bested Santa Clara 1-0 for the 1999 title, UCLA, and five-time champion Virginia are among the perennial men's powers.

North Carolina regained the 1999 women's crown, besting Notre Dame, 2-0. Santa Clara, Connecticut, and Portland are among the teams to beat in women's soccer.

North Carolina: Home of the soccer dynasty

There has not been more success in a college soccer program than the University of North Carolina, where coach Anson Dorrance has amassed an astounding 442-17-11 record.

After capturing the 1999 title, the Tar Heels have accumulated an incredible 15 national titles in 18 years, making it easier to list the years North Carolina did not win — 1985 (George Mason was champion), 1995 (Notre Dame), and 1998 (Florida).

North Carolina also has produced 49 first-team All-Americans and the core of the U.S. Women's National Team that dominated international soccer during the 1990s — defender Carla Overbeck, midfielders April Heinrichs, Kristine Lilly, and Tisha Venturini and forwards Mia Hamm and Cindy Parlow, among a host of others.

NCAA Division II

While the quality of play isn't as consistent as Division I after the top ten schools, Division II colleges have produced some professional players. Division II has slightly more liberal rules because many of the top schools have used foreign players.

Southern Connecticut successfully defended its national title — its sixth overall — behind a 2-1 win over Fort Lewis College — in 1999. Lynn, South Carolina-Spartanburg, and Seattle Pacific have been among the most successful programs.

Franklin Pierce stopped Cal Poly Pomona, 3-1, to take home the women's crown. The women's division has been dominated by Franklin Pierce, Lynn, and Sonoma State.

NCAA Division III

Athletic scholarships are forbidden in Division III as players choose to attend colleges for academics over soccer in many instances. They can earn academic scholarships and grants-in-aid.

St. Lawrence finished the 1999 season unbeaten and untied, downing Wheaton College in the men's championship game.

The University of California-San Diego, which downed defending champion Macalester, 1-0, for its fourth national title in five years, won the women's crown in 1999.

NAIA

The quality of players and teams are more of the Division II level, although the ranks of this division, named the National Association of Intercollegiate Athletics, has shrunk to 350 member schools in recent years.

Lindsey Wilson College (Kentucky) edged the University of Mobile (Alabama), 2-1, for the 1999 men's championship while Westmont registered a 3-0 victory over Transylvania (Pennsylvania) for the 1999 women's title.

NCCAA

The National Christian College Athletic Association, which is not associated with the NCAA, includes about 100 Christian-oriented colleges across the country and competes in its own leagues, regions, and national championship.

East Texas Baptist won the 1999 men's Division I crown, besting Mount Vernon Nazarene College, 4-1.

Indiana Wesleyan outlasted Western Baptist College, 3-2, in overtime to capture the 1999 women's title.

Junior colleges

Two-year schools, which are for players who need to improve their grades, to prove themselves as a player, or need a financial break, is an excellent springboard to the Division I ranks. Probably the best example of this was U.S. national coach Bruce Arena, who was a junior college All-American at Nassau Community College (N.Y.) in 1970 before he transferred and became an All-American at Cornell.

The Walsh Cup

There may not be a more innocent, endearing, and enduring soccer tournament than the Walsh Cup. Operated every year since 1990 by the family of New York/New Jersey MetroStars midfielder Billy Walsh in their oversized backyard in Chatham, N.J., the tournament attracts professional, high school, college, amateur, and women soccer players, including a couple of coaches as well. The Cup, which pits eight teams (five players a side) traditionally is played on the Saturday or Sunday before Christmas and has attracted such a following that stands from nearby Chatham High School had to be brought in.

And it's free for fans, although donations are accepted to fund a new nearby soccer field.

Several big-name players have participated in the cup, including former U.S. National Team defender Alexi Lalas, Kansas City Wizards goalkeeper Tony Meola, current National Team and Chicago Fire goalkeeper Zach Thornton, and D.C. United and National Team midfielder Ben Olsen, and several of Walsh's MetroStars teammates, including goalkeeper Mike Ammann, defenders Mark Semioli and Mike Petke, and midfielder Miles Joseph.

The best thing about the Walsh Cup is that you never really know what might happen.

In the 1998 championship game, 12-year-old Patrick Walsh scored the game-winning goal, beating the 6-foot-3, 210-pound Thornton, who only two months prior backstopped the Fire to the MLS title and won Goalkeeper of the Year honors himself.

In 1999, Darah Ross, a former University of Pennsylvania women's soccer player, scored the lone goal in F.C. Walsh's 1-0 win over Ebony and Ivory.

"It's something you have to do," said Semioli, who promised himself he would be a part of the tournament to see what all the hoopla was all about. "It's something you have to see to believe."

"This is what soccer's all about," added Olsen, who has managed to win one championship in three years at the Walsh Cup, although he hasn't received anything to put on his mantle. "You get a year of bragging. Everyone knows who won."

Chapter 19

Pro Soccer in the United States

- -

In This Chapter

▶ Watching the birth of major league soccer

▶ Understanding the ever-expanding minor leagues

▶ Entering the great indoors

▶ Knowing the best places to watch games

▶ Seeing the U.S. cup runneth over and over

- -

*W*hile they don't get near the salaries of their counterparts in baseball, football, basketball, and hockey, professional soccer players can earn a living in the U.S. these days. In fact, there have never been so many professional teams in this country — 12 in Major League Soccer, 28 in the A-League, and 26 in the D3 Pro League. Add the primarily amateur Premier Development Soccer League, and the U.S. has a four-tier structure, not unlike other countries.

The Birth of Major League Soccer

Major League Soccer (MLS), born December 1993 to serve as a legacy for the 1994 World Cup, was different from any other soccer league in the United States: It was organized as a single-entity league. *Single entity* sounds like a science-fiction creature out of something like *Star Trek,* but the league's founders, operators, and investors — that's their way of calling them owners — have a reason for this. Trying to avoid repeating the history of out-of-control salaries that doomed the NASL (see sidebar), the league's founders wanted to control the purse strings. That meant centralized control by the league office, which is in New York, and a salary cap for the league. The cap began at $1.131 million in its inaugural 1996 season and was around $1.8 million for the 2000 season, although it is considered a *soft cap.*

Annual player salaries range from a minimum $24,000 to a maximum $260,000. The lower paid players can supplement their income with modest endorsement agreements, while the players earning the maximum can make even more from league sponsors.

The league, which started out with ten teams, added two more for the 1998 season. The original ten included the Columbus Crew, Colorado Rapids, Dallas Burn, D.C. United, Kansas Wizards, Los Angeles Galaxy, New England Revolution, New York/New Jersey MetroStars, San Jose Earthquakes, and Tampa Bay Mutiny. The Chicago Fire and Miami Fusion were the league's two expansion teams in 1998.

The regular season begins in mid-March and ends at the beginning of September. The playoffs run through the middle of October and culminate in the MLS Cup. Each of the 12 teams is allowed four foreign players on its 19-man player roster, and plays a 32-game schedule, 16 at home and 16 on the road.

The quality has been compared to of that of Second Division clubs in Europe. Being a relatively young league and with the forever spiraling transfer fees and salaries overseas, MLS cannot afford to compete with European clubs for the top players in the world. So, for the most part, MLS settles for popular players on the other side of 30, such as Colombia's crafty playmaker Carlos Valderrama, or players who are trying to make a name for themselves, such as Trinidad & Tobago forward Stern John, who went on to star in the English First Division.

The single-entity concept has been most controversial, giving the league total control over player contracts and salaries. In fact, the league can mandate trades if it wants to. In 1999, former commissioner Doug Logan decided on his own to move Valderrama from Miami to Tampa Bay after the Colombian got into a major argument with Fusion coach Ivo Wortmann. Logan's logic was that it wasn't doing Valderrama or the team any good that such a talented player wasn't playing.

Teams can acquire players in several ways. The league can allocate a player — usually a U.S. National Team player or a foreigner. Teams also can pick players in what is now called the SuperDraft. The SuperDraft is a combination of the college and supplemental drafts (players from the A-League and D3 Pro League are available; see section later in this chapter) or high school or college players who have decided to become Project 40 players (see sidebar). Teams also have a third option, finding a local player who impresses their coach and general manager as a discovery player.

The league has hopes of expanding to 14 teams in 2001 and to as many as 18 by the end of this decade. Cities and regions being considered for expansion include Philadelphia, Houston, the Pacific northwest (either Portland or Seattle) and a second team in the New York market, in New York City.

After a solid first season in which teams averaged 17,562 spectators a game, attendance has dipped to a healthy plateau of approximately 15,000 per match. It is up to the team general managers and MLS officials, including new commissioner Don Garber, to find ways to increase that figure.

A very brief history of U.S. pro soccer

While Major League Soccer has been around since 1996, there have been several predecessors who have tried to make a go of it during the 20th century.

Three leagues have called themselves the American Soccer League. The first incarnation lasted from 1921 to 1933 before major internal problems destroyed the league. The second ASL enjoyed a much longer life, from 1934 to 1983. More internal problems forced the league to disband and reform as the United Soccer League, which also lasted all of one season (1984).

The modern professional era as we know it began in 1967. Several millionaires and owners of sports teams were inspired by the 1966 World Cup. Two groups decided to form leagues of their own — the United Soccer Association, which brought over club teams from Europe and South America to play as local club teams — the National Professional Soccer League.

After 1967, these two leagues merged to form the North American Soccer League, which enjoyed some incredible high notes before going out of business after the 1984 season. The Cosmos, which included Pele, Beckenbauer, and perennial scoring champion Giorgio Chingalia, were the class of the league.

For three years, U.S. pro soccer went through its version of the Dark Ages before the third version of the ASL, primarily an East Coast league, was born in 1988. After a merger between the Western Soccer League and ASL in 1991, the American Professional Soccer League was formed. In 1995, it switched its name to the A-League for marketing purposes and has been considered a Second Division league to MLS ever since.

How the teams break down

MLS breaks down into three divisions: the Eastern, Central, and Western. The Eastern Division is made up of three-time defending champion D.C. United, Miami Fusion, and New York/New Jersey MetroStars, New England Revolution. The Columbus Crew, Chicago Fire, Dallas Burn, and Tampa Bay Mutiny form the Central Division, while the Colorado Rapids, Kansas City Wizards, Los Angeles Galaxy, and San Jose Earthquakes comprise the Western Division.

Here are the teams that make up the Eastern Division:

✔ **D.C. United:** D.C. United is the class of the league, winning the first two MLS Cups, reaching the final of a third, and winning the last championship of the millenium with a 2-0 victory in MLS Cup '99. Even though United has been forced to deal players every year to get under the salary cap, the team, under coach Thomas Rongen, and before him Bruce Arena, has managed to keep a high level of excellence that is admired by its foes but difficult to duplicate. Bolivian midfielder Marco Etcheverry is still the heart of the team, although young American midfielder Ben Olsen is an up-and-coming talent.

✔ **Miami Fusion:** Despite having a multimillionaire — Ken Horowitz — at the helm, the Fusion has experienced more front-office woes in its first two seasons than most teams confronted in their first four. The team is named Miami, but plays in Fort Lauderdale because a deal to perform at the Orange Bowl fell through.

✔ **New England Revolution:** The Revs, as this team is also called, have reached the post-season only once — 1997. They have arguably the best fans in the league — they support the team even though it has has never finished above .500. Sunil Gulati, the former MLS deputy commissioner named managing director of Kraft Soccer Properties, which includes the Revs and San Jose Earthquakes, oversees the team's much-needed rebuilding.

✔ **New York/New Jersey MetroStars:** The less said about the MetroStars the better, because they set futility standards in 1999 for the league's worst record (7-25) and fewest points (15). Entering the 2000 season, they had used 81 players, including 19 foreigners, and five coaches during the first four seasons. Current head coach Octavio Zambrano is the sixth. For MLS to survive, let alone thrive, it needs a strong, competitive team (not necessarily a championship team) in the New York market.

Here are the teams that make up the Central Division:

✔ **Chicago Fire:** Talk about a fairy tale season. In its very first season of existence, the Chicago Fire not only was a competitive team in 1998 (20-12), but wound up as MLS and U.S. Open Cup champions. Behind coach Bob Bradley and general manager Peter Wilt, the Fire is built around veteran Eastern European players, a strong defense, and an opportunistic attack. The Fire has several young, promising, and exciting Americans for the future — DaMarcus Beasley, who won the Silver Ball as the second most valuable player at the Under-17 world championship in 1999, and forward Josh Wolf, who plays with the Under-23 National Team.

✔ **Columbus Crew:** The Columbus Crew, which calls itself the "hardest working team in America," had been frustrated by United in its quest to reach MLS Cup when the two teams were in the same conference. Under the new setup, the likelihood of the Crew meeting United early in the playoffs is not as great as before (see new rules part later in this section). U.S. National Team forward Brian McBride is expected to be the main attacking force after the team lost Trinidad & Tobagan striker Stern John in a transfer to Nottingham Forest of the English First Division.

✔ **Dallas Burn:** Built around American rather than well-known foreign players, the Dallas Burn, coached by David Dir, has reached the playoffs in each of its first four seasons. The Burn, however, have only been to the conference finals once and more, swept by the Los Angeles Galaxy in 1999. Forward Jason Kreis, the first player to crack the 15-15 barrier (18 goals, 15 assists), was the league's most valuable player in 1999. Ecuadoran newcomer Ariel Graziani's ability to find the back of the net will help him.

✔ **Tampa Bay Mutiny:** After a great 20-12 maiden season, the Tampa Bay Mutiny has struggled to regain its lofty status. The team was almost gutted in 1997, losing former Colombian World Cup captain Carlos Valderrama to the expansion Miami Fusion in a league-mandated deal before he was returned to the team in yet another league-mandated transaction. The acquisition of El Salvadoran Raul Diaz Arce has given the Mutiny a solid goal scorer up front.

Here are the teams that make up the Western Division:

✔ **Colorado Rapids:** Thanks to a couple of talented foreign players, solid American performers, and one of the top American coaches in Glenn Myernick, this team reached the MLS Cup '97 final and '99 Open Cup final. Panamaian forward Jorge Dely Valdes, who is excellent in the air, and newcomer Henry Zambrano, a Colombian forward, are expected to pull the Rapids out of their scoring doldrums.

✔ **Kansas City Wizards:** After reaching the playoffs in their first two seasons and scaling the heights of a then record 20-12 regular season in 1997, the Wizards barely managed to equal that win total over the 1998 and 1999 seasons. A slow start in 1999 cost veteran coach Ron Newman his job. Former U.S. national coach Bob Gansler was brought in to repair the damage. U.S. National Team goalkeeper Tony Meola, who missed most of the 1999 season with a knee injury, and midfielder Preki, the 1997 league MVP, need to have solid seasons if the Wizards are to make some headway in the Western Division.

✔ **Los Angeles Galaxy:** The Galaxy has been so close, yet so far away from winning it all twice. The Galaxy enjoyed a 2-0 lead after D.C. United in the 1996 MLS Cup, but squandered the lead and lost in overtime, 3-2. In 1998, the Galaxy set a league-scoring record (85 goals) and finished at a sterling 24-8, but the Chicago Fire eliminated the Galaxy in the Western Conference finals. After a slow start in 1999, the team rebounded under former UCLA coach Sigi Schmid to reach the MLS Cup. But the Galaxy, led by El Salvadoran midfielder Mauricio Cienfuegos and Cobi Jones, fell to United again, 2-0.

✔ **San Jose Earthquakes:** Like the MetroStars and Revolution, the Earthquakes — they were renamed from the Clash during the off-season — have grossly underachieved. It brought many San Francisco Bay favorites back for the 1996 season, but the team never jelled. Former U.S. National Team coach Lothar Osiander, who also coached the Galaxy and the Project 40 team (see the section later in this chapter) in the A-League, was hired to turn things around. The Earthquakes' best players are on offense including El Salvadoran forward Ronald Cerritos, the team's leading goal scorer.

How the MLS season and playoffs work

MLS teams play a 32-game regular-season schedule, which begins in mid-March and should finish around the end of September. Each team gets three points for a regulation or overtime win, one point for a tie.

Starting in the 2000 season, the three division champions automatically qualify for the playoffs, and the next five teams with the highest point totals also will reach post-season play, regardless of where they finish in the standings. For example, the Tampa Bay Mutiny could finish fourth in the Central Division, but could go to the playoffs instead of, say, the New England Revolution, which finished second in the Eastern Conference because it had more points. It is highly unlikely that scenario would occur, but it's mathematically possible.

The eight teams will be seeded in order of the number of points they accrued for the playoffs. The first and second rounds will be best-of-three series, and the MLS Cup will be a one-shot deal. The teams vie for the Alan I. Rothenberg trophy, named after the founder and original chairman of the league. The 2000 MLS Cup will be played at RFK Stadium in Washington, D.C., and the 2001 championship game is set for Columbus Crew Stadium.

The most important change for the 2000 season was the elimination of the controversial shootout. All tied games were decided by the shootout during the league's first four seasons, even though that method was despised by players, coaches, and many fans.

Players' and coaches' dislike for the shootout was three-fold. They felt it was an artificial way to decide matches. The league did not adhere to the rest of the world, where tied matches are common. And the losing team would walk away empty-handed, without a point. The winning side was awarded one point even though it played to a draw in regulation.

The shootout worked like this: Each team would pick five players. Each player would start his run from 35 yards out and have five seconds to beat the goalkeeper. The team scoring the most goals after five rounds would be declared the winner. If it was still tied after five rounds, a sudden-death shootout round was used to determine the winner.

The shootout also made for some deceptive records. For example, the San Jose Clash — the team is now called the Earthquakes — finished with what looked like a very competitive 19-13 record in 1999, but finished in fifth place in the Western Conference and considerably out of the playoff picture. Ten of those victories came through the shootout. The Clash accrued only 37 points, 11 out of a playoff berth.

Some things you should know about MLS

As it entered its fifth season in 2000, Major League Soccer already had established some intriguing trends and facts. Among the most interesting:

✔ How difficult is it to be a consistent goal scorer? Only three players managed to crack double figures in goals in each of the first four seasons — Roy Lassiter, Raul Diaz Arce, and Giovanni Savarese.

✔ How important is it for teams to win at home? Teams win at home 60.6 percent of the time, with a 427-277 record through the 1999 season.

✔ How important is it to score the first goal? Teams have won 77 percent of the time when they connect first, according to statistics through 1999. Teams that score first have a 507-168 record.

✔ Who are the most successful teams? Only four teams have reached the playoffs in each of the first four seasons — D.C. United, Columbus Crew, Dallas Burn, and Los Angeles Galaxy.

✔ Who are the least successful teams? Four teams have never finished above .500 in a season — New York/New Jersey MetroStars, New England Revolution, San Jose Clash, and Miami Fusion.

✔ How important is it to have an American coach? No foreign coach has posted a winning record. The best mark was by Portuguese native Carlos Queiroz, who guided the MetroStars to a 12-12 record.

✔ How often do coaches get fired or replaced? Very. Only one coach survived with the same team through the first four seasons — David Dir of the Dallas Burn. The MetroStars, in contrast, went through five coaches, the New England Revolution four. Some coaches get recycled, while others coach in the A-League.

✔ Can American soccer players score goals? They sure can! An American has led the league in scoring in three of its first four seasons — the Tampa Bay Mutiny's Roy Lassiter (27 goals, five assists for 59 points) in 1996, Kansas City Wizards's Preki (11 goals, 17 assists for 41 points), a naturalized citizen, and Dallas Burn forward Jason Kreis (18 goals, 15 assists for 51 points), the league's first 15-15 player, in 1999.

✔ Can American players create goals? Well, some can. Steve Ralston became the first American to lead the league in assists (18) in 1999.

Now, if a game is tied after regulation, teams will play a 10-minute overtime (broken into a pair of five-minute periods) to determine the winner. The first team that scores will be declared the winner, scoring the "Golden Goal," which is soccer talk for a sudden-death overtime goal. If the game is still even after overtime, it will end in a draw, and each team will receive one point in the standings.

Some words of advice to playoff-bound teams: Securing the first game of a playoff series is mandatory for long-term survival. MLS sides have swept their opponents in 14 of 19 playoff series.

The Ever-Expanding Minor Leagues

The United Soccer Leagues could very well be the best-kept soccer secret in the United States.

The USL, which boasts three men's leagues and an amateur women's league, has set up an extensive minor-league system in which players can develop and play for pay, not unlike minor league baseball. They have playoffs and championship games. In some cases, these leagues have been a feeder system to MLS. Unlike MLS, the USL has no salary cap in any of its leagues. The USL has expanded into 40 states. (It once had a team in Hawaii, but the travel costs were too restrictive.)

The A-League

The 25-team A-League is broken down into two conferences and four divisions. Each division has six teams, except for the Atlantic Division, which has seven clubs. The top six teams in each conference qualify for the playoffs.

Many A-League teams can compete on an even basis with many MLS teams. In fact, not all the best players perform in MLS. Some players can earn more money playing outdoor soccer in the spring and summer and indoor soccer in the winter compared to the MLS's paltry minimum. (See the indoor soccer section later in this chapter.)

Since joining the A-League in 1996, the Rochester Raging Rhinos have enjoyed incredible success, reaching the league championship game three times and winning the title once (1998) and reaching the final of the Lamar Hunt/U.S. Open Cup twice and winning it once (1999). Not surprisingly, the Rhinos, who attract an A-League high average of 11,500 fans to their games, have visions of playing in Major League Soccer someday. To join MLS, they would have to play in a soccer-specific stadium instead of at Frontier Field, which is a minor-league baseball stadium.

Here's the league alignment (each division in alphabetical order):

- **Western Conference:** *Pacific Division* — Bay Area Seals (San Francisco), El Paso Patriots (Texas), Orange County Zodiac (California), San Diego Flash, Seattle Sounders (Washington), and Vancouver 86ers (Canada). *Central Division* — Cincinnati Riverhawks, Indiana Blast (Indianapolis), Milwaukee Rampage (Wisconsin), Minnesota Thunder (Blaine), Tennessee Rhythm (Franklin), and U.S. Pro-40 (no home field; see the Project 40 section later in this chapter).

✔ **Eastern Conference:** *Atlantic Division* — Atlanta Silverbacks, Charleston Battery (South Carolina), Hampton Roads Mariners (Virginia), Hershey Wildcats (Pennsylvania), Raleigh Capital Express (North Carolina), and Richmond Kickers (Virginia). *Northeast Division* — Boston Bulldogs, Connecticut Wolves (New Britain), Long Island Rough Riders (New York), Montreal Impact (Canada), Rochester Raging Rhinos (New York), and Toronto Lynx (Canada).

Like the MLS, the A-League decided to switch from the shootout to leaving games tied for the 2000 season. The A-League continues to have a pair of 10-minute sudden-death overtime periods to decide matters and still awards four (and not three) points for a victory and only one point for a tie. The playoffs are two-game, total goal series. If they're still tied, the victory goes to the higher seed.

In its fourth attempt in the title game, the Minnesota Thunder defeated the Rochester Raging Rhinos for the 1999 championship, 2-1.

The D3 Pro League

The D3 Pro League, the third division in the U.S. pro soccer pecking order, is for players who are still developing, those who aren't quite ready to play at a more demanding level, or for players who are winding down their careers. While the pay can be sparse — from $50 to several hundred dollars a game — many players just play for the love of the game.

Some teams have visions of joining the A-League, while others could not meet the more demanding financial burdens (higher player salaries and traveling expenses) of playing in the higher league. D3 Pro League teams, which play in college or even high school stadiums, range from suburban areas (northern Virginia) to small cities (Reading, Pennsylvania) to even a big city (Houston).

The Utah Blitzz, which will play in Salt Lake City, is an expansion team for the 2000 season.

The league has 22 teams. Here's the league alignment:

✔ **Western Conference:** Arizona Sahuaros (Carefree), Chico Rooks (California), Riverside County Elite (California), Stanislaus County Cruisers (Modesto, California), Tucson Fireballs (Arizona), and Utah Blitzz.

✔ **Southern Conference:** Austin Lone Stars (Texas), Carolina Dynamo (High Point, North Carolina), Charlotte Eagles (North Carolina), Houston Hurricanes (Texas), Northern Virginia Royals (Annandale), Roanoke Wrath (Virginia), Texas Rattlers, and Wilmington Hammerheads (North Carolina).

✔ **Northern Conference:** Cape Cod Crusaders, Delaware Wizards (Wilmington), New Hampshire Phantoms (Manchester), New Jersey Stallions (Toms River), North Jersey Imperials, Reading Rage (Pennsylvania), Rhode Island Stingrays (Providence), South Jersey Barons (Ocean City, New Jersey), and Western Mass Pioneers (Ludlow, Massachusetts).

How would you like to have a team that included Tony Meola in goal, Chris Armas in midfield, and Giovanni Savarese at forward? Well, the Long Island Rough Riders did in 1995, when they captured the U.S. Interregional Soccer League championship. The USISL, which was the forerunner to D3 Pro League under the USL umbrella, was able to attract such well-known players because it was a year before Major League Soccer kicked off.

The Premier Development League

The Premier Development Soccer League is a way to develop young and college-age players. In fact, it was reorganized as an Under-23 league for the 2000 season. Players do not get paid at all. The PDSL gives players a chance to compete in a national league while they can maintain their college eligibility.

Because of no player salaries, the cost to run a team in the league is low. The main expense usually is road trips. Teams, which play in college or high school stadiums, are less likely to be found near major metropolitan markets. Instead many teams play in the suburbs (northern New Jersey), the heartland (Des Moines, Iowa), or in smaller cities (Lexington, Kentucky).

If you really want to get technical, the PDL doesn't belong in this chapter, but rather in Chapter 16 about amateur soccer because players don't get paid. But because the PDL is a springboard to go to other leagues under the USL umbrella, it is more appropriate in this chapter.

The PDL has 42 teams. Here's the league alignment:

✔ **Western Conference:** *Northwest Division* — Abbotsford 86ers Select (British Columbia), Cascade Surge (Salem, Oregon), Seattle Sounder Selects (Washington), Spokane Shadow (Washington), Willamette Valley Firebirds (Vorvallis, Oregon), and Yakima Reds (Washington). *Southwest Division* — Central Coast Roadrunners (San Luis Obispo, California), Nevada Zephyrs (Reno), San Fernando Valley Heroes (Sun Valley, California), and San Gabriel Valley Highlanders (Glendale, California). *Rocky Division* — Boulder Nova (Colorado), Colorado Comets, Colorado Springs Ascent (Colorado), Kansas City Brass (Kansas City), and Wichita Jets (Kansas).

✔ **Eastern Conference:** *Northeast Division* — Brooklyn Knights (New York), Central Jersey Riptide (New Brunswick, N.J.), New Brunswick Brigade (New Jersey), New York Freedoms (Long Island), North Jersey Imperials (Montclair, New Jersey), Vermont Voltage (Montpelier), and Westchester Flames (Mamaroneck, New York). *Southeast Division* — Bradenton Academics (Florida), Broward County Woldpack (Florida), Central Florida Kraze (Oviedo, Florida), Cocoa Expos (Florida), Miami Breakers (Miami Beach, Florida), Palm Beach Pumas (Florida), South Florida Future, Tampa Bay Hawks (Florida).

✔ **Central Conference:** *Heartland Division* — Chicago Sockers (Illinois), Des Moines Menace (Iowa), Rockford Raptors (Illinois), Thunder Bay Chill (Ontario, Canada), Twin Cities Tornado (Blaine, Minnesota), and Wisconsin Rebels (Menasha). *Great Lakes Division* — Dayton Gems (Ohio), Indiana Invaders (South Bend, Indiana), Kalamazoo Kingdom (Michigan), Lexington Bluegrass Bandits (Kentucky) Mid Michigan Bucks (Saginaw), and West Michigan Explosion (Grand Rapids).

The Alabama Saints and Lousiana Outlaws, who are expected to join the league full time for the 2001 season, played a provisional schedule in 2000 and were not eligible to make the playoffs.

Project 40: An MLS Team in A-League Clothes

In a unique twist, a team with MLS players participates in the A-League — dubbed Nike Pro-40 Select, which is better known simply as Pro-40. It is made up of Project-40 players — players who have decided to turn pro immediately after high school or while in college.

These players train during the week with an MLS team and get called for two A-League games on each weekend. They never play for the same team twice in a week.

Most of the Project 40 players earn the minimum salary of $24,000. They can't return to college as soccer players because they have given up their NCAA eligibility. But they can come back as students and not give up their college education; each player is given a five-year tuition package not to exceed $37,500.

The ultimate goal of Project 40 is to develop players at a much faster pace than at the present. College players see three months of action, while Project 40 players could wind up participating in as many as 40 to 60 matches over the course of a year.

The best places to watch soccer in the U.S.

Because not many soccer teams have a stadium they can call their own, there aren't many classic grounds, as they like to say overseas. However, a few do stand out in terms of site lines for the spectator and the atmosphere for everyone. Here's my pick of the five best stadiums in the U.S. to watch a soccer game:

✔ **RFK Stadium:** The old stadium in Washington, D.C., may be showing her age, but thanks to the curvature of the roof and the closeness of the stands to the field, you actually believe that you are in a typical European stadium rather than at a D.C. United game.

✔ **Columbus Crew Stadium:** MLS's first soccer-specific stadium was completed in 1999 for a mere $28 million, which was funded by Crew owner Lamar Hunt. The prototype for future MLS stadiums, the Crew park certainly has its advantages over using football stadiums. No divots or lines from football are left behind to spoil the fans viewing pleasure.

✔ **Frontier Field:** Yes, the Rochester Raging Rhinos (A-League) play on a converted baseball field, with grass covering the infield at the downtown stadium. Because the Rhinos sell out at virtually every game, the electric atmosphere is second-to-none, although the field is not as wide as it should be.

✔ **Lockhart Stadium:** It has seen better days and it is a converted high school stadium, but the stadium projects a cozy feeling — when spectators show up. The first soccer-specific stadium built in the U.S., the stadium is home to the Hampton Roads Mariners (A-League). This stadium was supposed to be the site of the 1998 Lamar Hunt U.S. Open Cup championship game, but Hurricane Bonnie had other ideas, forcing the organizers to postpone the match (which was eventually held at Soldier Field in Chicago).

✔ **Rose Bowl:** And we can't forget the Rose Bowl, which plays host to U.S. National Team games, the Women's World Cup, and the L.A. Galaxy.

Because not every Project 40 player is available for every game, the roster of the team changes dramatically from week to week. Sometimes players 23 and younger from MLS teams are called in. Players rehabilitating from injuries also have performed for Pro-40.

Through the first two years, Pro-40 had no home field as it played every game on the road, first under coach Tim Hankinson and then Lothar Osiander. The team reached the playoffs in 1999, finishing second in the Central Division with a creditable 16-12 record. Alfonso Mondelo, former coach of the New York/New Jersey MetroStars (MLS) and Long Island Rough Riders (A-League), will coach the Project 40 team in 2000.

Entering the Great Indoors

Indoor soccer has been a part of the American sports fabric since 1978, when the Major Indoor Soccer League launched with six teams. While it is played with the same ball and same players, many observers feel that it is an entirely different game than outdoor soccer.

It is played in a ice hockey rink with dasher boards, so errant shots can rebound back into play and into dangerous scoring opportunities. Six players, including a goalkeeper, are on each team. The rules are similar to the outdoor version, but the indoor game is much quicker as teams are allowed free substitution. Think of the indoor game as a sprint compared to the marathon-like qualities of outdoor soccer.

The MISL, which eventually dropped the I in its name, had as many as 14 teams. Steve Zungul, nicknamed the "Lord of All Indoors" because of his scoring prowess, was the top player for many seasons, leading the powerful New York Arrows to four consecutive titles before the San Diego Sockers became the dominant team, winning 10 titles in 11 years from 1982 to 1992. The league went out of business after the 1992 season.

The National Professional Soccer League (not to be confused with the NPSL outdoor circuit that was formed in 1967) was formed as the American Indoor Soccer Association in 1984 and has been around since, mostly in Midwestern cities. The 1999–2000 league, which runs from October through May, includes 12 teams in the American and National Conferences. The teams are as follows:

- ✔ **American Conference:** *Eastern Division* — Baltimore Spirit, Harrisburg Heat, and Philadelphia Kixx. *Central Division* — Buffalo Blizzard, Cleveland Crunch, and Montreal Impact.

- ✔ **National Conference:** *Northern Division* — Detroit Rockers, Edmonton Drillers, and Milwaukee Wave. *Midwest Division* — Wichita Wings, St. Louis Storm, and Kansas City Attack.

Chapter 20

U.S. in International Soccer and the World Cup

Soccer is not just dedicated to the youth, amateur, college, and professional ranks in this country. There is literally a whole world out there at the international level, with a seemingly endless number of championships and mountains to climb for several age classifications and for both sexes. The granddaddy of all soccer tournaments is the World Cup, which is played every four years.

Who's the Boss? Soccer's Governing Organizations

As in youth and amateur soccer in the United States, international soccer also has a certain pecking order. It starts with your country's federation. In this case, it's U.S. Soccer, the governing body for the sport in the United States. U.S. Soccer belongs to both CONCACAF and FIFA. CONCACAF, which stands for Confederation of North, Central American, and Caribbean Association Football, governs soccer in that part of the world. CONCACAF answers to FIFA, Federational Internationale de Football, which runs soccers worldwide. There is no higher authority than FIFA.

U.S. Soccer

The United States Soccer Federation, better known as U.S. Soccer, is the governing body of the sport in this country. Anyone and everyone who wants to perform in a sanctioned competition must play for an affiliated league or team. U.S. Soccer's national headquarters are located in Chicago, where more than 100 staff members are employed.

U.S. Soccer is essentially broken into three divisions — youth, amateur, and professional.

- ✔ The U.S. Youth Soccer Association (USYSA), whose members number more than 2.5 million, makes up the core of the youth division, with the American Youth Soccer Organization (AYSO) adding another million children.

- ✔ The U.S. Amateur Soccer Association (USASA) is for adults — men and women — who want to play the game after they have graduated from high school or college, although there is generally no age restriction on how young a player has to be.

   A number of unaffiliated adult leagues are out there, mostly in and around major metropolitan areas, but they have been brought under the U.S. Soccer umbrella during the past several years.

- ✔ The professional division is ruled by Major League Soccer and United Soccer Leagues, which is the umbrella organization to several leagues, including the A-League (Division II pro), D3 Pro League (Division III pro), Premier Development League (amateur), and W-League (amateur). For more on these leagues, see Chapters 18 and 19.

CONCACAF

The Confederation of North, Central American, and Caribbean Association Football (CONCACAF) is the governing body of soccer in this region of the world, including the United States, Canada, and Mexico. Thirty-seven countries belong to CONCACAF.

CONCACAF runs all qualifying tournaments for those 37 countries, whether it be World Cup, Olympics, Women's World Cup, or youth world championships. It is headquartered in New York City, where Chuck Blazer is secretary general, or the individual who runs the organization on a day-to-day basis. Jack Warner of Trinidad and Tobago is president. CONCACAF is one of six confederations that report directly to FIFA. The others are from Europe (UEFA), South America (CONMEBOL), Africa, Asia, and Oceania.

What if FIFA was the United Nations?

FIFA's membership totals 203 countries, which is more members than the United Nations has (188) and for the 2002 World Cup, has 197 entries. In fact, if FIFA were the UN, there would be no, or few wars. All battles and arguments would be settled on the soccer field. If a country does not like a FIFA decision, it could quit the organization and sacrifice playing the sport on an international level. In 1973, for example, the Soviet Union refused to play Chile in a World Cup qualifying match because of political reasons. The Soviets were fined $50,000, and Chile was awarded a forfeit. Had it been in the UN at the time, the Soviets might have gotten away without paying their dues.

FIFA

FIFA stands for the Federation Internationale de Football Association (FIFA), the world governing body of soccer. If your country's federation is not a member or is not in good standing with FIFA, then your nation might not be allowed to participate in the major world tournaments, including the World Cup. (For more on this major soccer event, see the section later in this chapter.)

FIFA officially started on May 21, 1904, when representatives of seven countries — France, Belgium, the Netherlands, Spain, Sweden, Switzerland, and Denmark — met in Paris. A number of statutes were laid down, and FIFA was formed. In 1932, FIFA was moved to Zurich, Switzerland, where it is still headquartered. Its current president, Swiss native Sepp Blatter, was elected to a four-year term in 1998. He succeeded Brazilian Joao Havelange, who concluded a 24-year reign in that year. A 24-member executive committee that meets regularly runs FIFA. Among its duties is to select the host of World Cups and dictate the laws and game rules to the game.

FIFA runs several world championships, including the World Cup, the Under-17 and Under-20 youth world championships, the Club World Championship, and the Women's World Cup. It is considering adding an Over-35 world championship to its growing competition list so that the heroes of yesteryear can compete against their peers.

A top priority of FIFA is to establish a harmonized international calendar. It is a daunting task because so many leagues and competitions are played at various times of the year. It has been difficult to get confederations and countries' federations on the same page. Blatter has stated that he hopes to have a global calendar in place by 2004, in which all World Cup qualifying games would be played on the same date or weekend and that many of the world's leagues would begin and end their seasons at the same time. FIFA also wants to limit the number of international friendlies National Teams can play in a year, as well as establishing a bloc of time in which there is no football so players can rest.

FIFA also has several representatives on the International Football Association Board (IFAB), the body which is responsible for the Laws of the Game. The IFAB meets annually in Great Britain to vote on, consider, and discuss rule modifications. At its meeting in Cliveden, Taplow, England, in February 2000, the board voted to speed up the time it takes goalkeepers to release the ball. Instead of being allowed four steps before throwing or kicking the ball to a teammate, goalkeepers will have only six seconds to put the ball into play. The 115th meeting is expected to be held in February or March 2001.

The World Cup: The Greatest Show on Earth

Just think of the World Series, Super Bowl, and Olympics all rolled into one, and you will begin to understand the magnitude of the World Cup. No other sports tournament is like the World Cup, which captures the imagination of the majority of the sports world every four years. The 32 National Teams that qualify every four years meet for a month to determine who is the very best on this planet. While the worldwide television audience balloons to nearly two billion for the championship game, another five billion will watch the rest of the tournament.

Numbers can tell only part of the story. The World Cup is about passion, nationalism, beauty, history, and controversy. It is a month-long celebration of soccer.

The World Cup can thank its birth to the success of the Olympic tournaments in 1924 and 1928, when Uruguay dominated the international scene, earning back-to-back gold medals. FIFA's hierarchy felt it was time to stage an international tournament away from the influence of the other Olympic sports. In 1930, they chose the then soccer capital of the world — Uruguay, which also was celebrating its 100th anniversary of independence. Slowly, but surely, the World Cup grew in stature and importance.

It wasn't until television was invented that a 17-year-old Brazilian named Pelé captured the world's imagination, leading the South Americans to the world championship in Sweden in 1958 (the only time a country won outside of its hemisphere). The tournament really began to take off, as Brazil went on to capture three titles within four attempts over a 12-year span, and the world was hooked. Pelé forged his reputation as the world's greatest player and established the tournament as the largest single-sport event in the world. (For more on Pelé, see Chapter 21.)

The games have produced some of the highest drama and some of the most amazing performances in the history of sports, from the likes of Argentina's Diego Maradona, Portugal's Eusebio, West Germany's Franz Beckenbauer to the likes of Gerd Mueller, the Netherlands' Johan Cruyff, and England's Gordon Banks, to name a few stars and superstars (for more on these players, see Chapter 21).

The World Cup kicks off a good two years before the event with a series of qualifying tournaments run by those six confederations after a World Cup qualifying draw, which determines what countries face what countries in their confederation. For the 2002 World Cup, for example, the qualifying draw was held in Tokyo on Dec. 7, 1999, with qualifying in March 2000 because many countries will play between 12 and 16 qualifying matches each. A total of 197 countries entered the 2002 competition.

For the first time ever, the 2002 World Cup will not be staged in Europe or the Americas, but rather in Asia. No host country has ever failed to reach the second round. That could be a major challenge for cohosts South Korea and Japan, which have struggled outside of their continent in international matches and in the World Cup.

The 2002 World Cup in South Korea and Japan will break new ground for one important reason. Except for Brazil winning in Sweden in 1958, no other country has won outside of its hemisphere. The South Americans have always ruled in the Americas and the Europeans in Europe. With Asian teams considered weak, it's a longshot that teams from that continent will prevail.

Ch—ch—ch—changes in the World Cup

Every World Cup tries to bring something innovative to the table. The Pontiac Silverdome in suburban Detroit was the site of the first World Cup game in a domed stadium in 1994. The stadium, which has artificial turf, was fitted with grass for three first-round matches.

The World Cup was expanded from 24 to 32 teams for the 1998 competition in France (the competition was open to 16 teams until 1982). And instead of the top-seeded teams getting a home-field advantage by playing two or three of its three first-round matches at the same venue, every team was forced to play in three different stadiums.

The 2002 World Cup will feature its own unique twist. The Cup will be cohosted by two countries for the first time — Japan and South Korea, from June 1–30 of that year. Despite warnings from the president and general secretary of FIFA and against some conventional logic, the organization's executive committee voted to give two countries the hosting chores. The differences in culture and currency and the difficulty of getting from one country to another could make this World Cup into a logistical nightmare. In contrast, the 1998 World Cup in France was fairly easy to traverse because of the country's extensive commuter train network.

The site of the 2006 tournament, which is contested between England, South Africa, Germany, and Brazil, will be determined in July 2000. The Cup is expected to return to the U.S., which held a successful tournament in 1994, in either 2010 or most likely in 2014.

While there have been 16 World Cups, only seven countries have won the competition — Brazil (four times), Italy (three), Germany/West Germany (three), Argentina (two), Uruguay (two), England (one), and France (one). In fact, only 11 teams have competed in the championship game. The other countries have been Czechoslovakia, Hungary, Sweden, and Holland.

A well-traveled trophy

It has been hidden under a bed, stolen twice, and possibly even melted down. The World Cup trophy, the most sought after piece of hardware in all of sports, has enjoyed a well traveled and intriguing existence. On June 30, 2002, the second incarnation of the trophy will wind up in the hands of the captain of a fortunate National Team and be paraded around a Yokohama stadium.

The first trophy, the Jules Rimet Trophy, was retired after Brazil captured its third World Cup in 1970. During the final years of World War II, FIFA vice president Ottorino Barrassi of Italy hid it in a shoe box under his bed to safeguard it from raids of Germans retreating from his country. FIFA named the cup the Jules Rimet trophy after the Frenchman who made the most significant contribution to the founding of the competition.

Only months before the 1966 World Cup in England, the trophy was stolen while on display at a stamp exhibition in the Central Hall of Westminster. Authorities were baffled over its whereabouts, although Pickles, a black-and-white dog of undetermined pedigree, found the trophy buried under a tree.

In 1983, thieves broke into the Brazilian Soccer Confederation and stole the cup. Authorities feared it was melted down, because it was never found. Kodak Brazil of Sao Paulo paid for its replacement.

In 1974, a new 18-karat, solid-gold trophy — called the FIFA World Cup trophy — was designed by a Milanese sculptor. With the names of six countries already inscribed on the base, there is enough room to honor the champions until the 2038 World Cup. Then a third trophy will be made.

The best teams in the world

If you're trying to figure out the best National Teams in the world, all you have to do is remember what Claude Reins said in the classic movie Casablanca, "Round up the usual suspects." Year in, year out, the same teams seemingly dominate international soccer and the World Cup.

Once in a while a team such as Croatia, which finished a surprising third at the 1998 World Cup, will enjoy a superb generation of players, excel, do well in a World Cup or two, and then drop back into the pack as an average team. The real test is whether a country can continue its success over 20 or 30 years or longer.

There have been only a handful of teams that have passed that test of time. Among the countries that are considered world powers:

- ✔ **Brazil:** The World Cup could be held on the moon, and the Brazilians still would have to be considered one of the favorites because of their enormous skills, talent, and history. They are the only country to have participated in all 16 World Cups and are the only nation to have paraded around with the trophy as champions on four occasions (1958, 1962, 1970, and 1994). Anything less than an appearance in the championship game is considered a huge disappointment.

- ✔ **Italy:** The Italians, who have won the Cup three times (1934, 1938, and 1982), traditionally boast some of the best defenses and top goalkeepers in the world, but have trouble scoring goals. The reasons: The fastest Italian players usually are put on defense, rather than attack, when they are youth players. And because the Italian Serie A — its First Division — attracts some of the best offensive players in the world, many Italian midfielders and forwards are not given an opportunity to play and develop their skills to the fullest potential in the country's highest league.

- ✔ **Germany:** Even though the Germans have aged in recent years and have not been as dominant since capturing the 1990 World Cup, they still must be considered a formidable team because of their World Cup history of a never-say-die attitude. They have made a number of memorable comebacks in the World Cup. Their most famous was overcoming a 2-0 deficit to favored Hungary in the 1954 to record a 3-2 triumph, the first of Germany's three World Cup championships (the Germans also won in 1974). Their most recent was spotting Mexico a 1-0 lead in the second round of the 1998 World Cup before rallying for a 2-1 win.

- ✔ **Argentina:** Considered the second-best South American team behind Brazil, the cunning Argentines have combined South American flair with European tactics to win a pair of World Cup since 1978 (they also won in 1986) and to finish second in 1990. Every four years they put together a competitive team that survives at least until the quarterfinals.

- ✔ **Netherlands:** The Dutch have produced some of the best players and teams in the world, particularly for a country of their size (15 million people). But they have yet to win a World Cup, having finished second twice. They still are given the utmost respect and must be a considered a contender for 2002 and beyond.

The pride of wearing your country's shirt

When an American player puts on the red, white, and blue in an international competition or World Cup, what goes through his mind?

"It makes you feel more proud that you are representing your country," defensive midfielder Chris Armas said. "It's more than just another game. You're playing for your country, and they for theirs. When you put on your club jersey, it's an honor, but this is more special."

"I've always felt that way. You can't take it for granted. You don't know if you're always going to be there."

✔ **England:** The English, who won their only world championship on their home soil in 1966, seemingly find a way to shoot themselves in the foot and break their fans' hearts in one controversial way or another. Take, for example, what transpired in a second-round match against Argentina in 1998 in France. While he was on the ground, star midfielder David Beckham raised a leg and kicked Argentine midfielder Diego Simeone. Beckham was red carded, and England was forced to play the rest of the match with 10 players. England was eliminated in a penalty-kick tiebreaker.

✔ **Other countries to consider:** The French National Team, the reigning world champion, is made up of several ethnic groups. That is a lesson to the rest of the world to take to heart. It is not known, however, whether the French can recapture the magic that made it so special when it hosted the 1998 World Cup, because that team will be four years older. Spain produces some of the most exciting and talented players in the world, although it has never gotten its act together in the World Cup. The Spanish captured the 1992 Olympic gold medal in men's soccer, but that wasn't good enough for a demanding public and media. Croatia turned out to be the surprise team at the 1998 World Cup, but it is not known whether it can continue its winning performances at this level, having failed to qualify for the European Championship in 2000.

The U.S. in soccer's promised land

While the United States doesn't have a long, glorious history in the World Cup, it certainly has enjoyed its moments. Mexico usually has been the roadblock in qualifying, although the playing field between these two archrivals has become a lot more even over the years.

Here's a quick look at how the U.S. has fared when it has reached soccer's promised land:

✔ **1930 (Uruguay):** As one of the invited teams, the U.S. enjoyed the best World Cup performance in this country's soccer history. (Only 13 countries participated because of the huge amount of travel — three-week boat ride from Europe.) The U.S. reached the semifinals before it was dismantled by Argentina, 6-1, after trailing 1-0 at halftime. Argentina met its match in the final, losing to Uruguay, 4-2.

✔ **1934 (Italy):** The U.S. earned a 4-2 qualifying victory over archrival Mexico on Buff Donelli's four goals, only to meet Italy in the first-round knockout competition. The Italians prevailed, 7-1. As it turned out, it would be the last time the U.S. would defeat Mexico in a World Cup qualifying competition for 46 years, or until a 2-1 triumph in Fort Lauderdale on Nov. 23, 1980, which broke a 15-game winless streak to the neighbors to the south.

✔ **1950 (Brazil):** This was another first-round elimination as the World Cup went to group play, but one game stands out. Sandwiched between a 3-1 loss to Spain and a 5-2 defeat to Chile was one of the greatest upsets in soccer, if not sports history — the U.S.'s incredible 1-0 triumph over England in Belo Horizonte on June 29. Joe Gaetjens redirected a 25-yard shot by Walter Bahr into the net in the 37th minute for the only goal of the "David versus Goliath" match. The Americans made the lead stand up, handing the English one of their most humiliating setbacks.

✔ **1990 (Italy):** The Americans, essentially a group of recent college graduates, showed their inexperience against a veteran Czechoslovakian team in a 5-1 defeat as Eric Wynalda became the first U.S. player to receive a red card in World Cup play. They bounced back with a fine effort in a 1-0 loss to Italy before dropping a 2-1 decision to Austria.

✔ **1994 (United States):** A brilliant free kick by Wynalda helped the U.S. to a 1-1 draw with Switzerland before the Americans stunned Colombia, 2-1, as defender Andres Escobar accidentally redirected a John Harkes pass into his own net for an own goal and a goal by Ernie Stewart. A disappointing 1-0 loss to Romania set up a July 4 encounter with eventual world champion Brazil in the second round. Despite having a one-man advantage for a little more than half the game after Leonardo was ejected for fracturing the skull of Tab Ramos with his elbow, the Americans hardly attacked in what turned into a 1-0 loss.

✔ **1998 (France):** The less said about this Cup the better. Using the veteran core of players from the 1994 and little "new blood," the U.S. finished a disappointing last out of 32 teams, losing all three games — 2-0 to Germany, 2-1 to Iran, and 1-0 to Yugoslavia. Off the field, there was a lot of dissent under Head Coach Steve Sampson, some of which was generated by the dismissal of team captain John Harkes just two months before the actual tournament.

The legacy of 1994

Besides producing some fantastic soccer and a record attendance of 3.6 million, the 1994 World Cup left a legacy for the sport's growth — the U.S. Soccer Foundation.

The foundation was established in 1993 with $50 million of net proceeds from USA '94. Through investments, the foundation has increased its endowment to $75 million.

The foundation has awarded more than $10 million to over 150 national, state, and local projects, an average of about 40 grants totalling $2 million a year. All applications must be soccer specific and must be a not-for-profit endeavor. The grants range from helping inner-city teams and clubs to upgrading facilities and fields for youth and amateur leagues.

For more information or to obtain an application — deadline is Dec. 1 every year — write to the foundation at U.S. Soccer Foundation, 1050 17th St. NW, Suite 210, Washington, DC 20036 or visit the Web site at www.ussoccerfoundation.org.

The U.S. National Team today

After the disastrous showing in France, the U.S. National Team has undergone a major makeover under the guidance of new coach Bruce Arena. Hired in October 1998, Arena has added some needed new blood to the team as several veterans of international play have been pushed for starting jobs or replaced.

The team has responded well to Arena, but there are a number of concerns, particularly in scoring. Arena is still looking for a forward who can score consistently. Among the players who have stood out during the early days of the Arena regime are goalkeeper Kasey Keller, defensive midfielder Chris Armas, midfielder Cobi Jones, and forward Brian McBride, who is an excellent target man due to his superb heading ability.

The U.S. is expected to start its CONCACAF qualifying run for the 2002 World Cup in the fall of 2000. Qualifying runs through November, 2001. Three teams from CONCACAF will reach the World Cup.

The Women's World Cup: "The Future Is Feminine"

In the late '80s, FIFA felt it was the right time to add women's soccer to its ever-growing list of sanctioned events in the form of a world championship. Current FIFA President Sepp Blatter has even said, "The future is feminine."

Blatter felt that the greatest growth in number in international soccer in the 21st century would come from girls and women.

Three women's world championships were held in the 1990s, with the United States winning two (1991 and 1999) and finishing third in another (1995) as Norway secured the title. For marketing purposes, the event was called the Women's World Cup for the 1999 tournament in the United States and expanded to 16 countries to encompass more teams.

USA 1999: A ground-breaking event

Not only did the U.S. women take home the title in 1999, they captured the hearts of the American public, playing before sold-out crowds. The final between the U.S. and China was watched by 90,185 at the Rose Bowl, the largest crowd to watch a women's sporting event worldwide, and 40 million people on television. That made the game the most-watched soccer game in American TV history.

The tournament attracted 658,167 spectators over 17 dates (all double-headers), an average of 38,716 per date.

As it turned out, the U.S. did not play its best soccer in the Cup, because it got off to several shaky starts, particularly on the defensive end. The Americans, however, prevailed over Denmark, 3-0, Nigeria, 7-1, and North Korea, 3-0, in the opening round. They then survived a tough encounter and an own goal against Germany in the quarterfinals, 3-2, a much-improved Brazilian team in the semifinals, 2-0, before overcoming China in a penalty kick tiebreaker in the championship game, 5-4, after playing to a scoreless tie in regulation and extra time.

The women of the hour, or perhaps we should say two hours because the game took 120 minutes, were goalkeeper Briana Scurry, who saved an important kick during penalties, and Brandi Chastain, who scored the game-winner.

While the U.S. is regarded as the best women's team on this planet, having also won the Olympic gold medal in 1996, China is right behind the Americans, having finished second in the last two major tournaments. They are expected to square off again in the 2000 Summer Olympics in Sydney.

Like the World Cup, the Women's World Championship is held once every four years, with the next competition set for 2003. Australia is said to be the leading candidate to host that tournament.

Project 2010

In an attempt to accelerate the growth of American soccer and increase success on the world stage, U.S. Soccer has instituted Project 2010, which has a goal of winning the World Cup by that year. Fueled by a $120 million contribution by Nike over 10 years, the United States is hoping to improve its lot in international soccer and in the World Cup.

The plan, which was unveiled in 1998, started with 14-year-olds in 1999. U.S. Soccer identified the top 1,000 players at that age group. The elite players attended Under-14 national camp. These 14-year-olds will be 25 in 2010, just getting into the prime of their careers. (To appreciate how far 2010 is off, a 20-year-old player who is participating in Major League Soccer's Project 40 in 2000 will be 30 by then.)

These players could become members of the U.S. U-17 team in qualifying for the U-17 world championship in 2001. (The goal is to make the semifinals, although the team reached that plateau at the 1999 tournament). They then would be on the U-20 team that would perform at the world championship in 2003. (Again, the goal is to reach the semifinals.) Then, as 19-year-olds, they would be a part of the U-23 team — the Olympic team — in 2004. (The goal, again, is to advance to the semifinals.) They would play for the U.S. World Cup team in 2006 (the goal is the semis), the Olympics in 2008 (the goal is a gold medal), and the World Cup squad in 2010. (The goal is winning the championship.)

The best of the best

Unlike the men, only a handful of women's soccer teams can be considered world class because the game is still in its infancy stage worldwide. The top countries:

- **United States:** The Americans are the undisputed world champions of the women's games in the 1990s, capturing the 1991 and 1999 world championships and finishing third in 1995. The team also took home the Olympic gold in 1996. Mia Hamm, the all-time leading worldwide scorer, is still the cornerstone of the attack, although a cast of talented players, including goalkeeper Briana Scurry, midfielder Julie Foudy, and forward Tiffeny Milbrett, shown in Figure 20-1, round out a tough side. How deep are the Americans? During a salary dispute with U.S. Soccer, a team of high school and college players won the Australian Cup in January 2000.

- **China:** Will the Chinese be forever the bridesmaid, having barely taken second place to the U.S. in 1996 and 1999 in championship matches that were played on American soil? China has too many talented players, including forward Sun Wen and goalkeeper Gao Hong, not to win a major title sometime in the near future.

International Sports Images, Pam Whitesell

Figure 20-1:
Tiffeny
Milbrett is a
member of
the talented
Women's
World
Cup '99
champion-
ship team.

✔ **Brazil:** After a stumbling start in international competition, the Brazilians are the most improved country, finishing fourth at the 1996 Olympics and third in 1999. Buoyed by players such as free-kick specialist Sissi, a new and talented generation of Brazilians are poised to continue their incredible rise in a short time and perhaps dominate the sport in the 21st century, not unlike their men.

That championship feeling

Only 19 men and women as captains of their respective National Teams have raised a World Cup trophy over their heads after a championship game. U.S. Women's National Team coach April Heinrichs was the captain of the American team that captured the very first world championship in 1991, and she knows that special feeling.

"I would liken it to winning the Super Bowl, or winning the World Series, or a major merger among major corporations," Heinrichs said. "It's an achievement of hard work. It's a reward of setting goals and then reaching it."

Project Gold

Along with Project 2010, U.S. Soccer also has a "Project Gold," which is designed to keep the Women's National Team as the top team in the world for the next decade and beyond. Despite the resounding success of the U.S. Women's National Team in the 1990s, the rest of the world is quickly catching up to the United States. With the retirement of several key players expected after the 2000 Summer Olympics, it is vital to find talented young players and discover new ways to keep in front of the pack.

- ✔ **Norway:** After being the U.S.'s archrival in the early and mid-1990s, the Norwegians appear to be in a rebuilding mode. But one thing the rest of the world has learned is to never, ever count out the gritty Norwegians. Linda Medalen is one tough cookie in the center of the defense, and Marianne Pettersen, considered one of the most dangerous forwards in the world, is just coming into her prime.

- ✔ **Germany:** The Germans are good and dangerous, but haven't displayed the consistency of a U.S. or China, reaching the championship match of a major competition only once (losing to Norway in the 1995 final, 2-0). They need to find a few more pieces to their puzzle, although Bettina Wiegman is one of the world's finest midfielders.

- ✔ **The pretenders:** There is a huge dropoff from the top five to the next level. For example, among the top 12 goal scorers in the 1999 Women's World Cup, only one player — Nigeria's Nkriu Okosieme — did not come from the top five countries. Sweden and Nigeria are at the next level, followed by a host of countries below them, including Russia and Italy.

The Cups Runneth Over

It almost seems as if international soccer has more Cups than actual teams. First, there is the CONCACAF Gold Cup, which is held every two years to determine the champion of that confederation. The winner qualifies for the FIFA Confederations Cup, an annual competition of the continental champions. The 1999 event, which included National Teams from the U.S., Mexico, Brazil, Germany, Bolivia, and Saudi Arabia, was held in Mexico and won by the hosts, with the U.S. taking third.

Every year since 1991 the U.S. has hosted the U.S. Cup, which pits the U.S. National Team against several of the top teams in the world in various venues in the United States.

Across the Atlantic, there's the European Championship — a quadrennial, 16-team tournament that determines the best National Team on that continent. The 2000 tourney will be cohosted by the Netherlands and Belgium in June and July. Portugal was selected to host the 2004 tournament. Copa America, the South American version of that competition, is played every two years in odd-numbered years (Brazil was the 1999 champion), although its stature has been somewhat diminished because it usually is overshadowed by World Cup qualifying. The U.S. was invited to Copa America twice, finishing a surprising fourth in 1995.

The African Nation's Cup, which brings together the best National Teams on that continent, is held every two years in even-numbered years. There is a similar Asian Cup as well.

Youth World Championships

To accelerate the progress of the development of players in Third World countries, FIFA decided to add a couple of youth world championships that could be hosted by nations that did not have the infrastructure to host a World Cup.

The first Under-19 World Cup was held in Tunisia in 1977, after which FIFA decided to repackage it as a U-20 tournament in 1985. It was considered a success, and an international tournament has been held every two years since then in such locales as Japan (1979), Australia (1981), Mexico (1983), Soviet Union (1985), Chile (1987), Saudi Arabia (1989), Portugal (1991), Australia (1993), Qatar (1995), Malaysia (1997), and Nigeria (1999). Argentine will host the 2001 championship.

The first Under-16 world championship was held in China in 1985 and was changed to a U-17 competition two years later in Canada. Like its U-20 cousin, it has been held every two years since. Scotland (1989), Italy (1991), Japan (1993), Ecuador (1995), Egypt (1997), and New Zealand (1999) have hosted this tournament. Trinidad and Tobago will hold the 2001 championship.

These youth tournaments have been plagued by accusations of older-age players, particularly concerning African players, who appear older and much more physically mature in their respective age groups. There is a valid reason for this. In many instances, African children aren't officially registered with their government until they are one- or two-years-old, because they live in such outlying rural areas, making for a discrepancy.

How the U.S. has fared in youth tournaments

The U.S. has advanced to the semifinals of two youth world championships, finishing fourth at both the Under-20 World Cup in 1989 (that team included Kasey Keller, who stars in the Spanish First Division) and at the Under-17 World Cup in New Zealand in 1999. In 1999, the Americans suffered a heart-breaking elimination by Australia in the semifinals. They overcame a 2-0 deficit in regulation, but lost in penalty kicks, 7-6. The U.S. did earn two individual honors as Landon Donovan and DaMarcus Beasley were awarded the Golden and Silver Balls, respectively, as the two best players of the tournament. That was an American soccer first and an international rarity.

The Olympics: Soccer's Proving Ground

Long before the World Cup was born in 1930, the Olympic soccer tournament was considered to be the premier event in the sport. The first such soccer tourney was held at the 1908 Summer Games in London and has been a staple of the Olympics since, although it was not part of the Los Angeles Games in 1932 because of the then growing professional influence and the emergence of the World Cup. There were difficulties defining what an amateur was for Olympic purposes. With no solution at that time, the International Olympic Committee decided not to hold soccer at the 1932 Los Angeles Games. But it returned as strong as ever in Germany in 1936 because the organizers needed the money generated by soccer.

While it hasn't received the publicity of the track and field, gymnastics, and swimming competitions, soccer has been among the best attended, if not the top spectator sport at the Games. In 1980, the Moscow Games set an Olympic standard of 1,821,624 million spectators, or 35 percent of the entire attendance. Four years later, the Los Angeles Olympics came close at 1,421,627 million fans, paving the way for the U.S. to host the World Cup in 1994. After a massive drop-off to 728,712 in Seoul in 1988 and another steep fall to 466,300 at Barcelona in 1992, the soccer tournament attracted an Olympics-best of 1,364,250 at the Atlanta Summer Games in 1996.

Through the years, the Olympic tournament has been one of controversy regarding who is an amateur. Before the advent of professional soccer throughout the world, it was much easier to define. But as more and more leagues started to pay players, it became more difficult to define what an amateur player truly was. It became impossible to define with the number of Soviet Bloc and Eastern European countries who claimed that all their players were amateurs, although they were playing at a high professional level.

Ten influential people who got their kicks off the field

In soccer, there are all sorts of players — on and off the field. While they were always behind the scenes, these ten people each placed their individual mark on the game in the United States.

Alan Rothenberg: As immediate past president of U.S. Soccer, chairman of the 1994 World Cup Organizing Committee, and a founder and first chairman of Major League Soccer, Alan Rothenberg's legacy will be felt for years.

Lamar Hunt: Multimillionaire Lamar Hunt put his money where his mouth is, as the owner of the Dallas Tornado (North American Soccer League) and as owner of the Kansas City Wizards and Columbus Crew (MLS). In 1999, Hunt became the first MLS owner to build a soccer-specific stadium, in Columbus.

Anson Dorrance: Anson Dorrance got the ball rolling for U.S. women on two levels. In college, Dorrance's North Carolina women's team won 15 of the first 18 NCAA Division I titles. Internationally, he led the U.S. to the first Women's World Cup crown. Dorrance's U.S. coaching record was 65-22-5. His current mark at UNC is an unreal 466-19-11.

Francisco Marcos: Francisco Marcos invented minor-league soccer—the three-tier United Soccer Leagues, which give hope to players aspiring to perform at the highest level possible. The 130-team USL includes the A-League, D3 Pro League, and Premier Development Soccer League.

Sunil Gulati: Sunil Gulati, a behind-the-scenes prime mover and shaker, was one of the MLS architects and the first deputy commissioner. He is the President of Soccer Operations for two MLS teams: San Jose and New England.

Bruce Arena: U.S. National Team coach Bruce Arena set standards of excellence in the college and pros, winning five NCAA Division I titles as coach of the University of Virginia and two MLS crowns with D.C. United.

Tony DiCicco: Tony DiCicco directed the U.S. women to a gold in the 1996 Summer Olympics and to the 1999 world championship. He resigned as coach in 1999 to spend more time with his family, leaving with an impressive 103-8-8 record.

Hank Steinbrecher: Hank Steinbrecher organized U.S. Soccer House in Chicago, the headquarters of the federation. U.S. Soccer has expanded to more than 100 employees since 1990. He stepped down in February 2000.

Marla Messing: As president of the 1999 Women's World Cup, Marla Messing presided over the most successful women's sporting event, attracting an average of 38,616 per date and a U.S. soccer record TV audience of 40 million.

Ron Newman: Ron Newman guided teams to titles in four leagues — Dallas Tornado (NASL), L.A. Skyhawks (American Soccer League), San Diego Sockers (NASL indoors), and Sockers (Major Indoor Soccer League, 10 crowns). Newman (753-296-27 record) also directed the Kansas City Wizards (MLS).

So, it should not be all that surprising that the Soviet and Eastern European countries dominated the Olympics from 1952 to 1980, winning 21 out of a possible 24 medals. It wasn't until 1984 that FIFA used a new definition of an Olympic performer — a player who had never made an appearance for his National Team — that a non-Communist country, France, captured Olympic gold. That has been refined over the years when, after many heated negotiations, FIFA and the International Olympic Committee (IOC) agreed to use the Olympic soccer tournament as an Under-23 tournament, as a proving ground for future stars.

The IOC wanted the Olympic tournament to be an open tournament, although FIFA saw that as a major threat to the marketability of its coveted World Cup. A compromise was reached for the 1996 Games, when FIFA allowed each team to use three players over the age of 23 in the 1996 Summer Games. Those rules will be followed at Australia 2000.

Many of the world's great players starred or got their start internationally in the Olympics, including France's Michel Platini, Mexico's Hugo Sanchez, Germany's Juergen Klinsmann, and Brazil's Ronaldo. Other players of note in the Summer Games included Soviet Union goalkeeper Lev Yashin, Hungarian forward Ferenc Puskas, Poland midfielder Kaz Deyna, and Uruguay's Jose Leandro Andrade, among others.

The 1996 Olympics, held in the United States, was not just a financial success, but an aesthetic one as well as underdog Nigeria became the first African country to earn an Olympic gold medal. The talented Nigerians topped favored Brazil in the semifinals, overcoming a 3-1 deficit to register a 4-3 extra time victory, and then defeated Argentina, 3-2, in the gold-medal match.

The Atlanta Olympics also produced another first — the first women's soccer tournament of its kind. The U.S. prevailed in a close battle with China, 2-1, when Tiffeny Milbrett scored the game-winning goal in front of more than 78,000 fans in Athens, Georgia, to earn the gold.

Part VI
The Part of Tens

In this part . . .

No *For Dummies* book is complete without the whimsical Part of Tens. In this part, you get several fun-filled chapters, each boasting ten soccer tidbits.

Chapter 21

Ten Players Who Made an Impact on Worldwide Soccer

· ·

*W*ith so many talented players performing in so many countries, it's not easy selecting the greatest players of all time. Pelé is an obvious choice. So are Franz Beckenbauer and Johan Cruyff. But who else has the credentials to fill out the list?

Pelé (Brazil)

Pelé is simply the greatest player of all time. Pelé, whose accomplishments are legendary, set standards that will be difficult to duplicate. He had it all — intelligence, speed, vision, agility, great instinct, and a passion for the game. The legend started to grow in 1958 as the 17-year-old Pelé helped Brazil to the first of its three World Cup titles within a 12-year span. In fact, he is the only player to have performed on three world championship teams. Born Edson Arantes do Nascimento on October 21, 1940, Pelé's playmaking and scoring prowess helped Santos become one of the great club teams as his name became a household word in virtually every country. A fantastic ambassador to the game during his playing days and especially in retirement, Pelé finished with 1,280 goals (an average of almost a goal per match), completing his career with the New York Cosmos in the North American Soccer League from 1975–77.

Who's soccer's top scorer? It's not Pelé!?!

Contrary to popular belief, Pelé has not scored more goals than anyone else. That honor goes to fellow Brazilian Artur Friedenreich, who scored 1,329 goals in a career that spanned from 1909 to 1935. Pelé wasn't too shabby himself, connecting 1,280 times, which is second all-time.

Franz Beckenbauer (Germany)

Franz Beckenbauer lived up to his "Kaiser" nickname by wearing a number of crowns for the titles his teams had earned in league, European, and world competition. Beckenbauer revolutionized the sweeper position, pushing up and attacking from the defense thanks to his vision, patience on the ball and passing ability. He also was the guiding force behind Bayern Munich's success in the German Bundesliga and in Europe (three consecutive European Cups from 1974–76) and was the backbone of the German National Team's near invincibility, climaxing with the 1974 World Cup championship. Beckenbauer, who is now Bayern president, played a vital role for the New York Cosmos in the latter years of his playing career. With all those accomplishments, it shouldn't come as a surprise that Beckenbauer became the first man to captain and coach a World Cup championship team as he directed Germany's win over Argentina in the 1990 final.

Johan Cruyff (The Netherlands)

Johan Cruyff, the centerpiece of the marvelous Dutch teams of the '70s, could play and excel at virtually every position on the field. His natural position was midfield, where he controlled the pace of the game and masterminded his team's attack with his vision and God-given skills. He starred for Ajax, Barcelona (to which he was transferred from the Dutch club for a then world record transfer price of $1.85 million in 1973), and the Dutch National Team, which lost to Germany in the 1974 World Cup final. In his later years, Cruyff was a standout for the Los Angeles Aztecs and Washington Diplomats in the NASL. He also went on to enjoy considerable success as the coach of Ajax and Barcelona, guiding the Spanish team to the 1989 European Cup crown and four consecutive domestic titles.

Alfredo DiStefano (Argentina)

Many Europeans consider Alfredo DiStefano the greatest player of his era, if not of all time, as he was an all-around and consummate team player. DiStefano could do it all, whether it was defending in his team's penalty area, organizing the midfield, or scoring a spectacular goal. He was best known for his scoring prowess as he became the most important player of the great Real Madrid teams of the '50s and '60s that captured the first five consecutive European Cups. DiStefano, born in Argentina, was lured to play professionally in Spain by Real Madrid in 1953. Real's fifth Euro title in 1960 is considered one of the greatest performances of all time. Not surprisingly, DiStefano played a vital role in that victory, scoring three goals in a 7-3 thrashing of Eintracht Frankfurt in Glasgow, Scotland.

Diego Maradona (Argentina)

As incredible as he was, you have to wonder how great Diego Maradona would have been had he avoided his dark side. For about a six-year span in the '80s, there was no better player in the world as he starred for Boca Juniors (Argentina), Barcelona (Spain), and Napoli (Italy). In fact, no player has dominated a World Cup as Maradona did in 1986, leading Argentina to the World Cup crown over Germany. One game in that Cup defined the cunning Maradona. That's when he accidentally punched the ball into the English net with his hand for one goal — yes, the game officials incredibly allowed it to stand — and when he ran around six players during a 50-yard jaunt to score one of the greatest goals ever in Argentina's 2-1 quarterfinal win. Sadly, Maradona also will be remembered for his suspensions for drug usage, first with Napoli for failing a cocaine test in 1991 and then for being booted from the 1994 World Cup for using a cocktail of stimulants.

Ferenc Puskas (Hungary)

Was there a better left-sided attacking player than Ferenc Puskas? The "Galloping Major," as he was known, had a lethal left foot that ripped the back of the net many times, first starring for Honved and the Hungarian National Team (83 goals in 84 matches) in the early '50s. That's when Hungary, nicknamed the Magic Magyars, captured the Olympic gold medal in 1952 and almost took home the World Cup trophy two years later. But Puskas and his teammates could not hold a two-goal lead in what turned into a 3-2 defeat to the gritty West Germans in the 1954 final. He escaped his native land during the Hungarian Revolution in 1956 and went to lead the Spanish First Division in scoring four times, teaming with Alfredo DiStefano to give Real Madrid a lethal one-two punch. He connected four times in the 1960 European Cup final, a 7-3 victory over Eintracht Frankfurt.

Lev Yashin (Soviet Union)

Lev Yashin was known as the Black Spider, Black Panther, and Octopus, among other names, because he was the goalkeeper who dressed in black and had an amazing ability to stretch and deny a player a certain goal with a spectacular save. He is considered the greatest goalkeeper of all time. He participated in three World Cups, won an Olympic gold medal at the 1956 Summer Games, and helped the Soviet Union capture the first European Championship title in 1960. Yashin probably is best remembered for his penalty kick saves. It is believed he saved 150 penalties. When he passed away in 1990, the news agency Tass called Yashin "the most famous Soviet sportsman ever."

Eusebio (Portugal)

Also nicknamed the Black Panther for his speed and ability to pounce on the opposition and to strike quickly, Eusebio brought Portuguese soccer to dizzying heights it hasn't seen since. Born Eusebio Da Silva Ferreira in Mozambique on January 25, 1942, he eventually joined Portuguese giant Benfica in 1961, starting an incredible string of success. He scored twice in Benfica's 5-3 win over Real Madrid in the 1962 European Cup final, was voted the 1965 Euro player of the year, and connected for nine goals in the 1966 World Cup, leading Portugal to a third-place finish. By 1969, he had led Benfica to the Portuguese title seven times. In his waning years, Eusebio performed for the Boston Minutemen and Toronto Metros-Croatia in the NASL, leading the latter to the 1976 championship.

Sir Stanley Matthews (England)

English players usually don't come to mind when you think of great dribblers, but Stanley Matthews was a special case. Considered the first great player of the modern era (after World War II), Matthews dazzled spectators, teammates, and the opposition for years with his skilled moves down the right wing. He had endurance as well, playing professionally for 33 years until he was 50. Matthews starred for Stoke City and Blackpool in the English First Division, but the grand prize of that time, the English Football Association Cup, had eluded him for most of his career. That is, until 1953, when as a 38-year-old, Matthews led Blackpool from a 3-1 deficit to a stirring 4-3 comeback victory over Bolton. Matthews passed away at the age of 85 on Feb. 23, 2000.

Bobby Charlton (England)

Take a look at old films of Bobby Charlton in his prime for England and Manchester United. It seems that every one of his goals came from booming 25-yard shots. Few players could unleash such fury from their feet as Charlton finished with 48 international goals in 106 appearances as a midfielder and withdrawn center forward. Beyond his goal-scoring ability, Charlton brought a certain level of class and leadership to his teams and even in retirement as a spokesman for a credit card company. Charlton was a key player of England's World Cup championship team in 1966, a surviving member of the horrific plane crash that all but wiped out United's talented side in 1958, and played for United's 1968 European Cup championship side as well.

Chapter 22

Ten American Players Who Made a Unique Impact

· ·

*T*he history of the U.S. Men's National Team spans almost the entire century, since the Americans defeated Sweden in Stockholm on Aug. 20, 1916. Since then, more than 558 players have proudly worn the red, white, and blue colors of the United States.

On the other hand, the U.S. Women's National Team is not yet 15 years old, but it has made an impact not only domestically, but internationally as well, setting standards and records that might never be duplicated or surpassed.

In this chapter, I talk about players — ten men and ten women — who have left their unique mark on the game.

Paul Caligiuri, Midfielder-Defender

A solid midfielder and defender throughout his career, Paul Caligiuri is best known for one goal he scored in a 1-0 victory against Trinidad & Tobago, securing a spot in the 1990 World Cup ending the U.S.'s 40-year absence from the world's greatest sporting event. Had the U.S. not qualified, then American players would not have had the opportunity to impress scouts at the World Cup and eventually go overseas to hone their craft and skills. Then the 1994 World Cup team most likely would have experienced a difficult time getting to the second round. And perhaps Major League Soccer might not have gotten off the ground. Caligiuri played professionally in Germany before returning to the states to play for the Columbus Crew and Los Angeles Galaxy in MLS.

Joe Gaetjens, Midfielder

Joe Gaetjens literally scored the shot heard around the world in 1950, the lone goal of the U.S.'s 1-0 stunning victory over England in the World Cup in Belo Horizonte, Brazil. Unfortunately, Gaetjens did not live long enough to tell his grandchildren about his feat. He is presumed dead. Gaetjens was arrested and supposedly put to death as a political prisoner in his native Haiti in the early 1960s, although that has not been officially substantiated.

John Harkes, Midfielder

A modern pioneer, John Harkes became the first American player to perform in the prestigious English Premiership, the top league in that country, when he appeared for the team Sheffield Wednesday as a hard-working left-sided midfielder. He also was the first U.S. citizen to play in the Football Association Cup final at Wembley in 1993, as Wednesday lost to Arsenal, 2-1. Returning home in 1996, Harkes helped D.C. United capture the first two Major League Soccer championships before he was traded to the New England Revolution in 1999. As captain of the U.S. National Team, he was presumed to be going to France '98 before then-coach Steve Sampson, in a controversial decision, did not include Harkes on the team.

Kasey Keller, Goalkeeper

If John Harkes was a pioneer by going across the Atlantic, then Kasey Keller was the first *impact player* — a player who can make a difference in a match on a regular basis — to become respected in England. Keller skipped his final semester at the University of Portland to pursue a career in England and became one of the Football League's top goalkeepers, first with Millwall in the First Division and then with Leicester in the Premiership. He is more of a positional goalkeeper than one who constantly makes spectacular saves, although his marvelous performance in the 1-0 victory over Brazil in the 1998 CONCACAF Gold Cup is considered his best performance. Keller realized a major personal goal by playing on the continent, signing with and starring for newly promoted Rayo Vallecano of the Spanish First Division just before the 1999–2000 season.

Billy Gonsalves, Forward

Billy Gonsalves was called the "Babe Ruth of Soccer" during his playing hey-days of the '30s and '40s and for good reason. Very few players of his era could score goals like Billy Gonsalves, who at 6'2" and 210 pounds, terrorized defenses and goalkeepers for nearly two decades. Playing in various semipro leagues, Gonsalves took seven different clubs to nine consecutive final appearances and six championships in the U.S. Cup during the '30s. He went on to help Brooklyn Hispano to the American Soccer League crown in 1943 and the Open Cup titles in 1943 and 1944.

Tab Ramos, Midfielder

Probably the most gifted player of his generation, Tab Ramos never really reached his true potential due to injuries. A superb dribbler, Ramos sometimes was the lone U.S. player who wasn't afraid to take on opposing players one-on-one. Ramos, part of the Kearny, N.J., connection of midfielder John Harkes and goalkeeper Tony Meola, suffered a fractured skull as Brazilian midfielder Leonardo elbowed him in a World Cup second-round game in 1994. He was never the same player, twice suffering major injuries to his left knee. Ramos played with teams Real Betis and Figueres in the Spanish Second Division and Tigres in the Mexican First Division before becoming the first American player to sign with Major League Soccer.

Eric Wynalda, Forward

Eric Wynalda proved U.S. players could score at the international level, connecting 34 times in 106 appearances to make him the all-time leading goal scorer in U.S. history. While not a classic power shooter, Wynalda used his speed and finesse to beat opposing defenses and goalkeepers. He played for the U.S. in all three World Cups in the 1990s. His most memorable moments? Becoming the first American to be ejected in the World Cup in 1990 and scoring a spectacular free kick against Switzerland in the 1994 competition. Wynalda, who played several seasons in the German Second Division, returned home as a star to play in MLS with the San Jose Clash (now Earthquakes) and then Miami Fusion.

Marcelo Balboa, Defender

While Alexi Lalas and his red goatee got the lion's portion of the spotlight during the 1994 World Cup, it was Balboa who helped organize a tough U.S. defense. Although he saw only a few minutes of action in the 1998 World Cup, Balboa did not complain publicly as several benched veterans had. In fact, he was among a handful of players who performed well after he returned from France. Balboa has played a vital role in the revival of the Colorado Rapids as a defensive midfielder and central defender.

Kyle Rote Jr., Forward

A generation ago, Kyle Rote Jr. made all the headlines, becoming the first American to lead the now-defunct North American Soccer League in scoring, totaling 10 goals and 10 assists for the Dallas Tornado in 1973. While he never became a superstar as so many fans had hoped for in a seven-year career, Rote did turn some heads. He proved that Americans could actually play the game in a time dominated by foreign players. His wages in those days were so meager that Rote made the bulk of his living off money he won in the televised "Superstars" competition, which pitted big names from various sports against one another in several sporting competitions. Rote, who made five appearances with the U.S. National Team, went on to become a sportscaster and now is a sports agent.

Alexi Lalas, Defender

While there might be dozens or even hundreds of U.S. soccer players with more skill than Alexi Lalas, he made his mark as a recognizable figure and product endorser during a time when the general American public had trouble naming one soccer player. As a member of the U.S. National Team, the tall and lanky Lalas was probably best known for scoring a goal in the 2-0 upset of England in 1993 and helping solidify the backline during the 1994 World Cup. He became the first U.S. citizen to play in Italy's world-renowned Serie A for Padova for two seasons. He returned home to MLS to play for the New England Revolution, New York/New Jersey MetroStars, and Kansas City Wizards before retiring in 1999 to focus more on his musical career.

Michelle Akers, Midfielder-Forward

Michelle Akers, the first superstar and "Grand Dame" of women's soccer, has defined two positions (see Figure 22-1). As a forward, Akers was a scoring terror. At 5-foot 10-inches and 150 pounds, she looked slow, but she would gain on her opponents with her long strides, pass them, and fire a shot on goal. Akers, one of only four women to score more than 100 international goals, is probably best known for her goal in the final two minutes that secured the U.S.'s first world championship, in a 2-1 triumph over Norway in China in 1991. Chronic Fatigue Syndrome has limited Akers' role and slowed her down since that time. But she has become a standout defensive midfielder in a sport that did not have many, if any, players excel there. She was the tireless heart and soul of the 1999 world championship team, earning the Bronze Ball as the tournament's third most valuable player.

Figure 22-1: Michelle Akers, the "Grand Dame" of women's soccer.

Mia Hamm, Forward

Mia Hamm is easily the most celebrated of all American women soccer players, earning the respect of teammates, coaches, and fans and more than $1 million in endorsements in 1999. Hamm is considered the best women's player in the world today. She is probably most dangerous on the right side, but can score with either foot or her head. If you give her room, she will run into the corner and cross the ball into the middle to a teammate. If you cover her tightly, she will run around you toward the goal and try to score. While she is the all-time women's international scoring leader with an amazing 115 goals (at press time), Hamm is the consummate team player, whether she is called on to make a key pass to a teammate or come back and play defense deep in her team's territory. Hamm, who made her international debut at age 15, played for the juggernaut University of North Carolina team.

Carin Gabarra, Midfielder

In the early '90s, if you mentioned the name Michelle Akers, then Carin Gabarra was probably not far behind. Gabarra was the creative midfield force of those teams. She was at the top of her game at the 1991 Women's World

Cup, when she was awarded the Golden Ball, soccer's equivalent of MVP. Gabarra scored five goals and assisted on five others. A back injury forced her to retire prematurely.

Julie Foudy, Midfielder

As good an all-around player as Julie Foudy is, she probably is best known for a trip she made to Pakistan to tour factories that manufacture soccer balls. It raised public awareness about the plight of women and children over there and how conditions were improving. And, oh, she can play the game as well as a member of the two world championship teams and 1996 gold-medal winning Olympic team. For years Foudy was a standout defensive midfielder on the National Team, taking a backseat to her high-scoring teammates. When Michelle Akers took on more of a defensive role, Foudy was moved to an attacking position and acquitted herself very well. Known as the team joker and nicknamed "Loudy Foudy," she was the U.S. team's cocaptain from 1995–99. Foudy has also started to make a name off the field as the ESPN broadcaster and as the new president of the Women's Sports Foundation.

April Heinrichs, Midfielder

Talk about combining the qualities of tenacity, talent, and leadership, and you get April Heinrichs, who was the captain of the first world championship squad in 1991. While much has been made about her leadership abilities, it sometimes gets lost in the shuffle how effective Heinrichs was as a player. She scored 38 goals in 47 international appearances, one of the most prolific rates in women's international history, before a knee injury forced her to retire after the 1991 Women's World Cup. The first female player to be inducted into the National Soccer Hall of Fame (1998), Heinrichs was named the U.S. Women's National Team coach in January 2000.

Kristine Lilly, Midfielder

During the 1999 Women's World Cup, a commercial was aired showing a toddling child meant to resemble a very young Kristine Lilly taking her first steps and then running away from her parents (see Figure 22-2). Today, that isn't too far from the truth, as Lilly literally can run all day. Her never-say-die attitude and consistency at midfielder has earned Lilly the respect of coaches and players. It's not surprising Lilly has played in more international matches than any other player — man or woman — on this planet, as she is closing in on an amazing 200 matches. As it turns out, Lilly might be best remembered for a time when she actually stopped running, standing and jumping to head away an apparent goal by a Chinese player off the goalline in overtime of the 1999 Women's World Cup championship game.

Figure 22-2:
Midfielder
Kristine Lilly
is known for
her never-
say-die atti-
tude and
consistency.

Joy Fawcett, Defender

She is literally the quintessential soccer mom, raising two daughters while being a vital part of the U.S. backline and arguably the world's best defender of the late '90s. Thanks to a team nanny, Fawcett is able to take Katelyn Rose (born in 1994) and Carli (1997) around the country, whether its training camp or a game. In 1997, Fawcett juggled coaching at UCLA and for a youth team and playing for the National Team before she stepped down from the college post. Fawcett, one of the steadying forces and most experienced play-ers in the back, rarely lost her head in tight situations. She even scored the game-winner in the 3-2 comeback win over Germany in the quarterfinals.

Carla Overbeck, Defender

Another steadying influence on defense, Carla Overbeck was the on-field captain of the 1999 world championship team. And like Joy Fawcett, Overbeck is a soccer mom as well. In fact, before Jackson was born in 1997, Overbeck was the team ironwoman, playing in 63 consecutive matches against 19 countries. Overbeck's leadership and organizational skills in the Women's World Cup came through big time, especially in the championship match. Remember, the Americans surrendered only three goals in the Cup, and that included two in one game to Germany. Overbeck is the assistant women's coach at Duke University.

Briana Scurry, Goalkeeper

On a team that is known for its scoring prowess, the goalkeeper can sometimes get lost in the shuffle. Briana Scurry, however, took center stage in the two most important matches of the 1999 Women's World Cup, making several key saves to keep the U.S. alive in the 2-0 semifinal win over Brazil and then stopping a Chinese player's penalty kick during the tiebreaker that determined the championship. Scurry celebrated winning the 1996 Olympic gold medal by running through the streets of Athens, Georgia, naked — for a few minutes in the middle of the night. Scurry has been entrenched as the U.S. starting goalkeeper since 1995 and has been almost perfect. She leads all U.S. goalkeepers in all-time appearances, wins, shootouts, and goals against average.

Brandi Chastain, Defender-Forward

Brandi Chastain is a living, breathing example of how players get second chances by coming back from injuries to still excel. A member of the 1991 world championship team as a forward, Chastain failed to make the 1995 squad. A knee injury forced her to return as a defender as she became arguably the best left fullback in the world. Speaking of second chances, Chastain inadvertently kicked the ball into her own net early in the quarterfinals against Germany in WWC 1999, but rebounded with the tying goal later on. And of course, who can forget Chastain's game-winning penalty-kick in the championship game and then ripping off her shirt in celebration? Photos of Chastain were on magazines and newspapers all across the nation and has made her a household name along with Mia Hamm. With a nickname like "Hollywood," Chastain embraced the spotlight and has become the second most recognized female soccer player ever.

Chapter 23

Ten Players to Pay to Watch and Stand to Cheer

● ●

*W*ant to start an argument? Just get into a debate on which players are the best current players in any sport. In soccer, those discussions could last forever. But remember, there can be a giant step between talented players and ones who will bring fans in to fill the seats and then bring them to their feet. Here are ten-plus stellar players — men and women — who grace today's playing fields.

Rivaldo (Brazil)

The best soccer player in the world as we enter the new millenium? Many observers may claim it's Rivaldo rather than Ronaldo, who has gotten more of the publicity. Rivaldo, born April 19, 1972, plys his trade with Barcelona (Spain). He grabbed the international spotlight with his marvelous midfield play at the 1998 World Cup, although he underachieved in the final.

Rivaldo, whose full name is Rivaldo Vitor Borba Ferreira, later proved himself, helping Brazil win Copa America, the South American championship, in 1999 with two goals and an assist. Manchester United reportedly has offered as much as $40 million for Rivaldo's contract, but Barcelona knows a good thing when it sees one and has decided to keep the brilliant Brazilian for now — and for good reason, as Rivaldo was named the 1999 FIFA World Player of the Year.

Ronaldo (Brazil)

Ronaldo, whose full name is Ronaldo Luiz Nazario da Lima, is supposed to be this generation's version of Pelé. There is no question that he is gifted, but it is unfair to compare the two because they are such different players. Where

Pelé could wreck a defense with his magnificent runs and passes, Ronaldo is more of a pure goal scorer. There's nothing wrong with that. Just ask PSV Eindhoven (Netherlands), Barcelona (Spain), and most recently Inter Milan (Italy), for whom he has filled the net. After leading the Spanish First Division in scoring in 1996–97 and earning FIFA and European player of the year honors, Ronaldo was transferred to Inter for a then world-record $30 million.

Ronaldo's strength is his powerful runs in the open field. When he runs at a defense, opponents have difficulty displacing the ball. Although he scored four goals in the 1998 World Cup, Ronaldo was considered a major disappointment, particularly in the final. There was much mystery to his condition, whether it be from a nervous breakdown due to stress or drugs or an ankle injury. A year later it was revealed to the public for the very first time that Ronaldo had suffered convulsions. Ronaldo, who was born on Sept. 26, 1976, fears that his chronic knee injuries, which have plagued him since his arrival at PSV, might cut short his career before he reaches the age of 30.

Gabriel Batistuta (Argentina)

Combine talent and work ethic, and you have one of the world's great goal-scorers in Gabriel Batistuta, who has earned the nicknames Archangel Gabriel and Batigol. The Argentine-born forward — he was born Feb. 1, 1969 — has a history of filling the net. In his first five seasons in Italy's defensive-oriented Serie A, Batistuta had scored 145 times in 245 matches entering the 1999–2000 season. If there is one downside to Batistuta's career, it's that he has never scored a key goal during the normal tempo of a game against a top-echelon team in the World Cup, other than a penalty kick.

Michael Owen (England)

Michael Owen was only an 18-year-old when he scored an incredible goal after a 50-yard jaunt for England in the 1998 World Cup. He was so impressive that Joao Havelange, when he was president of FIFA (the sport's worldwide governing body) asked for Owen's No. 20 England jersey. For an encore, as a Liverpool player, Owen led the English Premiership in scoring the next season. Owen, who has been insured by his team for $100 million, could fetch a minimum of $45 million on the open market, according to some estimates. For stardom at such a young age — Owen was born Dec. 14, 1979 — the unflappable forward doesn't seem affected, although a series of pulled hamstring muscles has slowed down his progress.

Jose Luis Chilavert (Paraguay)

No one really comes to see the goalkeeper play, but tell that to Jose Luis Chilavert, who feels he is the No. 1 keeper in the world. He is some piece of work. Besides making key saves for the Paraguayan National Team, Chilavert probably is best known for his goal-scoring prowess, finding the back of the net as many as 14 times for his Argentine team, Velez Sarsfield, in one season through penalty and free kicks. In fact, Chilavert was the first goalkeeper to score three goals in a game.

He is also known for his outrageous conduct. Chilavert, born July 27, 1965, once walked out on the Paraguayan team, accusing an official of incompetence. He also was given a three-month suspended sentence for punching a ballboy during a First Division match, slapped a reporter who had the audacity to suggest Chilavert might be overweight, and once said he wanted to pursue a career as a kicker in the NFL. Known as the "Bulldog," his jersey bears the animal that best describes his temperament.

Zinedine Zidane (France)

The critics of Zinedine Zidane claim that he saves his best and most memorable performances only for the big games. If that's true, then he saved his very best for last at the 1998 World Cup in France. After missing two games due to a red-card suspension, Zidane returned to produce one of the most memorable championship performances ever. He scored on a pair of head shots off corner kicks to lead France to a surprising 3-0 victory over Brazil. Zidane, born June 23, 1972, has done quite well in "ordinary" games and competitions as well, most recently starring for Juventus in the Italian First Division.

Dwight Yorke (Trinidad & Tobago)

Not only does Dwight Yorke score goals in bunches, he scores some of the most beautiful ones in the game today. When he played for Aston Villa in the English Premiership, it seemed that Yorke had at least one goal among the nominations for goal of the month. Now starring with England and European power Manchester United, Yorke's goals make the weekly highlights for yet another reason — because of the high profile team he plays for. Born Nov. 3, 1971, Yorke is expected to play a vital role for Trinidad & Tobago in its quest for a berth in the 2002 World Cup.

Roberto Carlos (Brazil)

Like goalkeepers, few fans go to stadiums to watch defenders perform, unless they are Roberto Carlos. Carlos, whose birthday is April 10, 1973, was "discovered" by the rest of the world in 1997, when his magnificent 35-yard free kick defied all laws of physics and swerved its way into the back of the French net in a 1-1 draw at Le Tournoi de France. The Real Madrid defender once scored a goal in which the ball was clocked at 90 miles per hour and his throw-ins usually range close to 30 yards. Carlos's speed and the quality of his runs on the left side make him a constant threat to opposing teams.

David Beckham (England)

David Beckham just very well could be the best midfielder in the world today as a focal point for Manchester United and the English National Team. Beckham, born May 2, 1975, received worldwide headlines for the wrong reasons, and scorn and ridicule at home for his red card during the 1998 World Cup. After setting up Michael Owen for his magnificent goal in the opening half in the shootout loss against Argentina, Beckham was red-carded for fouling Diego Simeone in the 47th minute, although the Argentine player eventually admitted he faked falling to the ground. Little good did that do Beckham months later. Incidentally, he is married to Posh Spice, also known as Victoria Adams, of the Spice Girls. They named their first child, Brooklyn, after the place he supposedly was conceived when Beckham ran away to the United States to "hide" from the media and public ridicule after the World Cup. History repeated itself at the first Club World Championship in Brazil in 2000, when Beckham was red-carded in a match against Mexico, causing yet another uproar in England.

Christian Vieri (Italy)

Entering the millenium, Christian Vieri claimed the prize as the most expensive player in the world as he transferred from Lazio to Inter in Italy's Serie A for a world-record $50 million. After all, there aren't many Italian forwards who have the lethal finishing — scoring — ability that Vieri has. The *Times of London* called him "the most coveted footballer in the world." Vieri, a forward, came of age internationally during the 1998 World Cup, scoring in four consecutive games for Italy. Up until the 1998–99 season, Vieri had scored 62 goals over five seasons. He once scored 24 goals for Atletico Madrid in one season. Actually, soccer was not his first sport of choice; cricket was. He was born in Italy July 12, 1973, brought up in Australia, and returned to Italy when he was 15. Vieri eventually performed for Torino, Atalanta, and Juventus before moving to Atletico Madrid (Spain), Lazio, and on to Inter.

Raul (Spain)

The key to Raul — his full name is Raul Gonzalez Blanco — has been his consistency at the club level with Real Madrid (Spain) and at international level with the Spanish National Team. He has a reputation for literally making something out of nothing — that is, he has the unique ability to score a goal when there doesn't seem to be a chance at all. Born June 27, 1977, Raul scored a spectacular goal in the 1999 Intercontinental Cup final to boost Real Madrid to the title. Barring injuries, Raul promises to be one of the top players in the world for many years to come.

And That's Not to Forget . . .

A top-ten list is way too short to forget some other leading men who deserve to be mentioned. They include (club teams in parentheses): Danish goalkeeper Peter Schmeichel (formerly Manchester United, now with Sporting Lisbon in Portugal), Italian defender Paolo Maldini (A.C. Milan), Chilean striker Marcelo Salas (Lazio), and Croatian striker Davor Suker (Arsenal), the leading goal scorer at the 1998 World Cup.

Some Leading Women

Compared to the men, the women's game is barely taking its first steps internationally, having three World Cups to the men's 16. Yet, several players already have emerged as dominant forces, and they are not all necessarily from the United States.

Mia Hamm (United States)

By the time she retires, Hamm could finish with 150 international goals or more at the rate she is filling the net. Born March 17, 1972, Hamm is at home as either a playmaker or a goal scorer. Combine her fine-tuned skills, a work ethic that is second to none (watch how she comes back to play defense), and you have one of the great players of the world. Hamm has played for a pair of world championship teams (1991 and 1999) and an Olympic champion team (1996) as well.

Sissi (Brazil)

Because forwards in their 30s usually don't fare well or dominate tournaments, Sissi, who was age 32 at the 1999 Women's World Cup, may not be seen at that particular competition again. Sissi, born June 2, 1967, enjoyed a memorable tournament at USA '99, scoring 7 goals and helping set up another 3 as she shared the scoring title with Sun Wen of China. Sissi is best known for her accurate and lethal free kicks. Just ask Germany, which paid dearly on Sissi's amazing talent. Or ask Nigeria, whose incredible quarterfinal comeback was dwarfed after Sissi's free kick in extra time.

Sun Wen (China)

During the summer of '99, Sun Wen proved that she could just about do it all. Even though she endured a sub-par performance in the championship match, Sun — Chinese last names are listed first — enjoyed a fabulous Women's World Cup. Sun, who was born April 6, 1973, shared Golden Boot honors as the leading scorer (7 goals, 3 assists) with Sissi of Brazil and won the Golden Ball outright as undisputed Most Valuable Player of the tournament.

Marianne Pettersen (Norway)

The scary thing about Marianne Pettersen is that she is only reaching her prime as a goal scorer. Pettersen, whose birthday is April 12, 1975, managed to find the back of the net three times for the Norwegians at USA '99, seemingly popping up everywhere on the field to make life miserable for the opposition by taking a dangerous shot.

Michelle Akers (United States)

If we were kids selecting soccer teams, Akers would be one of our first picks, because even on her worst days, she always plays to win. At the 1991 Women's World Cup, Akers set incredible standards for a forward, connecting for a record 10 goals. Today, she is doing the same as a defensive midfielder with her never-say-die, hard-hitting performances. Akers, born Feb. 1, 1966, is a real, honest-to-goodness legend of the game.

Kristine Lilly (United States)

Thanks to her seemingly endless running and great positioning, it seems that Kristine Lilly is everywhere on the field. Born on July 22, 1971, Lilly has earned a reputation as being the U.S.'s best all-around midfielder. She can score and defend with the best of them. Lilly, who is expected to become the first player ever — man or woman — to reach 200 international appearances, was the first American player to break the 100-match barrier with the National Team.

And that's not to forget . . .

Bettina Wiegmann is the creative force of a tough German side. She also scored 3 goals at the 1999 Women's World Cup and was one of only two players who solved the American defense during the tournament (the third was Brandi Chastain's own goal).

The women's game is not necessarily known for its defense, but Wen Lirong has stood out from the crowd. Excellent in the air and a very good distributor of the ball, Wen was the cornerstone of a defense that allowed only 2 goals in six games and also blanked the U.S. on its home soil at USA '99.

Canadian Charmaine Hooper did not fare as well as other forwards in the Cup. She is, however, one of the most dangerous and fastest forwards in the world. She suffered from a sub-par supporting cast, which allowed the opposition to focus on her.

As one of the veterans of the women's game, Norway's Hege Riise may be a step slower these days. But she still can rocket a shot toward the goal, having totaled nearly 50 international scores. She was the star of the 1995 Women's World Cup, capturing the Golden Ball and Silver Boot awards as the best player and second leading goal scorer, respectively. Teammate Linda Medalen has made the transition from a high-scoring forward to a hard-nosed defender.

Chapter 24

Ten Dream Teams That Gave Opponents Nightmares

· ·

Countless championship teams — club and national — have taken the victory lap around the field, but only a few have left an indelible impression in the minds of soccer fans.

In this chapter, I highlight six intriguing National Teams that stood out at the international level and six super Club teams that grabbed the spotlight and headlines and found time to entertain the fans during their glory days.

National Teams

Many National Teams have enjoyed a marvelous World Cup, European Championship, or Copa America. Few have enjoyed a dynasty of at least four years. Here are some talented National Teams who have withstood the test of time.

Brazil (1958-1970)

Brazil won three World Cups in four tries, an achievement that will be almost impossible to surpass. With the great Pelé as the focal point, Brazil dominated international soccer, becoming the first country to win the soccer's most coveted prize three times (1958, 1962, and 1970), and the only team to emerge victorious out of its hemisphere (Sweden in 1958). Pelé, however, was far from a one-man show as he and his talented teammates ran circles around the opposition. Its supporting cast included Vava, the only man to score in two consecutive championship games, Garrincha, a crafty winger, and Carlos Alberto, the captain of the 1970 team who went on to play for the New York Cosmos, and Rivellino and Tostao, who were key attacking players on that 1970 team.

Hungary (1950-1954)

Hungary just might be the best National Team never to win a World Cup. Known as the Magic Magyars, the Hungarians were the dominant European soccer team in the early '50s. Fueled by the feared quartet of Ferenc Puskas, Nandor Hidegkuti, Sandor Kocsis, and Zlotan Czibor, they captured the gold medal at the 1952 Olympics. But they fell to Germany in the World Cup championship game in 1954, losing a two-goal advantage in a crushing 3-2 loss. After the 1956 Hungarian Revolution, many players left the country, and soccer in Hungary was never quite the same again in this once proud soccer nation.

Netherlands (1974-1978)

If Hungary isn't the best National Team not to win a World Cup, then the Netherlands could lay claim to that title. The Netherlands finished second in successive World Cups, watching hosts Germany (1974) and Argentina (1978) take the victory lap in their respective home stadiums. This Dutch team introduced "Total Football" to the world — in which every player had to be able to play every field position in a pinch. This team also was fun to watch, packed with such talented players as the great Johan Cruyff, Johan Neeskens, and Rudi Krol.

Uruguay (1924-1930)

Uruguay's incredible success as the first world power set in motion the World Cup, which was spawned out of its overwhelming performances at the 1924 and 1928 Olympics, in which it earned gold medals in each competition. In 1930, the first World Cup was held in Uruguay, and not surprisingly, the host team came out on top behind the likes of Guillermo Stabile, Pedro Cea, and Hector Scarone. The Uruguayans came from behind to defeat archrival Argentina in the final, 4-2.

Italy (1934-1938)

How difficult is it to defend a world championship? Besides Brazil, Italy is the only country to win back-to-back World Cups, at home in 1934 and in France in 1938. While some critics claim that Italy "recruited" several Argentine players from the South American country's 1930 World Cup squad, Italy had more than its share of world-class players, including Giuseppe Meazza, who had the Milan stadium named after him, Luigi Colaussi, and Juan Schiavio.

U.S. women (1991 to present)

Few National Teams, men or women, have enjoyed the success of the American women within a decade. Of the four major international tournaments of the 1990's, the U.S. won three of them — world championships in 1991 and 1999 and the Olympic gold medal in 1996. The Americans' only disappointment was a third-place finish in 1995 as Norway captured the world championship. Mia Hamm, Michelle Akers, Kristine Lilly, Julie Foudy, Carla Overbeck, and Joy Fawcett have formed the core of this wonderfully talented side.

Club Teams

Any First Division club team in the world can have an excellent season. But how many can dominate their domestic leagues with flair and majesty that goes beyond just winning? Here are a number of teams that have stood out over the years.

Real Madrid, Spain (1956-1960)

Barring a billionaire buying the best players in the world, no club team will be able to match what Real Madrid accomplished in the late '50s and early '60s. The Spanish team won five consecutive European Cups — now called the Champions League — to claim undisputed club soccer supremacy during its era. The team boasted five stars from as many countries — Alfredo DiStefano (Spain), who scored in each of those finals, Ferenc Puskas (Hungary), De Stefano's partner in crime up front, Raymond Kopa (France), an excellent playmaker, Didi (Brazil), and Jose Santamaria (Uruguay).

A.C. Milan, Italy (1988-1992)

With salaries skyrocketing and players moving around at a rapid pace these days, will A.C. Milan be the last great super team in modern times? Owned by media magnate Silvio Berlusconi before he became Italian prime minister, Milan captured three Italian First Division titles, two European Cups, and two World Club Cups during its amazing five-year reign. Milan boasted several players who formed the nucleus of not one, but two National Teams. The Dutch connection of high-scoring striker Marco Van Basten, creative midfielder Ruud Gullit, and defender Frank Rijkaard formed the heart of this much feared and respected team. Italian world-class players such as midfielder Roberto Donadoni and defenders Franco Baresi and Paolo Maldini provided the soul.

Ajax, Netherlands (1971-1973)

The seeds of the marvelous Dutch National Teams were planted and harvested in this Amsterdam-based team. Coach Rinus Michels perfected his "Total Football" in which players could play various positions. Not only was Ajax effective, but entertaining as well. The team revolved around Johan Cruyff, and when he left for Barcelona (Spain) after the third consecutive European Cup crown, it took nearly a decade before Ajax could relive its European glory again. Ironically, it was with Cruyff as coach.

Bayern Munich, Germany (1974-1976)

Bayern Munich is one of only three clubs to win the European Cup three consecutive times, including capturing it in the same year — 1974 — as West Germany earned the World Cup. Franz Beckenbauer, the only man to captain and coach a team to the World Cup title, was the attacking sweeper. He was joined by superb goalkeeper Sepp Maier and Gerd Mueller, better known as "Der Bomber" for his lethal shots at goal.

Santos, Brazil (1956-1974)

During Pelé's heyday, there might not have been a better known team in the world than Santos. Thanks to its off-season tours, Pelé and Santos performed in friendlies — exhibition games — in front of capacity crowds in virtually every country and turned on the fans to the game. Santos did win many important games in actual competition, capturing five successive Copa Brazil crowns, two South American club crowns, and two World Club Championships.

Manchester United (1990 to present)

Manchester United, the world's most popular and profitable pro sports team, has an extensive history as the best team in one of the world's top leagues. Under the guidance of Sir Alex Ferguson, United had won five English Premiership titles and four Football Association Cups in the 1990s, but the really big prize — the European Champions Cup — eluded the team until 1999. In that magical spring, United won the *treble*, capturing the two domestic competitions and the European title. In December 1999, United took home a fourth trophy, earning the Intercontinental Cup after a victory over Palmeiras (Brazil).

United sometimes seems like an international all-star team, boasting a roster that includes Dwight Yorke (Trinidad & Tobago), Roy Keane (Ireland), Ryan Giggs (Wales), Jaap Stam (Netherlands), Ole Gunnar Solskaejer (Norway), and of course, David Beckham (England).

Chapter 25

Ten Matches Made in Soccer Heaven

• •

*E*veryone has his or her favorite games, regardless of the sport. It might be your daughter's youth game in which she scored her first goal. Or perhaps it was your favorite MSL team winning its fifth consecutive game on a last-second goal. Here's a list of the greatest and most dramatic soccer matches that had an historical impact or made headlines around the world. By the way, it's only a coincidence, but German teams were involved in seven of these games.

Germany 3, France 3 (Germany Advances on Penalty Kicks, 5-4)

July 8, 1982: This World Cup semifinal confrontation in Seville, Spain, had all the elements for an epic: two great teams (Germany and France), a superstar (French midfielder maestro Michel Platini), a villain (German goalkeeper Toni Schumacher), and an incredible comeback (Germany). Both teams left everything on the field, which almost included the body of French midfielder Francois Battison, who was leveled by Schumacher while on a breakaway. Battison's injury forced him out of the game, while the German goalkeeper was allowed to remain in the game and did not even get a yellow card. It changed the course of the game, which ended in regulation at 1-1. The French managed to take a 3-1 advantage on goals by Marius Tresor and Alain Giresse in the first extra time period. But the relentless Germans refused to surrender and equalized behind Karl-Heinz Rummenigge (102nd minute) and Klaus Fischer (107th). Germany eventually prevailed in penalty kicks, 5-4, as Schumacher saved an attempt by Maxime Bossis.

Real Madrid 7, Eintracht Frankfurt 3

May 18, 1960: Real Madrid won the first five European Cups as the perennial Spanish power put on one of the most memorable displays of soccer and a huge exclamation point on its last championship with a fabulous performance before 127,621 spectators at Hampden Park in Glasgow, Scotland. Two legendary players registered hat-tricks en route to a 7-3 triumph over Eintracht Frankfurt of Germany. Ferenc Puskas connected four times, and Alfredo Di Stefano had three goals.

Hungary 6, England 3

Nov. 25, 1953: It was only a friendly, but the result shook the soccer world. England had never lost at home at Wembley. Hungary, fresh off its gold-medal triumph in the 1952 Olympics and 30-1-1 in its last 32 matches, took apart what was considered one of the top teams in the world. The final score: Hungary 6, England 3, before a stunned crowd of 100,000. The Magic Magyars, who lined up in an ultra-offensive 4-2-4 formation (see Chapter 9), ripped apart the English defense with goals from Nandor Hidegkuti (hat-trick, including a goal in the opening minute), Ferenc Puskas (2), and Jozsef Boszik. In a rematch in Budapest six months later, Hungary left no doubt as to which was the superior team in a 7-1 demolition.

Italy 4, Germany 3

June 17, 1970: Looking at the final score, it may be difficult to believe that Germany and Italy battled to a 1-1 deadlock in regulation — the Germans were barely alive thanks to Karl-Heinz Schnellinger's 90th minute goal — in the 1970 World Cup semifinals in Azteca Stadium in Mexico City. The teams then broke loose for 5 goals in only 30 minutes of extra time. The Germans had enough troubles as Franz Beckenbauer was forced to play 60 minutes with a dislocated shoulder because Coach Helmut Schoen had used all his substitutions. Striker Gerd Mueller took advantage of a defensive error for a 2-1 German lead five minutes into the extra session. Italy rallied as Giovanni Rivera put in a free kick and Luigi Riva scored for a 3-2 advantage. With 10 minutes left in the second extra period, Mueller struck again — his 10th goal of the Cup — for a 3-3 tie. But barely a minute later, Roberto Boninsegna set up Rivera for the game-winner.

France 1, Brazil 1 (France Advances on Penalty Kicks, 4-3)

June 21, 1986: Back and forth they went, two great teams looking for holes in the opposition's defense in this World Cup quarterfinal in Guadalajara, Mexico. Careca had given France a 1-0 lead 18 minutes into the match, but the French equalized with four minutes remaining in the half on a Michael Platini goal. The second half was end-to-end action, but no goals. Zico had a grand opportunity to put the Brazilians ahead in the 74th minute, but his penalty kick was saved by Joel Bats. After extra time came the drama of penalties, where Luis Fernandez dramatically converted the game-winner as France prevailed in the tie-breaker, 4-3.

Nigeria 4, Brazil 3

July 31, 1996: Despite outplaying Brazil in the Olympic semifinal in Athens, Georgia, Nigeria found itself with a 3-1 deficit early in the second half. The Africans then missed a penalty kick in the 62nd minute and then went into a funk. Then, suddenly in the 77th minute, Nigeria came alive. First it was Victor Ikpeba, who scored from 22 yards. Then Nwankwo Kanu scored in a scramble with 23 seconds remaining in regulation before putting in the game-winner in the fourth minute of sudden-death overtime for an improbable 4-3 victory. "I'd have to stay this was the greatest (Olympic) game," said FIFA president Sepp Blatter, who has attended seven Olympics. "It had all that defines our sport, our game. It had technical and tactical. Again, we produced passion. We had drama." Three days later, Nigeria overcame a one-goal deficit late in the game to up-end Argentina for the gold medal, 3-2.

England 4, Germany 2

July 30, 1966: Perhaps the most legendary and controversial of all World Cup finals was England's 4-2 extra time win over Germany at Wembley. England enjoyed a 2-1 advantage, thanks to a Martin Peters goal in the 78th minute, before Wolfgang Weber equalized with 15 seconds remaining in regulation. Geoff Hurst struck for one of the most controversial goals in soccer history when his shot bounded off the crossbar and directly down behind the goal line. Or did it? The Germans claimed it wasn't a goal, but Soviet Union lines-man Tofik Bakhramov did. Hurst added a third goal in the waning minutes.

Denmark 2, Germany 0

June 26, 1992: Hans Christian Andersen could not have written a better fairytale. The Danes were a last-minute replacement in the 1992 European Championship for Yugoslavia, which was thrown out of the tournament because of international sanctions imposed on that war-torn country. Entering the 1992 European Championship final in Gothenberg, Germany was heavily favored and threw everything it had at the Danes. Goalkeeper Peter Schmeichel, who would go on to star for Manchester United, literally stood on his head. The Great Dane made nine saves, some of them spectacular enough to keep his team in the match. John Jensen scored early and Kim Vilfort late — their only goals of the tournament — in one of the biggest upsets of the century.

Germany 3, Hungary 2

July 4, 1954: How would you like to be down 2-0 only eight minutes into a World Cup final? Germany found itself with that challenge against the heavily favored Hungarians in Berne, Switzerland. These two talented teams had met earlier in the Cup as Hungary registered to a 8-3 victory because the Germans used many second-line players to get an easier route to the final. Ferenc Puskas and Zoltan Czibor had given the Magic Magyars the advantage. But in a game that established the German tradition of never saying die, Maxmillian Morlock scored in the 10th minute, and Uwe Rahn tied it at 2-2 eight minutes later. The score remained tied at 2-2 until Rahn connected again in the 84th minute. Hungary thought it had equalized on a Puskas goal with two minutes left, but it was ruled offside.

Manchester United 2, Bayern Munich 1

May 26, 1999: With time running out on its bid to make history, English club Manchester United incredibly pulled off a 2-1 comeback victory over German club Bayern Munich to capture the European Champions League title, incredibly scoring twice in four minutes of stoppage time in Barcelona. United earned the English version of the treble — winning the English Premiership title, English Football Association Cup and the European crown, although the team gave its supporters some heart-pounding moments. Mario Basler had given the German team the lead in the sixth minute and hit the crossbar twice in the second half. But United equalized 40 seconds into stoppage time as substitute Teddy Sheringham found the back of the net. About two minutes later, another late game substitute, Ole Gunnar Solskjaer, scored the game-winner.

Chapter 26

Ten Goals That Will Give You Goosebumps

• •

*T*here is nothing more beautiful in soccer than a goal that is well taken and superbly executed. In the past century, there have been tens of millions of goals scored. Some were magical. Others were dramatic. Others made history.

Diego Maradona (Argentina, 1986)

Many soccer observers claim that Diego Maradona's famous 1986 goal was the greatest of all time. Only four minutes after he used his chicanery to bat the ball into the English net with his hand — the Hand of God goal — in Argentina's 2-1 World Cup quarterfinal victory in 1986, Maradona commenced an amazing 60-yard run. He took possession of the ball 10 yards into Argentine territory, whirling around 180 degrees, which left two players in their tracks. He then raced down the right side into English territory past Ray Wilkins. Terry Fenwick tried to knock Maradona down at the top of the penalty area, but Maradona shrugged him off. Goalkeeper Peter Shilton came out of the net, committed himself, and fell to the grass eight yards out. Terry Butcher tried a last-ditch effort with a sliding tackle under Maradona, who pushed the ball into the unattended net. Total time: 10 seconds. Number of touches: 9.

Michael Owen (England, 1998)

Ironically, 18-year-old Michael Owen pulled off his amazing individual run for England against Argentina in the 1998 World Cup, 12 years after Diego Maradona's marvelous goal (see preceding section). He used skill, strength, speed, vision, and poise under pressure en route to his 16th minute score. Owen utilized his speed several times, first to accelerate away from Argentine defenders to catch up to David Beckham's finely placed pass. He then used his vision, cutting to the right before the penalty area to make space for himself. He then used his strength to ward off a challenge by defender Jose Chamot at the top of the box before combining his skill and poise to calmly fire a right-footed shot from 10 yards into the left corner past goalkeeper Carlos Roa. Ironically, Roa was the hero in the penalty-kick tiebreaker that Argentina won.

Pelé (Brazil, 1958, 1961)

Pelé has scored so many goals that it would be a crime to have only one spotlighted. Pelé said the most important goal of his career was his very first World Cup score in 1958. He had sat out the entire opening round before he made his debut against Wales in the quarterfinals. As it turned out, it might have been one of the uglier goals of his career as the 17-year-old superstar-to-be scored on a deflection off a defender in front of the Welsh net in the 73rd minute of a 1-0 victory. Pelé surmised that if he hadn't scored, Brazil would not have won the match and perhaps the World Cup, the first of three in four tries.

On March 5, 1961, Pelé scored "Gol De Placa," one of the most amazing goals of his career. Translated from the Portuguese, it means Goal of the Plaque. He dribbled from his penalty area past six Fluminense defenders and the goalkeeper for a goal à la Maradona at Maracana Stadium in Rio Janeiro. The goal so entranced the media that Sao Paolo newspaper *O Esporte* had a plaque made and mounted at the entrance of the stadium commemorating the most beautiful goal ever scored.

Geoff Hurst (England, 1966)

England forward Geoff Hurst's goal in 1966 is probably the most controversial goal in the history of the World Cup, if not the sport. Hurst fired a shot that bounded off the crossbar and into the German goal 11 minutes into extra time in the 1966 World Cup final. Linesman Tofik Bakhramov of the Soviet Union ruled the ball had indeed crossed the line, and the goal stood. Hurst connected for his third goal in the waning minutes to secure a 4-2 triumph to become the only player to score three goals in a championship game.

Leonidas (Brazil, 1930s, 1940s)

While not one single goal comes to mind, Leonidas deserves to be mentioned because he is credited with perfecting the bicycle kick — shooting with his back to the goal and kicking out of the air over his shoulder — with not one, but two feet. (See Chapter 6 for more on the bicycle kick.) Word has it that opposing goalkeepers would congratulate Leonidas because his goals were so pretty. Remember, Leonidas performed his goal-scoring feats before the age of TV and video in the '30s and '40s.

Mohammed "Nayim" Amar (Morocco, 1995)

Few players had tried to loft a long, high lazy shot over the goalkeeper until Real Zaragoza midfielder Mohammaed Amar, better known to the international soccer community as Nayim, pulled off the feat in the final seconds of the 1995 European Cup Winners Cup against Arsenal and goalkeeper David Seaman. As the final minute wound down at Parc des Princes in Paris, Nayim, standing some 45 yards out on the right side, noticed that Seaman was off his line. So, he floated a long looping shot that eluded the astonished keeper for a 2-1 victory for the Spanish club.

Joe Gaetjens (U.S., 1950)

Outside of the United States and Haiti, very few soccer fans knew of Joe Gaetjens — that is, until June 29, 1950. That's when the Haitian-born Gaetjens put in a head shot off a long pass by Walter Bahr for one of the most improbable goals in soccer history to give the U.S. a 1-0 upset of England in the 1950 World Cup in Belo Horizonte, Brazil. The English claimed the goal was an accident.

Marco Van Basten (Netherlands, 1988)

When he was 12 years old, Marco Van Basten wrote down the various ways a player can score a goal. It is not known whether Van Basten, an obvious student of the game, described the goal he scored in the 1988 European Championship game — a superb volley shot — in a 2-0 victory over the Soviet Union. Van Basten scored 24 goals in 58 appearances for the Netherlands, before a severe ankle injury prematurely cut short his career at the age of 29 in 1993.

Raymondo Orsi (Italy, 1934)

Forward Raymondo Orsi scored a spectacular equalizer for Italy to send the game into extra time in its 2-1 win over Czechoslovakia in the 1934 World Cup final. His right-footed shot curled the ball into the net. A day later, Orsi tried 20 times to repeat the shot for photographers and 20 times he failed.

Dennis Bergkamp (Netherlands, 1998)

Few World Cup matches have experienced the dramatic ending that occurred in Marseille on July 4, 1998. Dennis Bergkamp put in a precision, cross-field 50-yard pass from teammate Frank DeBoer with 14 seconds remaining to lift the Netherlands to a 2-1 quarterfinal win over Argentina. Bergkamp gathered in the pass with grace on the right side, beat defender Roberto Ayala, and placed a right-footer past goalkeeper Carlos Roa. Bergkamp then fell to the ground with his arms raised to the heavens, almost as though he thanked God for that goal.

Roberto Carlos (Brazil, 1997)

Regardless how the rest of his career turns out, Brazilian defender Roberto Carlos forever will be associated with what is considered one of the greatest, or perhaps the greatest, free kick. He accomplished that feat at Le Tournoi de France, a dry run for the World Cup, a year before the event kicked off, in June 1997. Carlos combined raw power, skill, and flair to fire in a 35-yard free kick past French goalkeeper Fabien Barthez in a 1-1 tie in Lyon, a goal that earned praise from teammates and foes alike. Unfortunately, Carlos could not duplicate this fantastic goal during the 1998 World Cup. But that score could wind up as a once-in-a-lifetime goal.

Mia Hamm (U.S., 1998)

Mia Hamm has scored so many goals that we could write an entire chapter (or even a book) describing them. One memorable goal that showcased Hamm's soccer smarts, vision, and skill came during the Goodwill Games in Uniondale, N.Y., on July 27, 1998. After securing a hat-trick in a rout of Denmark, Hamm scored both goals in the U.S.'s 2-0 triumph over archrival China in the championship game. Noticing that Chinese goalkeeper Gao Hong was standing off her line in the 87th minute, Hamm floated in a marvelous chip shot that eluded her opponent to cap off a memorable one-woman show that U.S. coach Tony DiCicco called a "Michael Jordan-like performance."

Part VII
Appendixes

@RICHTENNANT

I hate when my English teacher referees a soccer match. She gives red cards for 'bad language', and 'poor grammar'.

In this part . . .

This part has all the extras. Forgot what a touchline is? Then check out the Glossary in this part. Want to know who to contact for youth soccer? Then don't skip Appendix B.

Appendix A

Soccer Speak

● ●

Advantage: Instead of stopping play when the attacking team has a serious offensive penetration after the opposition has committed a foul, the referee allows that team to play on. Stopping play would give an unfair advantage to the defending side.

A-League: A 28-team coast-to-coast league that comprises the Second Division of American soccer, although Canadian franchises exist in Toronto, Montreal, and Vancouver.

Amateur: A player who plays for the fun of it and doesn't get paid.

Assessors: USSF officials who attend games to grade referees, assistant referees, and fourth officials on their performance.

Assistant coach: Helps the coach run the team. While not a glamourous position, an assistant coach can shoulder a lot of responsibility. Depending on the level of play, a team can have several assistant coaches, with some specializing in a particular skill, such as goal-keeping.

Assistant referee: Actually a linesman (the old term to describe this game official) who stands and runs up and down the sidelines or touchline to determine whether a ball is out of bounds, which team last touched it, and whether a player or team is offside. The name was switched from linesman by FIFA in an attempt to be politically correct.

Back heel pass: A ball played with the back of the foot to a teammate.

Back pass: A pass that goes toward the player's own goal. It is usually a pass from a defender to the goalkeeper.

Bicycle kick: Potentially the most spectacular of all maneuvers because timing is such a vital component of the kick, in which the player jumps and moves his legs as though he is pedaling a bicycle. It is also a dangerous maneuver because the player has his back to the net and must land properly after the kick to avoid injury.

Boots: An English term for soccer shoes or cleats.

Box: This term can have two meanings — the penalty box or area or when a goalkeeper boxes or punches the ball.

Captain: The on-field player designated by the coach (although teams are sometimes allowed to vote) who is allowed to talk with the referee. The captain is sometimes considered an extension of the coach.

Caution: Another way to refer to a yellow card. The referee can hand out a yellow card for dangerous actions on the field, such as kicking an opponent, handling the ball, and dissenting with the game officials.

Center spot: A mark at the center of the field that is used for kickoffs.

Chip shot: Attempted when a player lofts the ball over the defense to pass to a teammate or to try to score by catching the goalkeeper out of the net.

Clean sheets: A British term for a goalkeeper recording a shutout.

Clearance: When defenders kick the ball away from in front of the net.

Club: The umbrella organization that most European and South American teams — youth, amateur, and pro — belong to. In Europe, for example, a club will have a first team and a reserve team at the pro level and a number of amateur and youth clubs from Under-10 to Under-19. Virtually every pro club in the U.S. does not have several teams below the first team, although that could change in the not-too-distant future. American youth clubs, however, have several age groups — boys and girls — usually from Under-10 to Under-19.

Coach: The person who runs the team on the field, from practices to lineup and tactical decisions. In England, a coach is a person who trains a team on the field, while a manager makes all the key strategic and tactical moves.

Coin toss: A midfield ritual before the opening kick. The toss determines which direction a team may choose to attack or defend in a particular half. This is important especially if there are unique weather conditions, such as an extremely windy day.

CONCACAF: Confederation of North, Central American, and Caribbean Association Football, which is the governing body of soccer in the Western Hemisphere, excluding South America. The United States is a member of CONCACAF and must play its World Cup qualifying matches through this confederation.

Corner flags: These flags are at each of the four corners of the field to help game officials determine whether a ball has crossed the goal line or sideline and to signify from where corner kicks must be originated.

Corner kick: A kick is given to the attacking team when the defending side clears the ball over the end or goal line. The kick is taken from the left or right corner on the side of the field in which it went out of bounds.

Cross: When a player on the left or right wing lofts the ball to a teammate standing in front of the goal or on the other side of the field.

Dead ball: This situation occurs when the ball is not in play while on the field, which is usually on free kicks, corner kicks, penalty kicks, and throw-ins.

Defender: A defender plays in front of the goalkeeper and his primary duty is to stop the opposition from scoring or getting shots — quality and quantity. Assignments and responsibilities can vary from man-to-man coverage or zone defense, in which he defends a particular area. Outside fullbacks play on the left and right wings and patrol the flanks and rarely move from their sides of the field. Central defenders play in the middle of the field and usually cover the opposition's leading goal scorer or center forward(s).

Direct kick: These free kicks are awarded when a player kicks, trips, charges, jumps at, strikes or holds an opponent or handles the ball with his hand. The defending team must stand at least 10 yards away from the ball prior to the kick.

Dissent: When a player complains, yells at, or even swears at the referee and is awarded a subsequent yellow card.

Draw: This term has two definitions. When teams finish regulation or over-time with the same amount of goals, it's called a draw. Another way to describe a tie game. It is also a term that is used to determine seedings for a tournament or an international competition such as the World Cup.

Dribble: The primary way a player moves and controls the ball with her feet while running.

Drop ball: One of the rarest plays of soccer, it is used after an injury stops play or after play has been stopped without the ball going out of bounds. The referee drops the ball where the play stopped. The ball must bounce once before a player can touch it.

Dummy run: When a player without the ball makes a run toward the goal to draw defenders away from the dribbler or passer.

End line: Also known as the goal line. It is the line that runs from sideline to sideline, with the goal placed in the middle, and forms the width of the field.

Equalizer: A goal that is scored to tie the game.

Expulsion: Another way to say red card or ejection. The British also use the term "sending off" or a player "getting his marching orders."

Extra time: Another way to say overtime. This usually comes in the form of a 15-minute "sudden death" or "Golden Goal" period in which the first team to score wins. Extra time shouldn't be confused with injury time or stoppage time.

Fair play: A term that is used to describe sportsmanship by a player or team. FIFA has an annual Fair Play Award that is awarded to a player or a team that demonstrates exemplary and rare sportsmanship.

Far post: The goalpost that is farthest from the ball.

FIFA: Federational Internationale de Football Association, the sport's governing body, which is headquartered in Zurich, Switzerland. If a country is not a member of FIFA, it cannot play sanctioned international matches, including the World Cup.

Final whistle: When the referee blows the whistle to signify the end of a half, regulation, or game.

Finish: Another way to describe scoring a goal.

Flagposts: Another way to describe corner flags.

Formation: The tactical setup a coach chooses for his team. The most popular formation these days seems to be a 4-4-2. That translates into four defenders, four midfielders, and two forwards. Goalkeepers are not used in the numerical formations because they are considered a given quantity.

Forward: A forward's primary job is to score goals or to create them for teammates. There are several types of forwards. Wings play on either the left or right side and usually run up and down the sides of the field. They can either take the ball into the penalty area for a shot or keep it on the flank and try to pass it to a teammate in the area. Center forwards play in the middle of the field, but they are allowed to wander if open space is there. A center forward, also known as a striker, should be a team's leading goal scorer and most dangerous player up front.

Foul: A foul is a result of an infraction of the rules by a player or even team official. A free kick — direct or indirect — is awarded to the attacking team. See Chapter 4 for more info on fouls and rules of the game.

Fourth official: This official sits or stands on the sidelines, keeps a written record of the game, oversees substitutions, makes sure that the players and coaches on both benches aren't getting out of line, and announces the amount of stoppage time for each match.

Free kick: A kick that is taken by the attacking team after a player is fouled. Teams must give the kicker a minimum of 10 yards before the ball is put into play. Also see direct kick and indirect kick.

Friendly: A term that is used to describe an exhibition game that will not count in official standings.

Fullback: Another way to describe a defender, usually one who plays on the right or left side.

Game officials: Another way to describe a referee, assistant referees, and fourth official.

General manager: The person who makes player personnel decisions on trades and player signings for a professional team.

Goal: A goal is scored when the ball completely crosses the goal line and goes under the goalposts. A goal is worth 1 point.

Goal kick: The goalkeeper takes this kick after a shot or pass by the attacking team sails over the end line.

Goal line: The line that runs from sideline to sideline at the end of both sides of the field, with the goal in the middle. Also known as the end line.

Goal mouth: The area directly in front of the goal.

Goalkeeper: The only player allowed to use his hands, and that activity is restricted to an 18-x-44-yard area called the penalty area. If a goalkeeper handles the ball outside of the box, he should be awarded a red card and the attacking team given a free kick from that spot.

Goalkeeper's box: A 6-yard box directly in front of the goal in which the goalkeeper is supposed to be king. If an opposing player fouls the goalkeeper in the box, he may be given a yellow card.

Golden Goal: A more popular and positive term for an overtime or sudden-death goal. It was added to soccer terminology in 1996.

Ground: This term has two descriptions — the field surface and, in England, a stadium.

Half volley: A kick or shot that is made immediately after the ball hits the ground on the short hop.

Halftime: The time between the first and second halves. Also known as the interval. Usually lasts 15 minutes.

Hand ball: When a player other than the goalkeeper touches the ball with his arm or hand on purpose. If the ball hits the player's hand or forearm by chance, the referee determines whether it was intentional or not. Goalkeepers can be called for hand balls if they venture outside of the penalty area.

Hat trick: When a player scores three goals in a game.

Head shot or header: When a player hits the ball with her head.

Indirect kick: This free kick is awarded if a player performs in a dangerous way, obstructs an opponent, or stops the goalkeeper from releasing the ball from his hands. A goalkeeper can be called for an indirect free kick if he takes more than four steps before releasing the ball, touches the ball with his hands after it was thrown or kicked by a teammate, or wastes time. Two players, the shooter and a teammate or opponent, must touch the ball before a goal can be scored.

Injury time: Time added on by the referee after the end of the half and/or game due to injuries, arguments, or stoppages of play. Also known as stoppage time.

Inswinger: This is a shot, pass, or corner kick in which the ball curves toward the goal.

Interval: Another way to describe halftime.

Keeper: A shortened term for goalkeeper.

Kickoff: A free kick that is used to start the game, half, overtime, or play after a goal. Unlike gridiron football, however, the kicking team does not have to boot the ball to the opposition. Instead, they are allowed to pass it to their own team.

Linesman: The old term for game officials who run up and down the sideline even with the ball to determine offside, whether a ball is in or out of bounds, and who last touched it.

Major League Soccer: The First Division league in the United States that kicked off its first season in 1996. It has 12 teams in three divisions — Eastern, Central, and Western. D.C. United, Miami Fusion, New England Revolution, and New York/New Jersey MetroStars are in the Eastern Division. The Chicago Fire, Tampa Bay Mutiny, Columbus Crew, and Dallas Burn are in the Central Division, and Los Angeles Galaxy, Colorado Rapids, San Jose Earthquakes, and Kansas City Wizards are in the Western Division.

Manager: A British term for the equivalent of the coach in the U.S.

Man-to-man marking: When each defender is responsible for covering a specific opponent.

Match: Another term for a game.

Midfielder: This player is the link between the defense and attack. Midfielders must be the most physically fit players on the field because they are expected to run the most in a game. They should be able to penetrate deep into enemy territory on attack and make the transition to defense when the opposition retains possession of the ball. Midfielders can specialize as an attacking player or defensive midfielder.

NCAA: National Collegiate Athletic Association, the governing body for most of college soccer in this country. It is broken into Division I, II, and III. There is also the National Association of Intercollegiate Athletics (NAIA), National Christian Collegiate Athletic Association (NCCAA), and the National Junior Collegiate Athletic Association (NJCAA).

Net: Another way (although uncommon) to say goal.

Near post: The goalpost that is nearest to the ball.

Nutmeg: A type of pass in which a player kicks the ball between the legs of an opponent. It is one of the most difficult passes to attempt and one of the most embarrassing moments for a defender. Also known as the tunnel pass.

Obstruction: When a player blocks an opponent with her body. Obstruction results in an indirect free kick for the attacking team.

ODP: Olympic Development Program, which brings together the top boys and girls in different ages groups in each of the youth state associations.

Officials: Also known as game officials, they run the show on the field. They include the referee, two assistant referees (linesmen), and a fourth official on the sidelines.

Offside: A player is offside when he is nearer to his opponents' goal than the second to last opponent, when the ball is played. The key phrase is "when the ball is played." Sometimes a play or pass happens so quickly that it is difficult to determine whether a player is onside when the ball is played.

Offside trap: A defensive tactic used to pull an attacking player or team offside repeatedly. Players move away from the goal in unison to create an offside situation for the attacking player or team.

Olympics: A festival of sports that is played once every four years. Soccer is one of 33 sports in the competition, so a lot of great players and matches get lost in the shuffle. The men's tournament is open to Under-23 players, although countries are allowed to use three players over that age limit. The women's tournament is an open competition with no age limit. The next Olympics is scheduled for Australia in September 2000, followed by the 2004 Summer Games in Athens, Greece.

One touch: When a ball is kicked on a player's first touch on a pass or shot.

Outswinger: This is a shot, pass, or corner kick in which the ball curves away from the goal. If it is a corner kick, for example, the ball is kicked toward the top of the penalty area. That is in contrast to an inswinger, which is aimed for the front of the goal mouth.

Overlap: When a defender runs forward on the left or right flank to become part of the attack.

Overtime: If the game is tied, teams play a certain amount of predetermined time until a goal is scored. Not every league has overtime. Also known as extra time.

Own goal: When a player accidentally kicks, heads, or knocks the ball into his own net. The goal is awarded to the attacking team.

Pass: How a player moves the ball to a teammate, kicking it with his feet or hitting it with his head.

Penalty arc: That half-moon that is positioned at the top of the penalty area, which is exactly 10 yards from the penalty spot. All players must stand behind that arc when a player attempts a penalty kick.

Penalty area: An 18-x-44-yard part of the field in front of each goal in which the goalkeeper is allowed to touch the ball with his or her hands.

Penalty kick: A free kick that is taken in the penalty area after a foul is incurred in the penalty area. The only person defending the net is the goal-keeper, who stands 12 yards away on the goal line.

Penalty-kick tiebreaker: Also known as a shootout or penalty-kick shootout around the world, this tie-breaking method involves penalty kicks taken by five players on both teams against the opposing goalkeeper. If the procedure is still tied after five kicks, it goes into a sudden death.

Penalty spot: The small circle that is 12 yards from the goal, from which a player will attempt a shot after a defensive foul in the penalty area.

Pitch: A British term for a field.

Professional: A player who gets paid and earns his living from playing soccer.

Punt: When goalkeepers distribute the ball down field toward the opposing goal by booting it high in the air.

Red card: A card the referee awards for violent action on the field, such as tackling from behind, a vicious kick or action, and spitting. Two yellow cards in a game are equivalent to a red card.

Referee: The official who runs the game and awards fouls.

Restart: Another way to describe a free kick, corner kick, throw-in, goal kick, or kickoff.

Save: A shot that is blocked, caught, or parried by the goalkeeper, which otherwise would have gone into the net.

Scrimmage: Another term for a practice game.

Semipro: A player who gets paid for playing, but cannot support himself on the salary so he retains his regular job. Many of the top amateur leagues in the United States pay their players.

Set piece: A free kick, corner kick, throw-in, or goal kick. Also known as a dead-ball situation.

Shootout: Depending on your vantage point, it can have two meanings. The shootout was invented by the North American Soccer League in 1977 to decide tie games. Used to settle MLS games that were tied after regulation (from 1996–99), each team uses five shooters who have five seconds and 35 yards to score against the opposing goalkeeper. In recent years, the term has been used worldwide to describe a penalty-kick tiebreaker.

Shot at goal: When an attacking player tries to score, but his shot fails to go into the net as he kicks or heads it wide left or right or over the crossbar.

Shot on goal: When an attacking player tries to score, and the goalkeeper is forced to save it or it goes into the net.

Shutout: When a team limits its opposition to no goals.

Side: Another way to describe a team.

Sideline: The line that runs the length of the field on both sides, from goal line to goal line.

Square pass: A pass by a player to a teammate standing beside him.

State association: The organization — youth or amateur — that runs soccer in each state. There are 55 state association because five states were split into two because of huge population or geographical differences.

Stoppage time: The time added on by the referee after the end of the half or game due to injuries, arguments, or stoppages of play. It also is known as injury time.

Striker: A forward whose main responsibility is to score goals.

Substitute: When a player replaces another during a match. The number of substitutions will vary, depending on the level of play. In youth soccer, teams are allowed to sub freely. In the pros, three substitutions are allowed per team, although a fourth, for a goalkeeper, is allowed in Major League Soccer. In some international friendlies, as many as five substitutes are allowed, if both teams agree before the match.

Tackle: A defensive tactic in which a player uses his foot to take the ball away from his foe.

Target player: A forward, usually a tall one, who is the target of passes, crosses, and corner kicks.

Through pass: A medium or long pass that goes through or between at least two defenders to a running player.

Throw-in: This action is taken when a player sends the ball out of bounds over the touch line, or sideline. The ball is awarded to the opposing team. The player throws the ball in from out of bounds, the only time she is allowed to handle the ball with her hands.

Tie: When both teams end the game or overtime with the same amount of goals. Also known as a draw.

Time wasting: Usually done by the winning team late in a game in an attempt to take some time off the clock. This usually happens when a team takes the maximum time in dead-ball situations. An alert referee notices this tactic and will award the guilty party a yellow card for delay of game.

Touch line: The lines that run on both sides of the field from goal line to goal line. For older youth, amateur, college, pro, and international matches, its length can vary from 100 to 120 yards.

Trainer: Depending in what part of the world you are in, a trainer can mean two things. American sports fans are accustomed to a trainer in the medical sense, keeping players healthy before, during, and after matches. In Germany, the trainers are considered to be the coach of the team because they train the team.

Trap: When a player receives the ball with his foot, thigh, chest, or head.

UEFA: European Football Union, which governs all of Europe, plus Israel. Israel was placed in UEFA years ago to avoid playing against its Arabic neighbors, which would be a security nightmare no matter where the game would be played.

United Soccer Leagues: The umbrella league for two professional leagues and three amateur ones. The two pro leagues are for men — the A-League, which is the Second Division in the United States, and the D3 Pro League, which is the Third Division. The Premier Development League, which is the Fourth Division, is for amateur and college-age players. Women play in the W-League, which has two divisions. The USL also sponsors the Super Y-League, which is a league full of youth teams.

Unsportsmanlike behavior: Conduct by a player that brings disgrace to the game. It could be anything from kicking a player when he is on the ground to arguing with a referee to spitting on an opponent to throwing off his shirt after he has left the game.

USA '94: Another way to refer to the 1994 World Cup, which was hosted by the United States. You take the name of the host country and the year it was played in. For example, the Women's World Cup is called USA '99, while the 1998 World Cup, played in France, is called France '98.

U.S. Amateur Soccer Association: The governing and sanctioning body of amateur soccer in the United States. A division of U.S. Soccer.

U.S. Soccer: The popular name for the United States Soccer Federation, which administers soccer in the United States. Dr. Bob Contiguglia is the president; his four-year term is up in 2002. Founded in 1913, the national governing body (NGB) of the sport in this country. Based in Chicago, Illinois.

U.S. Youth Soccer Association: The governing and sanctioning body of youth soccer in the United States. A division of U.S. Soccer.

Volley: Kicking the ball while its in the air with the foot.

Wing: A way to describe a player who plays on the left or right sides, or flanks, of the field, either as a forward or midfielder.

W-League: Another part of the United Soccer League, it is the top league — an amateur league — for women in the United States. It is comprised of two divisions — W-1 and W-2 — depending on the level of play and the financial resources of the owners.

Women's World Cup: The world championship for women, which was started in 1991 and played every four years since. The U.S. captured the 1991 and 1999 titles, while Norway earned the 1995 crown.

World Cup: The largest single-sport tournament in the world, which is held every four years. The World Cup kicked off in Uruguay in 1930. Brazil is the only country to capture the title four times and France became only the seventh nation to win the coveted trophy, in 1998. The 17th World Cup will be co-hosted by South Korea and Japan in 2002.

Yellow card: The referee can hand out a yellow card for dangerous actions on the field, such as kicking an opponent, handling the ball, and dissenting with the game officials. Two yellow cards are equivalent to a red card, which carries automatic ejection from a game.

Youth player: A participant of the game — boy or girl — between the ages of 4 and 19.

Zone defense: When defenders cover a designated area instead of man-to-man coverage.

Appendix B

Soccer Associations

· ·

*W*ant to know who you need to call in the world of soccer? Then you've come to the right place. In this appendix, I give you contact information for all levels of soccer, from international to youth associations.

International

You never know when you're going to see the address or phone number of FIFA — Federation Internationale de Football Association — and CONCACAF — Confederation of North American, Central, and Caribbean Association Football.

FIFA, P.O. Box 85, 8030 Zurich, Switzerland, Phone: (41) 1-384-9595, Fax: (41) 1-384-9696, Web site: www.fifa.com

CONCACAF, 725 Fifth Ave., New York, NY 10022, Phone: (212) 308-0044, Fax (212) 308-1851,Web site: www.footballconfederation.com

National

American soccer is governed by several national bodies. Here is a list of the most important ones.

U.S. Soccer, 1801 South Prairie Ave., Chicago, IL 60616, Phone: (312) 808-1300, Fax: (312) 808-1301, Web site: www.us-soccer.com

U.S. Youth Soccer Association, 899 Presidential Drive, Suite 117, Richardson, TX 75081, Phone: (800)-4-SOCCER, Web site: www.usysa.com

American Youth Soccer Organization, 12501 South Isis Ave., Hawthorne, CA, 90250, Phone: (800) 872-2976, Fax: (310) 643-5310, E-mail: webmaster@ayso.com

Soccer Association For Youth, 4050 Executive Park Dr., Suite 100, Cincinnati, OH 45241. Phone: (800) 233-7291, Fax: (513) 769-0500, E-mail: sayusa@ saysoccer.org, **Web site:** www.saysoccer.org

U.S. Amateur Soccer Association, 7800 River Road, North Bergen, NJ 07047-6221, Phone: (800) 867-2945, Fax: (201) 861-6341, E-mail: usaussf@aol.com

Professional

Two organizations run professional soccer in the U.S. — Major League Soccer and the United Soccer Leagues, which is the umbrella organization for the A-League, D3 Pro League, Premier Development Soccer League, and W-League.

Major League Soccer, 110 East 42nd St., New York, N.Y. 10017, Phone: (212) 450-1200, Fax: (212) 450-1300, Web site: www.mlsnet.com

United Soccer Leagues, 14497 North Dale Mabry Highway, Suite 201, Tampa, FL 33618, Phone: 963-3909, Fax: (813) 963-3807, Web site: www.usisl.com

U.S. Amateur Soccer Association

Need to find an adult amateur team to play on in your state? Then you have come to the right place. The following are the state offices of the 55 adult state associations.

Alabama Amateur Soccer Association, P.O. Box 731, Helena, AL 35080, Phone: (205) 424-0568, Fax: (205) 424-0569, E-mail: lotsocents@aol.com

Alaska Amateur Soccer Association, P.O. Box 92124, Anchorage, AK 99509, Phone: (907) 688-6867, Fax: (907) 522-3170

Arizona State Soccer Association, 7817 West Maui Lane, Peoria, AZ 85381 Phone: (623) 979-3978, Fax: (623) 979-3978, E-mail: dbtrain@goodnet.com

Arkansas State Soccer Association, 1100 East Kiehl Ave., Suite 1, Sherwood, AR 72120, Phone: (501) 833-0550, Fax: (501) 835-2176, E-mail: info@arkansassoccer.org

California Soccer Association North, 1348 Silver Ave., San Francisco, CA, 94134, Phone: (415) 467-1881, Fax: (415) 467-1934

California Soccer Association South, 2363 South Atlantic Blvd., Commerce, CA 90040, Phone: (323) 263-0472, Fax: (323) 263-7158

Colorado State Soccer Association, 9725 East Hampden Ave. #101, Denver, CO 80231, Phone: (303) 368-8000, Fax: (303) 338-5554, E-mail: eeid@sni.net

Connecticut State Soccer Association, P.O. Box 2213, 757 West Main St., New Britain, CT 06050, Phone: (860) 826-5000, Fax: (860) 826-5000, E-mail: cssa-adm@snet.net

Delaware Soccer Association, 122 Chadd Road, Newark, DE 19711, Phone: (302) 992-4127, Fax: (302) 992-5045, E-mail: kpritch@bellatlantic.net

Eastern New York Amateur Soccer Association, 2479 North Jerusalem Road, East Meadow, NY 11554, Phone: (516) 679-8672, Fax: (516) 679-9457, E-mail: sarah340@aol.com

Eastern Pennsylvania Soccer Association, 2 Village Road, Suite 7A, Horsham, PA 19044, Phone: (215) 659-1393, Fax: (215) 830-0483, E-mail: eastpasa@aol.com

Florida State Soccer Association, 2108 South Cortez Ave., Tampa, FL 33629, Phone: (813) 251-6483, Fax: (813) 254-2283, E-mail: reeffish@aol.com

Georgia Amateur Soccer Association, 3684 B-1 Stewart Road, Atlanta, GA 30340, Phone: (770) 452-0505, Fax: (770) 452-1946

Hawaii Soccer Association, P.O. Box 1072, Wailuku, Maui, HI 96793, Phone: (808) 244-0219, Fax: (808) 244-6964, E-mail: mauisoccer@aol.com

Idaho State Soccer Association, P.O. Box 190069, Boise, ID 83709, Phone: (208) 375-4911, Fax: (208) 375-4911

Illinois State Soccer Association, 5306A West Lawrence Ave., Chicago, IL 60630, Phone: (773) 283-2800, Fax: (773) 283-2869, E-mail: soccerissa@aol.com

Indiana State Soccer Association, 1126 Tealpoint Circle, Indianapolis, IN 46229, Phone: (317) 891-7572, Fax: (317) 891-0810

Iowa Amateur Soccer Association, 5406 Merle Hay Road, Johnston, IA 50131, Phone: (515) 252-6363

Kansas Adult Soccer Association, 2712 North Terrace, Wichita, KS 67220, Phone: (316) 683-2211, Fax: (316) 687-5913, E-mail: Mil492@feist.com

Kentucky Soccer Association, P.O. Box 5626, Louisville, KY 40255-0626, Phone: (502) 458-1177, Fax: (502) 485-0274

Louisiana Soccer Association, 2133 Silverside Drive, Suite G, Baton Rouge, LA 70808, Phone: (225) 766-0577, Fax: (225) 766-0623, E-mail: lsa_soccer@ premier.net

Maryland State Soccer Association, 1 Maple Ave., Baltimore, MD 21228-5569, Phone: (410) 744-5864, Fax: (410) 744-1994

Massachusetts State Soccer Association, 67 Bright Road, Belmont, MA 02478, Phone: (617) 489-3732, Fax: (617) 354-6939, E-mail: frisoli67@aol.com

Metropolitan D.C.-Virginia Soccer Association, 312 Bostwick Lane, Gaithersburg, MD 20878-1930, Phone: (301) 948-3623, Fax: (301) 527-9525, E-mail: soccersue3@aol.com

Michigan Soccer Association, 23077 Greenfield, Suite 510, Southfield, MI 48075, Phone: (248) 552-7240, Fax: (248) 552-7242

Minnesota Soccer Association, 5404 Landmark Circle, Mounds View, MN 55112, Phone: (612) 780-9159, Fax: (612) 786-2429

Mississippi Soccer Association, P.O. Box 13066, Jackson, MS 39211, Phone: (601) 982-5198, Fax: (601) 982-5297, E-mail: mysaoffice@aol.com

Missouri Soccer Association, 10260 Reavis Gardens Drive, St. Louis, MO 63123, Phone: (314) 544-0270, Fax: (314) 638-9528

Montana State Soccer Association, 850 Lobby Circle, Billings, MT 59714, Phone: (406) 254-1332

Nebraska State Soccer Association, 5616 South 85th Circle, Omaha, NE 68127, Phone: (402) 596-1616, Fax: (402) 596-0660

Nevada State Soccer Association, 1396 Betty Lane, Las Vegas, NV 89110, Phone: (702) 453-6214, Fax: (702) 452-2222

New Hampshire Soccer Association, 1600 Candia Road, Suite 2, Manchester, NH 03109, Phone: (603) 626-9686, Fax: (603) 626-9687, E-mail: nhadmin@nhsoccer.com

New Jersey Soccer Association, P.O. Box 9765, Trenton, NJ 08650, Phone: (609) 278-9765, Fax: (609) 394-2081, E-mail: patv@soccernjsa.com

New Mexico State Soccer Association, 1820 San Pedro NE, Suite 6, Albuquerque, NM 87110, Phone: (505) 346-0831, Fax: (505) 346-0831, E-mail: nmssoccer@aol.com

North Carolina Amateur Soccer Association, P.O. Box 29308, Greensboro, NC 27429, Phone: (336) 856-0702, Fax: (336) 856-0204, E-mail: ncasa@mindspring.com

North Dakota Soccer Association, 5805 Fourth St. NW, Moorhead, MN 56560, Phone: (701) 233-0777

North Texas State Soccer Association, 1740 South I-35, Suite 105, Carrollton, TX 75006, Phone: (972) 323-1323, Fax: (972) 242-3600, E-mail: mkaipus@ ntxsoccer.org

Ohio Soccer Association - North, 4107 Laurell Lane, North Olmsted, OH 44070, Phone: (440) 779-8596, Fax: (440) 779-8596, E-mail: john.p.gyekenyesi@ gre.nasa.gov

Oklahoma Soccer Association, P.O. Box 35174, Tulsa, OK 74153-0174, Phone: (918) 627-2663, Fax: (918) 627-2693, E-mail: okcsoccer@earthlink.net

Oregon Adult Soccer Association, 1750 SW Skyline Blvd., Suite 121, Portland, OR 97221-2553, Phone: (503) 292-1814, Fax: (503) 297-4513, E-mail: socceror@aol.com

Pennsylvania West Soccer Association, 855 MacBeth Drive, #2, Monroeville, PA 15146-3332, Phone: (412) 856-8011, Fax: (412) 856-8012, E-mail: stateoffice@pawest-soccer.org

Rhode Island Soccer Association, 17 Hall Ave., Newport, RI 02840-2132, Phone: (401) 847-5174, Fax: (401) 847-6723, E-mail: mrembisz@risa.org

South Carolina Amateur Soccer Association, Department of Recreation, Hampton Park, Charleston, SC 29403, Phone: (843) 720-3821, Fax: (843) 579-7574

South Dakota Amateur Soccer Association, P.O. Box 8143, Rapid City, SD 57709, Phone: (605) 341-3846

Southern Ohio Amateur Soccer Association, 2300 Lake Road, Medway, OH 45341, Phone: (937) 849-1123, Fax: (937) 849-1513, E-mail: kenc@erinet.com

Tennessee State Soccer Association, 161 Second St. NE, Suite 2, Cleveland, TN 37311, Phone: (423) 559-1150, Fax: (423) 476-9993, E-mail: tnsoccer@ tnsoccer.org

Texas State Soccer Association South, P.O. Box 1763, Deer Park, TX 77536, Phone: (281) 479-8221, Fax: (281) 479-8221, E-mail: tssa@tssas.com

Utah Soccer Association, 4476 South Century Drive, Suite B, Salt Lake City, UT 84123, Phone: (801) 263-8166, Fax: (801) 263-8966, E-mail: utahsoccer@aol.com

Vermont Soccer Association, 567 Longmeadow Drive, Shelburne, VT 05482, Phone: (802) 985-4131, Fax: (802) 985-4131, E-mail: portiz@together.net

Washington State Soccer Association, 7802 NE Bothell Way, Kenmore, WA 98028, Phone: (425) 485-7855, Fax: (425) 485-7386, E-mail: wssa@accessone.com

West Virginia Soccer Association, P.O. Box 3360, Beckley, WV 25801, Phone: (304) 252-9872, Fax: (304) 252-9878, E-mail: wvsa@citynet.net

Western New York Soccer Association, 44 Parkwood Lane, Hilton, NY 14468, Phone: (716) 392-6024, Fax: (716) 392-1280, E-mail: arman@eznet.net

Wisconsin Soccer Association, 10708 West Hayes Ave., West Allis, WI 53227, Phone: (414) 545-7227, Fax: (414) 545-7249

Wyoming Senior Soccer Association, 704 S Washington St., Casper, WY 82601-3454, Phone: (307) 261-7740

U.S. Youth Soccer Association

Here are the 55 state associations of the U.S. Youth Soccer Association.

Alabama Youth Soccer Association, State Office, 19220 Highway 280 W, Birmingham, AL 35242, Phone: (205) 991-9779, Fax: (205) 991-3736, E-mail: aysa@mindspring.com

Alaska State Youth Soccer Association, State Office, PMB 1187, 200 W 34th Ave., Anchorage, AK 99503-3969, Phone: (907) 789-7826

Arizona Youth Soccer Association, State Office, 1815 West Missouri Ave., Suite 101, Phoenix, AZ 85015, Phone: (602) 433-9202, Fax: (602) 433-9221, E-mail: azsoccer@amug.org

Arkansas State Soccer Association, State Office, 1100 East Kiehl Ave., Suite 1, Sherwood, AR 72120, Phone: (501) 833-0550, Fax: (501) 835-2176, E-mail: info@arkansassoccer.org

California Youth Soccer Association - North, 1040 Serpentine Lane, Suite 201, Pleasanton, CA 94566, Phone: (925) 426-5437, Fax: (925) 426-9473, E-mail: cysaoffice@aol.com

California Youth Soccer Association - South, 1029 South Placentia Ave., Fullerton, CA 92831, Phone: (714) 778-2972, Fax: (714) 441-0715, E-mail: cysa@pacbell.net

Colorado State Youth Soccer Association, 7375 East Orchard Road, #300, Englewood, CO 80111, Phone: (303) 770-6440, Fax: (303) 770-6958, E-mail: cheryl@csysa.org

Connecticut Junior Soccer Association, P.O. Box 2230, 757 West Main St., New Britain, CT 06050, Phone: (860) 224-2572, Fax: (860) 826-4400, E-mail: office@cjsa.org

Delaware Youth Soccer Association, P.O. Box 5325, Wilmington, DE 19808, Phone: (302) 731-4523, Fax: (302) 731-8972, E-mail: tqhawk@snip.net

Eastern New York Youth Soccer Association, 49 Front St., #2, Rockville Centre, NY 11570, Phone: (516) 766-0849, Fax: (516) 678-7411, E-mail: enyysa@worldnet.att.net

Eastern Pennsylvania Youth Soccer Association, 2 Village Road, Suite 3, Horsham, PA 19044, Phone: (215) 657-7727, Fax: (215) 657-7740, E-mail: epysa@erols.com

Florida Youth Soccer Association, 8 Broadway Ave., Suite B, Kissimmee, FL 34741-5712, Phone: (407) 847-2001, Fax: (407) 847-5974, E-mail: info@fysa.com

Georgia Youth Soccer Association, 3684 B-1 Stewart Road, Atlanta, GA 30340-2760, Phone: (770) 452-0505, Fax: (770) 452-1946, E-mail: gssa@mindspring.com

Hawaii Youth Soccer Association, 1442 Kona St., Honolulu, HI 96814, Phone: (808) 951-4972, Fax: (808) 955-5513

Idaho Youth Soccer Association, 2419 West State, Suite 2, Boise, ID 83702-3167, Phone: (208) 336-5256, Fax: (208) 367-9044, E-mail: iysa@micron.net

Illinois Youth Soccer Association, 1655 South Arlington Heights Road, Suite 201, Arlington Heights, IL 60005, Phone: (847) 290-1577, Fax: (847) 290-1576, E-mail: iysa@iysa.org

Indiana Youth Soccer Association, 5830 North Post Road, Suite 215, Indianapolis, IN 46216, Phone: (317) 377-3405, Fax: (317) 377-3428, E-mail: stateoffice@inyouthsoccer.org

Iowa State Youth Soccer Association, 5406 Merle Hay Road, Suite 300, Johnston, IA 51031-1209, Phone: (515) 252-6363, Fax: (515) 252-7676, E-mail: hkahler@netins.net

Kansas State Youth Soccer Association, 8220 Travis, Suite 201, Overland Park, KS 66204, Phone: (913) 648-6434, Fax: (913) 648-0564, E-mail: ksyouth@aol.com

Kentucky Youth Soccer Association, 443 South Ashland Ave., Suite 201, Lexington, KY 40502, Phone: (606) 268-1254, Fax: (606) 269-0545, E-mail: kriszander@aol.com

Louisiana Soccer Association, 2133 Silverside Drive, Suite G, Baton Rouge, LA 70808 Phone: (225) 766-0577, Fax: (225) 766-0623, E-mail: lsa_soccer@premier.net

Maryland State Youth Soccer Association, 303 Najoles Road, Suite 109, Millersville, MD 21108, Phone: (410) 987-7898, Fax: (410) 987-8707, E-mail: msysa@aol.com

Massachusetts Youth Soccer Association, 30 Great Road, Acton, MA 01720, Phone: (978) 287-5207, Fax: (978) 287-5212, E-mail: jim_gondek@compuserve.com

Michigan State Youth Soccer Association, 23077 Greenfield Road, Suite 510, Southfield, MI 48075, Phone: (248) 557-8220, Fax: (248) 557-8216, E-mail: msysoc@aol.com

Minnesota Youth Soccer Association, 11577 Encore Circle, Minnetonka, MN 55343, Phone: (612) 933-2384, Fax: (612) 933-2627, E-mail: steveolson@mtn.org

Mississippi Youth Soccer Association, P.O. Box 13066, Jackson, MS 39236-3066, Phone: (601) 982-5198, Fax: (601) 982-5297, E-mail: mysaoffice@aol.com

Missouri Youth Soccer Association, 1811 Sherman Drive, Suite 10, St. Charles, MO 63303-3976, Phone: (636) 947-8442, Fax: (636) 947-7626, E-mail: mysaoffice@netscad.com

Montana Youth Soccer Association, P.O. Box 1757, Kalispell, MT 59903-1757, Phone: (406) 752-1776, Fax: (406) 752-5015

Nebraska State Soccer Association, 5616 South 85th Circle, Omaha, NE 68127, Phone: (402) 596-1616, Fax: (402) 596-0660

New Hampshire Soccer Association, 1600 Candia Road, Suite 2, Manchester, NH 03109, Phone: (603) 626-9686, Fax: (603) 626-9687, E-mail: nhadmin@nhsoccer.com

New Jersey Youth Soccer Association, P.O. Box 848, Hightstown, NJ 08520, Phone: (609) 490-0725, Fax: (609) 490-0731, E-mail: office@njys.net

New Mexico Youth Soccer Association, 2300 Candelaria NE, Suite 110, Albuquerque, NM 87107, Phone: (505) 830-2245, Fax: (505) 830-2247, E-mail: nmysa@kozmail.com

New York State West Youth Soccer Association, P.O. Box 12, Corning, NY 14830, Phone: (607) 962-9923, Fax: (607) 962-0525, E-mail: office@nyswysa.org

North Carolina Youth Soccer Association, P.O. Box 29308, Greensboro, NC 27429, Phone: (336) 856-7529, Fax: (336) 856-0204, E-mail: ncysa@mindspring.com

North Dakota Youth Soccer Association, 3022 Walnut St., Grand Forks, ND 58201, Phone: (701) 775-2942

North Texas State Soccer Association, 1740 South I-35, Suite 105, Carrollton, TX 75006, Phone: (972) 323-1323, Fax: (972) 242-3600, E-mail: mkaipus@ntxsoccer.org

Ohio South Youth Soccer Association, 25 Whitney Drive, #104, Milford, OH 45150, Phone: (513) 576-9555, Fax: (513) 576-1666, E-mail: info@osysa.com

Ohio Youth Soccer Association - North, P.O. Box 367, Richfield, OH 44286, Phone: (330) 659-0989, Fax: (330) 659-0993, E-mail: oysan@aol.com

Oklahoma Soccer Association, P.O. Box 35174, Tulsa, OK 74153-0174, Phone: (918) 627-2663, Fax: (918) 627-2693, E-mail: okcsoccer@earthlink.net

Oregon Youth Soccer Association, 4840 SW Western Ave., Suite 800, Beaverton, OR 97005, Phone: (503) 626-4625, Fax: (503) 520-0302, E-mail: oysa@brigadoon.com

Pennsylvania West Soccer Association, 855 MacBeth Drive, #2, Monroeville, PA 15146-3332, Phone: (412) 856-8011, Fax: (412) 856-8012, E-mail: stateoffice@pawest-soccer.org

Rhode Island Youth Soccer Association, 116 Eileen Drive, North Kingstown, RI 02852, Phone: (401) 885-0379, Fax: (401) 885-9110, E-mail: rgoga@riysa.org

South Carolina Youth Soccer Association, 121 Executive Center Drive, #140, Columbia, SC 29210, Phone: (803) 798-5425, Fax: (803) 798-5425, E-mail: scysa@scysa.org

South Dakota State Soccer Association, 3701 Freda Circle, Sioux Falls, SD 57103, Phone: (605) 371-2255, Fax: (605) 371-2636, E-mail: sdsoccer@aol.com

South Texas Youth Soccer Association, P.O. Box 1370, Georgetown, TX 78627, Phone: (512) 863-4969, Fax: (512) 869-4785, E-mail: marilynt@stxsoccer.org

Tennessee State Soccer Association, 161 Second St. NE, Suite 2, Cleveland, TN 37311, Phone: (423) 559-1150, Fax: (423) 476-9993, E-mail: tnsoccer@tnsoccer.org

United Soccer Federation Of Maine, 35 Farvue Ave., Bangor, ME 04401, Phone: (207) 990-0662, Fax: (207) 990-0662, E-mail: usfm@ime.net

United States Youth Soccer Nevada, 5650 West Charleston Blvd., #13, Las Vegas, NV 89146, Phone: (702) 870-3024, Fax: (702) 258-8381, E-mail: usysnv@aol.com

Utah Youth Soccer Association, 4476 South Century Drive, Suite A, Salt Lake City, UT 84123, Phone: (801) 268-3365, Fax: (801) 268-3415

Vermont Youth Soccer Association, P.O. Box 90, Williston, VT 05495, Phone: (802) 859-9601, Fax: (802) 859-9602, E-mail: vysa@vtsoccer.orgVirginia

Virginia Youth Soccer Association, 2239 G Tacketts Mill Drive, Woodbridge, VA 22192, Phone: (703) 494-0030, Fax: (703) 551-4114, E-mail: vysa@aol.com

Washington State Youth Soccer Association, 33710 - 9th Ave. South, Suite 8, Federal Way, WA 98003, Phone: (253) 476-2237, Fax: (253) 925-1830

West Virginia Soccer Association, P.O. Box 3360, Beckley, WV 25801, Phone: (304) 252-9872, Fax: (304) 252-9878, E-mail: wvsa@citynet.net

Wisconsin Youth Soccer Association, 10708 West Hayes Ave., West Allis, WI 53227, Phone: (414) 545-7227, Fax: (414) 545-7249, E-mail: wysa@mail.gmtcom.com

Wyoming State Soccer Association, 7207 Bomar Drive, Cheyenne, WY , 82009-2017, Phone: (307) 637-2304, Fax: (307) 637-2305, E-mail: wssa@cheyenneweb.com

Index

● *D* ●

• F •

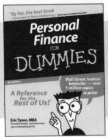

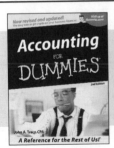

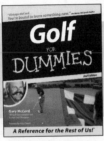
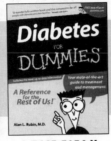
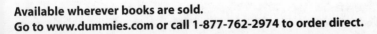

FOR DUMMIES®

A world of resources to help you grow

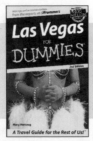

FOR DUMMIES®

Plain-English solutions for everyday challenges

COMPUTER BASICS

0-7645-0838-5

0-7645-1663-9

0-7645-1548-9

Also available:

PCs All-in-One Desk Reference For Dummies (0-7645-0791-5)

Pocket PC For Dummies (0-7645-1640-X)

Treo and Visor For Dummies (0-7645-1673-6)

Troubleshooting Your PC For Dummies (0-7645-1669-8)

Upgrading & Fixing PCs For Dummies (0-7645-1665-5)

Windows XP For Dummies (0-7645-0893-8)

Windows XP For Dummies Quick Reference (0-7645-0897-0)

BUSINESS SOFTWARE

0-7645-0822-9

0-7645-0839-3

0-7645-0819-9

Also available:

Excel Data Analysis For Dummies (0-7645-1661-2)

Excel 2002 All-in-One Desk Reference For Dummies (0-7645-1794-5)

Excel 2002 For Dummies Quick Reference (0-7645-0829-6)

GoldMine "X" For Dummies (0-7645-0845-8)

Microsoft CRM For Dummies (0-7645-1698-1)

Microsoft Project 2002 For Dummies (0-7645-1628-0)

Office XP For Dummies (0-7645-0830-X)

Outlook 2002 For Dummies (0-7645-0828-8)

Get smart! Visit www.dummies.com

- **Find listings of even more** *For Dummies* **titles**

- **Browse online articles**

- **Sign up for Dummies eTips™**

- **Check out** *For Dummies* **fitness videos and other products**

- **Order from our online bookstore**

Available wherever books are sold. Go to www.dummies.com or call 1-877-762-2974 to order direct.

FOR DUMMIES®

Helping you expand your horizons and realize your potential

FOR DUMMIES®

The advice and explanations you need to succeed

SELF-HELP, SPIRITUALITY & RELIGION

Sex
FOR DUMMIES
2nd Edition

0-7645-5302-X

Parenting
FOR DUMMIES
2nd Edition

0-7645-5418-2

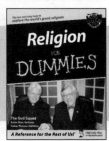

Religion
FOR DUMMIES

0-7645-5264-3

Also available:

The Bible For Dummies
(0-7645-5296-1)

Buddhism For Dummies
(0-7645-5359-3)

Christian Prayer For Dummies
(0-7645-5500-6)

Dating For Dummies
(0-7645-5072-1)

Judaism For Dummies
(0-7645-5299-6)

Potty Training For Dummies
(0-7645-5417-4)

Pregnancy For Dummies
(0-7645-5074-8)

Rekindling Romance For Dummies
(0-7645-5303-8)

Spirituality For Dummies
(0-7645-5298-8)

Weddings For Dummies
(0-7645-5055-1)

PETS

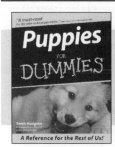

Puppies
FOR DUMMIES

0-7645-5255-4

Dog Training
FOR DUMMIES

0-7645-5286-4

Cats
FOR DUMMIES
2nd Edition

0-7645-5275-9

Also available:

Labrador Retrievers For Dummies
(0-7645-5281-3)

Aquariums For Dummies
(0-7645-5156-6)

Birds For Dummies
(0-7645-5139-6)

Dogs For Dummies
(0-7645-5274-0)

Ferrets For Dummies
(0-7645-5259-7)

German Shepherds For Dummies
(0-7645-5280-5)

Golden Retrievers For Dummies
(0-7645-5267-8)

Horses For Dummies
(0-7645-5138-8)

Jack Russell Terriers For Dummies
(0-7645-5268-6)

Puppies Raising & Training Diary For Dummies
(0-7645-0876-8)

EDUCATION & TEST PREPARATION

Spanish
FOR DUMMIES

0-7645-5194-9

Algebra
FOR DUMMIES

0-7645-5325-9

The ACT
FOR DUMMIES

0-7645-5210-4

Also available:

Chemistry For Dummies
(0-7645-5430-1)

English Grammar For Dummies
(0-7645-5322-4)

French For Dummies
(0-7645-5193-0)

The GMAT For Dummies
(0-7645-5251-1)

Inglés Para Dummies
(0-7645-5427-1)

Italian For Dummies
(0-7645-5196-5)

Research Papers For Dummies
(0-7645-5426-3)

The SAT I For Dummies
(0-7645-5472-7)

U.S. History For Dummies
(0-7645-5249-X)

World History For Dummies
(0-7645-5242-2)